Peace & Prosperity to you

Douglas James Cottrell

Sept 2015

THE NEW EARTH: A PROPHETIC VIEW OF OUR FUTURE

BASED ON THE REMARKABLE QUANTUM MEDITATION READINGS OF
DOUGLAS JAMES COTTRELL, PH.D.

CO-AUTHORED AND EDITED BY
DOUGLAS MATTHEW COTTRELL, B.A., M.A.

MANY MANSIONS PRESS
BURLINGTON, CANADA

WWW.MANYMANSIONSPRESS.COM

The New Earth: A Prophetic View of our Future

First edition: March 12, 2012
Previously published as *The New Renaissance: A Prophecy of 2012 and Beyond*

Second edition: April 2015

Copyright © 2012 Douglas James Cottrell, Ph.D.

Cover photo: Colourbox.com

ISBN 978-0-9919795-7-8

Published in Canada by
Many Mansions Press
www.manymansionspress.com

"THE MYSTIC BOND OF BROTHERHOOD MAKES ALL MEN ONE."

– THOMAS CARLYLE, "ESSAYS." *GOETHE'S WORKS* (1832)

"WHAT BEFALLS THE EARTH BEFALLS ALL THE SONS OF THE EARTH.
THIS WE KNOW: THE EARTH DOES NOT BELONG TO MAN,
MAN BELONGS TO THE EARTH. ALL THINGS ARE CONNECTED LIKE
THE BLOOD THAT UNITES US ALL. MAN DOES NOT WEAVE THIS
WEB OF LIFE. HE IS MERELY A STRAND OF IT.
WHATEVER HE DOES TO THE WEB, HE DOES TO HIMSELF."

– CHIEF SEATTLE, *LETTER TO THE PRESIDENT OF THE UNITED STATES* (C. 1855)

"I CELEBRATE MYSELF, AND SING MYSELF,
AND WHAT I ASSUME YOU SHALL ASSUME,
FOR EVERY ATOM BELONGING TO ME AS GOOD BELONGS TO YOU."

– WALT WHITMAN, "SONG OF MYSELF," *LEAVES OF GRASS* (1855)

DEDICATED TO THE MEMORY OF
CHERI-ANNE COTTRELL
1968 - 2006

CONTENTS

∂୨ ୧୨

PART TWO - THE NEW EARTH

THE APPENDICES

ACKNOWLEDGEMENTS

I wish to acknowledge and thank the many people who have helped or supported me in my career. First, my family: my parents, Thomas and Elinor; my wife, Karen; our children, Cheri-Anne, Douglas, Louise and Jason; my father-in-law, George; my brothers-in-law, David and Richard; and my sisters-in-law, Betty, Annette and Karen. Next, to all of the doctors, therapists, nurses, teachers, care-givers and support workers who helped Cheri-Anne through the thirty-eight years of her life. Their kindness added so much to her life and they are forever a part of our family. Next, to those who have supported me with their friendship and resources which have sustained me through hard times, and were instrumental in founding my spiritual centre in Hamilton, Canada: Maria A., Seymour A. Berger, Brenda Carlin, Dr. Carroll Vidhan Guérin, Jackie Novak, James Sinclair and Baroness Ursula von Diergardt. Next to my mentors, Ross Peterson and Rev. Alex Holmes, who guide me on the spiritual path which I continue to follow. Next, to my friends in the media who have promoted me and my work (especially in the early days), including John Gilbert, John Hardy, Jim Henderson, Peter Henderson, John Hesselink, Rob McConnell, Richard Syrett, Betty Thompson, and Paul Zuromski. And, last but not least, to my friends, colleagues, and associates around the world who have come into my life at pivotal times and who have made a contribution in my life, or provided inspiration. I am grateful for your support, love, and encouragement I received along the path.

PREFACE TO THE SECOND EDITION

by Douglas Matthew Cottrell, B.A., M.A.

In 2012, my father, Douglas James Cottrell, and I published *The New Renaissance: A Prophecy of 2012 and Beyond*. This was our second major work, after 2004's *Secrets of Life*, which focussed on spirituality, consciousness, the spiritual realms, and the abilities of the soul. In both cases, the information was gathered from a number of intuitive readings given by Dr. Cottrell, and edited by myself into a form that would be more easily read. To read more on that specific process, please see the introduction. It took as its focus the various predictions that have been made by various cultures regarding our present era.

Since publication of the first edition, *The New Renaissance* was translated into French, and then into Portuguese and Spanish. Thanks to the technology of digital publishing, it has been read by people in numerous countries around the world. Reviews have been overwhelmingly positive (an average of 4.8 out of 5 stars on Amazon, as of this writing). The most common complaint, however, is that the book is too short.

The opportunity to expand on the original edition came in 2015. This second edition, which you are now reading, has been re-titled *The New Earth: A Prophetic View of our Future*. It contains all the information from the first edition, augmented with roughly one hundred pages of new material, gathered from the Dr. Cottrell's

"Source" (sometimes called the Akashic Records) over a number of independent readings in 2013 and 2014. It is the most up to date information we have on predicted environmental and social changes.

One notable and fascinating addition to the material is the intriguing figure of "the Hallower." In a research reading on December 10, 2013, Dr. Cottrell was predicting economic changes in the United States, linked to a possible event involving China. Reference was made to the Hallower; a person who would be a harbinger of the changes to come. Thus far, there have only been a few references to the Hallower in Dr. Cottrell's work. We have collected all of them (to date) in this edition, for the first time.

Another addition to this book is an extended discourse on the Law of One, originally touched upon in the first edition. Readers asked for more information regarding the Law of One, and several research readings were done by Dr. Cottrell for this purpose. While many people understand the Law of One as the Golden Rule, it is more than that. It is the principle that lies at the heart of all of the world's great religions. It is the universal law imprinted upon our souls. We are all interconnected. We are all one.

I trust you will find this new and expanded edition to be useful and helpful for you and your loved ones. It is my sincere hope that readers will take the information and apply it in their own daily lives so that, if possible, the predicted hardships can be mitigated (or perhaps even avoided). Let us all come together as one, set aside our differences, and help build the new Earth.

"For those who have ears, let them hear…"

Douglas Matthew Cottrell, B.A., M.A.
Burlington, Ontario, Canada
March 2015

FOREWORD

by Robert Appel, B.A., B.C.L., L.L.B.

The year was 2001.

Two hard-working writers were putting the finishing touches on their respective book projects; projects about which they were totally passionate. These two writers had never met, neither was even aware of the other's endeavors, and, indeed, on the surface, the two projects seemed as far apart as chalk and cheese.

The first work was from the pen of investigative journalist, Lynn McTaggart. In an especially ambitious oeuvre, McTaggart had determined to take the recent complex, yet ground-breaking work in the field of Quantum ("small particle") Physics and explain it, in plain English, to average readers. It was a daring undertaking, but McTaggart ultimately nailed it. The result of her efforts, a worldwide best-seller entitled *The Field*, showed how fully-scientific, double-blind experiments from reputable scholars had established – for the first time in Western history! – a working, theoretical basis for a Unified Field that, effectively, joins everything and everyone into one single energy matrix.

This field, so-called, would be not merely a static or passive grid that existed within the boundaries of time and space as we understand them, but, astonishingly, a dynamic and innately intelligent grid that had the ability to transcend time and space, as and when needed. As McTaggart would ultimately explain to millions worldwide, following the very latest experiments in Small Particle Physics, the smaller the particle being studied, the more it tended to respond unpredictably to the subjective thoughts and expectations of the individual experimenter (as opposed to the objective, impersonal and otherwise predictable laws of Pure Physics).

So what precisely was this field? McTaggart, it should be understood, already had her plate full simply trying to deliver these complex concepts to the lay-person, and, amazingly, never actually specifically opined on what she was writing about. But reviewers of her work, academic professionals, and even the net bloggers, had no such inhibitions. "What McTaggart has presented," suggested a typical review blog on the book, "is nothing less than proof of an alert, interactive, central, core, intelligence that governs all matter at all levels. Science has finally achieved its ultimate nightmare. It has effectively proven the existence of God."

That very same year, 2001, a somewhat less-known writer was also compiling research on an (arguably) even more ambitious project – a book which, like McTaggart's, was destined to become the bellwether, the gold standard, if you like, for its niche. Called simply *Secrets of Life*, Douglas Mathew Cottrell had launched a multi-year project which attempted to take hundreds of hours of material delivered from a "deep meditative state" by his father, Douglas James Cottrell, and then soften the prose so that the complicated material would be more easily digestible by the layperson.

Some explanation, and even a little back story, is perhaps helpful here.

About a century ago, in the southern U.S.A., there lived an extraordinary individual named Edgar Cayce. Though barely educated himself, early in Cayce's life it was discovered quite by accident that, in an hypnotic trance, Cayce could somehow answer questions on virtually any topic or any person. For example – and this sentence should be read very carefully and literally – if, when Cayce was placed in an hypnotic state, he was given the name of an individual in Australia, he was then able to discuss in intimate detail every aspect of that person's physical, mental, and even spiritual state. His so-called 'medical' readings of this ilk, done remotely, were so accurate that even the New York Times of the day headlined that Cayce became a "doctor" when "asleep!"

Because Cayce's family had the foresight to bring in a stenographer to transcribe these unusual sessions, Cayce's legacy (he died in 1945) turned out to be a compilation of approximately fourteen thousand of these "readings," some twelve thousand of which were entirely medically-based. The balance, the remaining two thousand, spanned a potpourri of varied spiritual and esoteric topics, including (but not limited to) reincarnation, lost continents such as Atlantis and Mu, the missing years of Jesus, and several dozen very specific predictions on what might happen at the turn of upcoming century (which, of course, would be NOW).

Now in the ordinary course, these types of extraordinary claims (i.e. a man who under hypnosis could speak accurately about anything and anyone, and even discuss events that happened years or centuries prior, as if he were watching a movie) would be quickly dismissed as quackery. Save and except for the fact that every single Cayce client who later went to a doctor to verify his or her health reading (remember, there were some twelve thousand of these) seemed to get confirmation that the information provided was correct; and, moreover, in many cases, it was even more specific than what the best physicians of the day could offer. Not to mention they were done without any physical examination of any kind...

Although, as mentioned, Cayce himself died in the 1940s, in the 1960s a writer named Jess Stearn took upon himself the daunting task of reviewing all fourteen thousand readings left by Cayce, attempting to determine how accurate the medical portion actually was...?

What he determined, to his astonishment, was that not only were the medical sessions (done, in most cases, for clients thousands of miles from Cayce's own home, for people he had never met or seen) were accurate to the ninety-ninth-plus percentile. So accurate that, by Stearn's own era (the 1960s), actual clinics run by medical doctors had sprung up around the world which attempted to apply treatment protocols from the Cayce readings to patients at large. (For example, during the last century, a successful treatment for M.S. had continued to elude medical science. Yet the approximately one dozen individuals with M.S. who had sought a remote reading from Cayce, and faithfully followed the advice given, had achieved almost complete recoveries, fully documented, that traditional medicine simply could not explain.)

It was writer Stearn who first put forward the hypothesis that if, as had already been established, the twelve thousand or so medical readings by Cayce were seen to be accurate (albeit still inexplicable by modern science), did that not then lend credibility to the remaining two thousand...many of which, because of their esoteric subject matter, were otherwise impossible to prove or test...? Consider, Stearn argued persuasively in his writing, if Cayce's medical or health-related ability was established to be genuine – which it had been – did that not then suggest that the other topics Cayce had covered, springing from the very same (but still quite unknown) source, also deserved respect and consideration?

This was an argument that resonated well with the reading public at the time; which, in turn, was the beginning of a literary 'phenom' that present readers may perhaps not recall, but their parents or grandparents certainly will. Stearn's oeuvre, *The Sleeping Prophet,* became an international bestseller, translated into over one hundred and thirty languages. It was, indeed, so popular that it spawned dozens and dozens of follow-up books on Cayce. By the early 1970s, every single bookstore and drugstore in the U.S.A. had an entire Cayce "section" to entice browsers. An Off-Broadway play was done on Cayce's life, followed by two T.V. movies, and, later, countless mentions in documentaries on "Ancient Mysteries" and others.

So what, you ask, does this have to do with those two very special books being worked on in 2001 by authors McTaggart and Cottrell?

Everything.

Douglas Mathew Cottrell, in *Secrets of Life,* had attempted to condense into one single work years of sessions that his own father, Douglas James Cottrell, had also delivered from a state of deep meditation on a varied number of esoteric topics.

Early in his life, 1975 to be exact, the elder Cottrell, just like Cayce before him, accidentally discovered that, in a state of deep hypnosis, he could answer complex medical questions about people he had never met, living in places he had never been.

As was the case with Cayce, over the years, Cottrell ultimately completed thousands of these types of readings for clients from all over the globe; clients that included professionals, heads of governments and corporations, and even practicing medical doctors. Readings that were acknowledged, after much testing and verification, to be as good as or better than anything that modern medicine had to offer. (This writer is personally aware of a half-dozen medical doctors who have, over the years, sought Cottrell's help for difficult cases, all on the condition of anonymity, of course.)

By best calculation, Douglas James Cottrell, now in his sixties, has, so far, done well over twice as many sessions within his own lifetime as Cayce did in his, about some thirty thousand in all. And, as to the question of whether there are many competing individuals in this field, the answer appears to be a resounding "no." Those who have taken the time and trouble to study this phenomenon have, after thorough investigation, concluded that Cottrell's work is essentially one-of-a-kind. He has been called in the media, alternatively, "the living Edgar Cayce," and "the last of the Sleeping Prophets." At the time of writing, some three hundred-plus Youtube videos have, so far, been posted containing snippets of his work. Interestingly, none were posted by Cottrell himself; all by clients or students.

So it was that, back in 2001, Douglas Matthew, son of Douglas James, undertook the ambitious project of taking his father's meditation musings on key esoteric topics and turning them into a book. Following in the footsteps of Stearn before him, the postulate of the younger Cottrell was equally simple and straightforward. If the medical dicta from his father was so accurate that even medical professionals from around the world sought him out, was it not, therefore, logical that the non-medical material, covering spiritual and metaphysical topics, was equally well-founded and worthy of attention?

Published by a "boutique" or micro-publisher, *Secrets of Life* never generated sales in the millions. However, just as was the case with McTaggart's *The Field*, it, too, was a major hit with those specific readers who sought it out, and eagerly absorbed its material. ("Best book ever," read a typical review on Amazon.com, where the book earned a very rare five out of five stars from buyers.)

Which brings us full circle to the question we started with. What is the connection between McTaggart's book and Cottrell's?

What connects the work of two popular authors who, having never met, nonetheless were passionately pursuing their projects in approximately the same time frame?

The answer is....everything.

Ever since Stearn's work in the last century spawned a veritable "industry" tracking the work of Cayce, the largest problem that critics and skeptics have had with material delivered from the deep meditative state is...what is the scientific basis?

A question that no one had been able to even try to answer...until now.

Once you wrap your head around the very latest work in Quantum Physics – which was, please recall, why McTaggart started her book in the first place – you start to see a very different universe than the one you grew up with.

You start to see an awake and intelligent universe that contains, at the same time – in simultaneous time if you will – all knowledge that ever was and ever will be. Like the operating system on a computer, you start to see that, scientifically, there is a connection – a grid if you like – between everything that is, was, and will be. And you start to wonder if that grid can be accessed...? And then you start to wonder if the specific talent that has come to be known as the "Cayce phenomenon" – a talent only demonstrated, arguably, by two people in the last one hundred and fifty years – could actually be a manifestation of that field, or, at the very least, at least a unique form of access to it...?

This writer believes that answer is in the affirmative, although, it is acknowledged in the same breath, that one cannot please all the critics all the time. One can merely point to the road that McTaggart herself took and, say, follow that road, and you will finally have a basis to understand, and better appreciate, the amazing

work that emanates from Edgar Cayce and Douglas James Cottrell.

Such as, for example, the present work assembled and edited by Douglas Matthew Cottrell, a work which could not possibly be more timely or appropriate.

In this most current work, Douglas James focuses his astonishing ability on the question of the prophecies for this age, and what they mean to mankind.

The result is a work that is not only compelling, but reads like a good thriller. Douglas James not only provides readers with the correct and true background to the prophecies behind the key 2012 date, but, like Cayce before him, presents a series of incredibly specific and detailed expositions as to how our world will change in the next few decades – ultimately ushering in a "golden age" that is expected to last, we are told, at least five thousand years.

That said, the inquisitive reader is, no doubt, wondering by now just what precisely Douglas James Cottrell, from a deep meditative state, has to say about the coming epoch?

There is, as the T.V. comics like to say, both good news and bad news.

On the plus side, Mankind is entering an age of co-operation and mutual respect, long overdue:

> *Warfare will be coming to an end (for a time). Those souls that have been released upon the planet who have caused disturbances for the last five millennia will be corralled, and there will be a cessation of their disturbances. The heavens will open and there will be further visitations by the Divine. This will cause changes in the structures which you would call religion or belief, for there will be apparitions and appearances of saintly beings. For those*

*who are on the spiritual path, they will be enlightened
and enlivened. As such, there will be a moving towards
a single, world religion or belief system; not because it
will overpower or take away from others, but it will
be in accord, amalgamating the world's great religions.
The cessation of hunger, and the cessation of greed will
be on the way. There will, of course, be reductions of
the population, and there will be disturbances in
communications and transportation – and transportation may be established in a new venue, a new way –
and you will not see transportation as it now occurs,
ever again! You will find that the peoples of the world
will truly reach out to one another and, therefore, you
will see some cessation of indifference and prejudice;
this will take a little longer than a year or two, as
you might imagine. There will be a cessation to the
inhumanity that humans plague upon one another.
There will be an attempt, not in a utopian or euphoric
way, but in a realistic and logical way, for those upon
the planet to express themselves and to live their lives
fully; but in a new essence of art, education and knowledge and a new appreciation one for another.
Politics will change greatly as well, for those who are
now entering the field of politics to line their own
pockets or to find ways and means that they can be
selfishly rewarded, their time is at an end. Those who
are capable and able will come to the forefront, and
they will assist in an organized and intellectual,
practical way of ruling the people; the cooperation of
the people and the various groups. There will be a*

variety of individuals who will have authority.
They will be like governors over certain regions and
areas. They will, themselves, be personally responsible
for the implementation of their ideas and authority.
Therefore, political leaders who no longer are re-
sponsible, or accountable, these will end as well!

A golden age is coming, heralding major breakthroughs in the fields of health and medicine:

...frequencies about the body would be enhanced,
isolating disease in the body, amplifying the genetic
code or genetic vibrational rate in the body. This, too,
will come about in what would be considered the
Renaissance itself. For, even now, there is examination
of light therapy to remove disease from sores on the
mouth, to lasers being used for operative purposes, to
that that would be sonic scalpels, shall we say. Rough-
cut gemstones used for surgical purposes, like Flint,
or other waferous stones, suit the body much better, and
healing is much quicker than a steel, sharp blade, be-
cause it is non-intrusive on the body, where the steel is
more adverse. Using implements such as natural scalpels,
wafers of stone, you see, or crystal, sound and light,
medicine, as you know it, will not exist! It will be so
different that it would not even be close to what is tak-
ing place today! Why poison the body to try to cure it?!
Today's conditions in the body are usually due to illnesses
hiding out in the body, corralled or suppressed by medi-
cations, as if the medication would be a jailhouse and

*the disease would be an inmate. Disease does not
actually become eradicated or overcome in the body;
it is simply subdued until the death of the body, at
which time it consumes part of the body until it terminates itself. In the future, this will not be allowed, and,
indeed, looking back this time will be remembered as
a time of remorse and shame for those who would be
understanding. For those who have ears, let them hear.*

The bad news? Douglas James's prophecies on the years
ahead are eerily similar to, and moving in lockstep with, the predictions given a full century ago by Cayce himself on this post-millennial
period. There will be trials and tribulations, of this there is no doubt:

*This will be just prior to the greater collapse of those
landmasses on the west coast of North America and
those areas that would be on the eastern seaboard of
China and Japan; even the coastlines of the islands of
the Philippines, New Guinea, and Australia itself. Look
to Etna and Vesuvius, and you will see that when they
are in harmony with each other, it would be like the
key has been turned in the lock, the door has opened,
and the proverbial Pandora's Box has been released of
those difficulties into the world itself. For those who
have ears, let them hear. Move inland from the coastlines, or move up to higher land so you are not suffering
the intrusions when the oceans are rocked from their
basins. See? This would be the last, prior to the tipping,
or bobbing and weaving of the planet itself. Then there
will be a time in which it will settle, and the rotation*

would turn back to normal. There will be some scorching of the planet, from the rays of the sun, and there will be some freezing in places that will be furthest away from the sun. But this will be short-lived. People will live in caves, in some areas. Rather than fear, be prepared. Smoke, dust, and ash will cause breathing difficulties in some places in the Northern Hemisphere, and these would best be prepared against as well.

The bottom line? This writer was privileged to be asked by the author to write the introduction to the first printing of *Secrets of Life*, and is pleased to, once again, be offering to the enquiring reader another "must-read" from the Cottrells, father and son. Understand that if you Google the topic "2012," you will presently get over twenty-five billion hits. (Yes, that is BILLION, not a misprint). From this, one can safely presume there is widespread interest in this topic, which bridges continents, religions and even ethnicities. The writer can assure you, having read many dozens of these sorts of books on his own, that you will never encounter another work with more specific, or more explosive information on this important subject.

Whether one ultimately determines the content offered to be positive or negative is a choice left to the reader, and to the reader alone. But be assured that, regardless, you will not be bored. Ultimately, however, the choice, the final say, perhaps, belongs not so much to the reader as it does to the "field" itself, to that innate intelligence that includes us all. As Douglas James himself posits so eloquently:

There is no injustice in the world; the laws are perfect. This (age) will attempt to establish the spiritual laws,

*or the concepts, or the understandings which individuals
can live their life by, that will help to resolve conflicts,
that there will be no shortage of affection or love. And,
here, they will keep their peace and meet those things
that they must meet as life unfolds in front of them.
If there is any message, it would be that a critical mass
is forming, that groups of like-minded people are coming
together for the protection and benefit of each other, and
in particular, each individual in these groups. For that
that is done in the macrocosm is done in the microcosm; as above, so below.*

Robert Appel, B.A., B.C.L., L.L.B.
Toronto, Canada
January, 2012

INTRODUCTION

by Douglas Matthew Cottrell, B.A., M.A.

Think about this for minute: if you had a way of knowing what was going to happen in the future, what would you do?

For the sake of argument, let's assume that the source of the information was reliable, and by that I mean that you have some experience with that source, and over time you have come to trust in the source's reliability, based on a history of past performances of giving information that proved to be sound and true. If you were given some information about a future event, from a source you knew to be reliable, what would you do with it?

Being the thoughtful people that we are, most of us listen to the weather forecast in order that we can prepare ourselves for what will happen, and often we will change our plans based on the information that is given to us. If we know it is going to rain in the evening, we make provisions by packing an umbrella with us as we head to work in the morning; or we take a jacket with us if we know that conditions will turn cool later in the day.

And if the future event you were given fore-knowledge of was not just a rainstorm or a temperature drop, but a tornado, chances are you would take every precaution to ensure that you and your loved ones would be protected, should a tornado pass through your area. If you are a compassionate and caring person, you would probably let many others know about the information you had been privy to, in order to warn as many people as you could.

By having information, we can make informed choices, and we can prepare ourselves, and perhaps even assist others.

You are holding a book that contains information about events that have yet to happen, from a source that has been proven time and time again to be reliable and trustworthy. It is humbly offered so that you, too, can make informed decisions. This is not said lightly, nor is it an exaggerated claim made to inflate someone's ego and market some product that you do not need. It is a sincere belief that the information contained in these pages may help arm you, so that you can make provisions that will help others, and, of course, yourself.

Where did the information come from? It came through my father, Douglas James Cottrell, Ph.D., while he was in a deep state of meditation. It is information that is beyond his conscious knowledge and level of understanding, and information he did not receive through any rational evaluation, exploration or investigation. Some might say that it came "through" him, not from him, as he was in an altered state of consciousness at the time, and the words were inspired through a unique process that allows Dr, Cottrell the ability to get his own thoughts, emotions, biases and beliefs out of the way so that a direct communication from "the beyond" can come through (for lack of a better word).

Since 1975, Dr. Cottrell has gained a reputation for being able to put himself into a state of hypnosis or what he calls "Quantum Meditation" (previously, "deep trance"), from which he can gain information that is beyond his own perception (and often removed from him spatially and temporally); knowledge which, under scrutiny, proves to be incredibly accurate, especially as pertaining to people's health conditions. Those who seek his guidance do not do so lightly. In most instances, they seek Dr. Cottrell as a last resort after many failed attempts to find causes and solutions to their concerns from mainstream sources. These people are rational, thoughtful individuals who seek an alternative source of information out of desperation, and you can rest assured that in most cases, they follow up on the information given in this unorthodox manner with examination and scrutiny by qualified health professionals to know for certain that the information offered is genuine.

[Aside: Having witnessed literally thousands of such Quantum Meditation. sessions on topics as varied as health, finances, relationships, business, ancient history, karma, past lives and spiritual development, I am convinced of the ability of the human mind to go beyond the physical and to demonstrate the abilities of premonition, precognition, prediction, and prophecy. I do not believe in blind faith, but I believe that faith can be built upon belief, and that belief is built upon evidence. There is always room for skepticism, but with more and more evidence, we are able to have stronger and stronger belief.]

It was this same sense of desperation that introduced a young Dr. Cottrell to this phenomenon in the first place. Together with his wife, Karen, he sought the advice of a man who was reputed to possess genuine intuitive abilities. They were desperate to find answers about their daughter, Cheri-Anne, who had been placed in an institution for handicapped children six years prior, with little real hope of recovery. She was suffering from a convulsive disorder which was being managed with heavy medication therapy, and her physical and mental development seemed to have stopped. She was unable to crawl, walk, talk, or even feed herself; and medical doctors could not offer a cause, nor a solution to this condition.

The man who Douglas was led to was named Ross Peterson, and he had been the guest on a television show that Douglas happened to watch, called, "World of the Unexplained with Allen

Spraggett." Ross was reputed to be the legacy of an intuitive or metaphysical ability as demonstrated in the early part of the Twentieth Century by Edgar Cayce. Coincidentally, Douglas had been given the book, *There Is A River*, a biography of Cayce, a few weeks before, and he was so convinced of the claims regarding Cayce's ability to know about someone's health problems, that he searched for someone who could manifest this same ability to help Cheri-Anne.

To Douglas's relief, Ross turned out to be legitimate, and he gave Douglas and Karen hope for their daughter. He saw that an impairment in her neck caused by the birthing process was the cause for her varied troubles, left untreated for years, and exacerbated by heavy drugs which had made her body toxic. Douglas was so inspired by the information that was given, and based on the strength of that single intuitive session alone, he removed Cheri-Anne from the institution (against medical advice, of course) and began to administer a series of natural health treatments that effectively and immediately ceased the convulsive disorder, and chronic pain.

Unfortunately Cheri-Anne's condition had degraded so much during those early years that she never fully recovered, and she lived life in a wheelchair, assisted by family and health care workers on a daily basis.

In the course of the session with Ross, Douglas was not only given health insights into himself and his daughter, but information regarding past lives and karma. Ross also gave Douglas a remarkable piece of information that he had wondered about, but never investigated: that he, too, had the same ability to enter meditation and receive information. Said Ross (in deep meditative trance):

"Ye have been a prophet of old, and ye will be a prophet of new."

These words of inspiration put Douglas onto the path to develop any spiritual or intuitive ability he may possess, which took him literally around the world as he began to explore the mystical teachings of the world's great religions. He is now considered to be one of a select few to reliably demonstrate all of the spiritual abilities, including telekinesis, telepathy, remote viewing, prediction, and prophecy.

> *Prophet: From the Greek word profitis meaning "foreteller," a prophet is an individual who is claimed to have been contacted by the supernatural or the divine, and serves as an intermediary with humanity, delivering this newfound knowledge from the supernatural entity to other people. The message that the prophet conveys is called a prophecy. Claims of prophets have existed in many cultures through history, including Judaism, Christianity, Islam, the Sybilline and the Pythia, known as the Oracle of Delphi, in Ancient Greece, Zoroaster, the Völuspá in Old Norse and many others. Traditionally, prophets are regarded as having a role in society that promotes change due to their messages and actions.* (Source: *Wikipedia*)

What does it mean to call Dr. Cottrell a prophet? It means that repeatedly, and reliably on thousands of occasions over the years, Douglas has demonstrated the ability to foretell events and circumstances of the future, which have come true. What does this mean? It means that our minds have the ability to transcend the limitations of time and space and perceive situations which have not happened yet. Does this imply that the future is set in stone? I do not believe so. I believe that people such as Dr. Cottrell are perceiving information which represents the highest probability of an event taking place, provided that certain variables remain constant. If a loco-motive is going in a particular direction at a particular velocity, it can be predicted that at a certain time it will arrive in a certain location.

Dr. Cottrell has been very good at making predictions per-taining to future probabilities, from the outcome of a business meet-ing, to the success of a medical procedure, or the future price of a stock or commodity. Have all of his predictions come to pass? No, they have not. The complex set of circumstances surrounding any event and the ability to forecast the outcome of that event based on present circumstances is something that this book will explore.

The theme is that when someone knows that a certain course of action or pattern of behavior will lead to a particular outcome in the future, they can make choices that may affect the outcome, and perhaps even prevent that future predicted event from taking place.

Is Dr. Cottrell alone in what he does? No, he is not. Through his own Quantum Meditation consultations, he has counseled that many can learn to develop these same abilities. In fact, this is some-thing he encourages, and has opened a teaching facility in Hamilton, Ontario, Canada, for this very purpose.

That being said, I do believe that Dr. Cottrell is special. Only he can do what he can do, just as only you can do what you can do.

Can you be Mozart, or Michelangelo? No. But if you feel you have some artistic sensibility or ability, then it should be nurtured and developed to the greatest agree that you wish. Perhaps you are a Master in your own right. But even if you learn to paint or play an instrument, you will never be Mozart or Michelangelo. And no matter how developed someone else's intuitive abilities are, they can never be Dr. Cottrell; they can only be themselves. It was revealed recently in a research Quantum Meditation session, much like the ones which made up the book you are about to read, that Dr. Cottrell is, in fact, the reincarnation of the last oracle of Atlantis.

[N.B. for more information about Quantum Meditation, please see the appendices at the back of this book.]

What you are about to read is a series of questions and answers taken from a number of Quantum Meditation consultations given by Dr. Cottrell in 2011 and 2012. The questions were submitted to him by a group of people with a wide range of interests. The sessions were all recorded and transcribed, and then arranged by topic in this volume. I have done some editing of the material for ease of reading, as the communications tend to speak in an archaic way that lends itself better to listening than reading. In the editing, I have kept to the spirit of the communication, if not the letter.

What I was struck by in arranging the material are the common threads that weave throughout. Keep in mind that these sessions were done over a span of months, with questions being asked in a fairly random way by a number of different people from various locations. Once the information was re-organized, themes appeared that I was not consciously aware of. To me, this reinforces that the information is coming not from Dr. Cottrell, but truly from the infinite wisdom of the Divine. Someone once said to me that in the spiritual dimensions, this book already exists, and that my job as editor is to just to assemble it as it comes through Dr. Cottrell through the various communications. I like to believe that is the case!

I humbly present to you in *The New Earth* a depiction of the future as Dr. Cottrell has foreseen it. I do not believe in doom and gloom, but I believe in cause and effect. It is my belief that the prophecy described in these pages is a description of what will come to pass should we collectively continue in the way we are going; but if we make changes now, there is a chance we can avoid the troubles that lie in our path.

The purpose of these challenging times that lay ahead of us is to bring the people of the world together, united as one and in communion with the spiritual forces that are all around us.

The hope for the future is that we are entering a golden age, but in order to get from here to there, some changes need to take place, to shake things up a little. A revolution is taking place, a total change in the way we relate to one another, and a rebirth of arts, culture, ethics, politics, religion, education, and the sciences; truly a new Renaissance for a new Earth.

It is my sincere hope that all who read this book will take the information to heart and implement its suggestions in their own lives. What is clear is that cooperation is what is needed most in the world; and one way or another, we will have to learn to put aside our differences and cooperate with others in order to survive. The disasters that are predicted in this book are the end results of decisions made and activities carried out over a few thousand years, in disregard of the consequences. Now is the time to make a change, to correct these erroneous ways, and to make this world the amazing place it was meant to be. What you will do with the information you now have is a choice you will have to make. As Dr. Cottrell has said in many quantum meditation sessions, "There is no darkness, there is no night. There is simply love and light. Choose what you wish to choose. As for us, we would choose light and life!"

Douglas Matthew Cottrell, B.A., M.A.
London, Ontario, Canada
January 2012

[A note on the text: as you read this book, you will notice that questions are answered in the first person plural ("we," "our"). When asked in a

Quantum Meditation session who is speaking, the answer was, "you are communicating with the high self of Dr. Cottrell, which is in communication with the high self of the Conductor, the questioner, and any other minds who have an interest in the subject matter."]

PART ONE

THE END
OF AN AGE

CHAPTER ONE

❧❧

Prophecies of the Future

COULD YOU PLEASE DESCRIBE PROPHECIES WHICH PERTAIN TO OUR CURRENT TIME PERIOD AND BEYOND, AND EXPLAIN THEIR RELEVANCE?

As in all times, there are always those omens, occurrences, or events that forecast the timing of certain aspects or events in the Universe, the solar system, the Milky Way, and in the planet itself. For understand there is a vibration or a frequency that emanates out through all things. This frequency can be considered the communication frequency; not in the same sense as you would understand a telephone or a telegraph. But the vibration or frequency communicates with all things, through this vibration. You may call it "The Word," you may call it the original thought, you may call it whatever you please. But it is that binding, critical mass collecting, magnetic influencing, adhesive that keeps the most distant star in contact with the closest material thing of this world. See?

There is a thread that goes through all things. Although it is described somewhat differently, it is the universal mind, shall we call it, in which there can be the influence at the subatomic level. Subatomic particles can be influenced by thought or sound, as has been proven by McTaggart; and a professor in Japan has shown how vibration or words can be frozen in ice. You will find there are many ways to interpret, demonstrate or come upon this intrinsic bioelectrical/mechanical/metaphysical connection, shall we call it. Things can be influenced telekinetically; this is true. Information can go through books and you can contact another on the other side of the world for assistance, or help, or to be of service, as if you were side by side in the same room. There is always the connection. If you understand electrons, and how they move and flow from one proton to another, you would understand that in the subatomic world, which seems to be finite, you cannot find the ends. The point is that this particular connection, thread, or, more accurately, "current" flows through all things. When something dies or passes away, it is transmuted, transferred or transformed into a different form; but in essence, it has not. It has been reduced to what it once was: the smallest particles in movement, in relationship to one another. Think of this: if you take things apart, and you move to the subatomic world, are all things not the same?

As you would understand this concept, that there is an underlying communication, then you would understand that the prophecies that are made are visions of those things that would occur; the items, or circumstances, or events that would relate to the timing of the occurrence. Here, there is the large rock that has split in two. Here, there is the white buffalo or bison that has appeared. Here, there are anomalies, in other predictions, in which (if you would look for them) would have been stated a forecasting of this particular time; whether it would be the mathematical clock of the Maya in relationship to the Universal clock, or the forecasting of holy minds or beings by the Hopi themselves. The Hopi remember the origins of the world, and if you would examine their prophecies, you would find they have accurately given the forecast of the four worlds, or the previous four episodes. This would be the fourth destruction and the fifth new world we are referring to.

As you would examine far and wide, you would find many indigenous peoples who have lived in tribal huts, or caves, or who have, in their own way, persisted with their original memories or folklore. For instance there would always be a recalling of the Flood, which was basically the oceans rocking out of their basins when the world went through the last destruction. As you would examine the Hopi, they would tell of the world standing still, for days, and then the commencement of the rotation again! If you would examine these with an eye that would look for the planet flipping or rotating in an opposite direction (instead of the present, towards the east), you would see that there would be marked a memory of the rotation towards the west; although the poles were in a different place. The North Star was not always the North Star. In ancient times it would be referred to as the constellation of the Bear, for the Bear was the northern "pole," as you would understand it.

As you would look back in time, you would find these prophecies relate to this time by virtue of certain aspects, the timing of celestial occurrences, and also occurrences in the world itself (the appearance of certain things). If you would consult holy books such as *The Bible*, you would see that when Jesus the Nazarene came into the world, the sky was marked by certain stars. Likewise, you will find certain arrangements of constellations taking place, and the alignment of planets in the shape of a "V;" two larger planets on the left, one larger planet on the right, with the Earth at the end of the V, and the sun behind it. This is the time in which there would be the catastrophes in the planet itself that many will call chaotic. As you would look to the Mayans, look to that of the Milky Way and the saying that when the donkey dips its tail into the river, it would be, again, the time in which the world will change. You will see that now is the time that the Donkey is dipping its tail into the Milky Way river.

Such sayings or prophecies relate to this time, not a decade before, and not a decade after, but this time.

In the finite mind, time is measured by minutes, hours, days, weeks, months and years. But in the infinite mind, there is no such finite measurement! And therefore, a more simple way, a way of celestial evolution, arrangements, or events is necessary to provide the timing of a predicted event. The plagues that have infested the Earth have also been forecast by these far-sighted, highly-metaphysically-trained minds. The Rosicrucians have predicted this time for thousands of years, accurately predicting the cycles economically. As you would look to the Egyptians, you would also find times relating to this situation, mathematically instilled in the Great Pyramid's building itself, you see? Remember, frequency or vibration is mathematical!

Each of these prophecies offers that there will be times that will be difficult; "testing or teaching times" to test human nature, and to allow those to teach themselves through difficulties or what would be challenges at hand. The test provided will be the circumstances in which there will be difficulty, destruction, or change. Then, and only then will there be change in the hearts and minds of the peoples on this world, or this planet. Let us hope that their ignorance, darkness, or indifference can be altered before the critical point in time, which is now, you see.

Altering the attitude of those peoples that exist here on this planet may allow certain changes to occur very quickly, to the positive and benefit of the people who reside on the planet. The positive is that they will prolong their lives. The numbers of lives lost will be reduced, that there will be circumstances that will intervene from the Divine above, as well as the hearts and minds of those who reside in this world. As it was given by the Hopi many years ago, there comes a point when humankind may alter its path; not downward into despair, darkness, and more death and suffering; but that the planet itself, which is in harmony with the vibration or communication, can hear those prayers, and can tilt, or shift, or alter its future destiny, even by a degree. This would be immensely productive, and fortunate for those who live upon this world!

Therefore, there is the opportunity if humankind would change its materialistic and carnal ways. By "carnal," we are not speaking about sex, or lust. We are speaking of the inhumanity that is plaguing the world now, and which has for some time. If there can be compassion or reasoning, a sort of rationale that all should get along as best they can, then there will be a lack of judgment, a lack of criticism, a lack of want, and a lack of destruction. As such, the prophecies are given so that there can be an adherence, or, perhaps, a change towards compassion. For understand, actions always have consequences; positive, negative or otherwise. These signs or omens are given so there can be attention paid to these circumstances so there can be change. And as there is change, there is, perhaps, avoidance of the hard lessons, and then there may be acceptance of the soft lessons.

There exists in the world always those who can perceive the future, in a prophetic way. Some can see for centuries! These prophecies or predictions we refer to were seen by seers in the various groups, or tribes, or temples, many, many years ago. It is up to those who now hear these words whether they would wish to change their ways. In essence, this is the offering of the Hopi; if humankind alters or changes its ways, even by one degree, or but a few minds or hearts change to the better, then the benefits are enormous. There may be avoidance of destruction, and acceptance of construction, or what would be considered the compassion of the soul coming through, you see.

Therefore, for those who have ears, let them hear. Let them willfully alter their own lives, and the lives of others, so this can be carried forth like a ground swell, until there is the changing of those hearts and minds of those who are in authority; the world leaders who are not world leaders by chance, but they are there by their due presence, duty, or karma. Let them come together as they have in the past, and, perhaps, there can be changes in the world, as you know it. There is always an alternative, there is always an opportunity ... until a certain time, or point. After that time, no change can take place. This is why the prophecies have been given by the many tribes, seers, shamans, sensitives, clairvoyants and prophets in the past: so that there can be a preparation for these times, so this truth, or this knowledge can be given forth; to protect a few, perhaps; to protect many, more than likely; and to change the hearts and minds of the world, a high probability (and a duty also!).

Humans, as you know humans, usually do the right thing, but for the wrong reason. If they do the right thing for the right reasons, it could be assured that great changes will take place to the outcome of what is about to befall the world; for The Word, or the vibration can be altered or changed. The rearrangement of certain events can occur. The softening or the lessening of difficulties can occur. The human mind may not understand or comprehend the vibration or The Word that emanates through all things, but you should understand that all things are connected. They are all one. Yes, even those who are difficult to love still have love within them on some level. As it is said, "Does not the sun shine and the rain fall upon the good and the wicked alike?" So it is with the outcome of those influences, circumstances, or events that are taking place (and will continue to take place).

This world, this cinder in which the people live is important, but it is not unfeeling. It is not without its own soul, shall we say. It can be appealed to, and the planet can alter or heal itself. All of the people who live upon the world now, within one hundred years, will be gone, save for a few, and the world will be turned over to the next generation. Think of that when you understand the timelessness of this planet, and of those predictions and prophecies that were given by learned and humble people alike; by Chinese herbalists, shepherds, Mayans, Druids, the followers of Ra-Ta, the Sons of the Law of One, and even the Sons of Belgal in Atlantis.

Our elaboration is simply: does it not make sense that the Divine would send warnings to the peoples of the planet, to mend their ways when they are in error? For the peoples upon the planet have, through the industrial revolution, been quite destructive upon this place, and through the atomic age inflicted more destruction than benefit upon the world! The world changes every decade. The people upon the planet are like the captain that steers the ship; as they turn the rudder, they change the course and the ship follows the course. This juggernaut in space can be changed as well. If all the people would change the course, change the direction by changing the rudder, being compassionate, being caring, and attempting to be fair and to care, then the course will change, and the very same things that have been given forth will be returned. This is not a vengeful God, nor is this a vengeful time. It is a time of reflex of those things that have been given forth previously. The reflex now is that which is coming back. However, there is still yet an opportunity for people to change their ways, to change the course of this planet, and even the solar system in which they reside!

The seers see from the vastness of their soul minds; the peoples on the planet think from the littleness of their intellectual minds.

The macrocosm cannot be comprehended by the finite mind, but the finite mind can alter, incrementally, the steps that are taking place now, that may lead to a higher, better outcome (or to a lower, worse outcome). Take your steps. Encourage each other. Treat each other with humanity. Be humble. Be humane. You will overcome just about any difficulty, disaster, or extreme that is coming into this place. There are no injustices. Thy God is a loving and just God. But re-member the communication travels both ways. Whatever the word, whatever the sound, it has vast consequences. Let it be a sound of love and compassion.

Throughout the ages, there have been seers, guiding hu-mankind, helping to improve the human condition, to bring others closer to the God-head, to touch upon the face of God itself. They existed in the past, they exist in the present, and they will exist in the future. For those who have ears, let them hear. The way to tell the difference between a false prophet and a truly inspired one is simply to listen to their words, and from that you can determine if they are in harmony with God Almighty, the Universal membership, or if they are of their own accord, you see? It is as simple as that. If nothing they ever say comes true, then reject them. If things, how-ever, do tend to come true, then begin to accept them. Listen to their words. Are they words of compassion, healing, and caring? Then ac-cept them further. If not, reject them. There are no injustices. The prophecies are given to the wise man who listens. The prophecies are given to the wise people who partake of them and change imme-diately their actions or ways, and by doing so, the whole world is saved, you see? As then, as now.

WHEN A PREDICTION OR PROPHECY IS MADE, IT IS UP TO THE PERSON LISTEN-ING TO THE PREDICTION TO TAKE ACTION; NOW, ACCORDING TO THE LAW OF

ATTRACTION AND MANIFESTATION, WHAT YOU HOLD IN YOUR MIND YOU AT-
TRACT AND EVENTUALLY THIS IDEA BECOMES MANIFEST. SO IN THIS WAY OF
THINKING, TELLING SOMEONE A PREDICTION THEN HAVING THEM THINK ABOUT
IT, MAKES THE THOUGHT COME TRUE OR IN OTHER WORDS IT BECOMES A SELF-
FULFILLING PROPHECY. FOR THE SAKE OF CLARITY, COULD YOU PLEASE EXPLAIN
PROPHECY AND HOW IT FITS INTO THE LAW OF ATTRACTION AND MANIFESTA-
TION?

There are several factors that should be considered. Firstly, you assume that because people think of a thing, they make it happen; or
that when they are exposed to some information, they readily accept
it into their minds as being the truth. On occasion, do they not dis-
miss things that have come to them as frivolous, imaginary, or un-
true? Of course they do! The question touches upon several
philosophical concepts. For the finite mind, it is difficult to understand the infinite; and this question attempts to make finite the conclusion. As such, understand this: a prophecy is the future viewing
of an event that is destined to happen. If it were not so, many people
would not see the same thing. Many people do see future events from
different perspectives; a slight variance in how they observe things,
and they sometimes do this at various times in their lifetimes. Biblical
prophecies, which are now taking place, were given to certain people
more than two thousand years ago.

Understanding the Law of Attraction is to understand that
the person is attracted to the information in the first place, not that
they are attracted to the prophecy and making it fulfilled. When one
is exposed to a prophecy or information, at that moment in time they
have the opportunity to accept or reject the notion, the idea, the
facts, or the prophecy and they do. Those who adhere to the
prophecy, perhaps become prepared. The prophecy may be a proba-

bility, even a high one, until it actually occurs, at which time there is the fulfillment of the prophecy given or the destiny of the event, so to speak. But at that moment in time when the prophecy is given, they accept the possibility of the probability, take action, and become prepared. This is the reason why prophecy is given in the first place, that there might be some saving of lives or the avoidance of a difficulty or a circumstance in a person's life (or even in the nation's existence, or the world's evolution, you see).

To understand the Law of Attraction is to understand that the person is being attracted to information, not that he or she is bringing into the world terrible things, or even blessed things. These are going to happen on their own. In their own way, these events are predestined to happen. Understand the world is not by chance; for if you think it is by chance, then your statement would hold water, or be correct. But it is not by chance. There is a destiny, and there are certain things that must come into the world, for the world to evolve. There are cycles, and cycles within cycles. These guarantee certain events. This is a world of duality. That which is favorable and that which is unfavorable exist at the same time, and the meandering between the two is how the road is taken or the fulfillment of what would be the existence or the materialization of the existence occurs. After all, physical life has a purpose; it is not by chance or coincidence. Human minds do not make up certain things, unless they are in total agreement. These things are given by the Divine, and they are caused to come into the world.

With this understanding, then you can know the difference between what is destined and what is the probability of meeting destiny, and how it is done. For then free will and free choice occurs. One can approach a mountain from the left, or from the right. One may choose to go to the top, or perhaps only halfway. Whatever the case, that person is still at or on the mountain! Understanding the Law of Attraction is that you understand that you are attracting yourself towards that which is of benefit to yourself. How many would wish the world to go through difficult times? How many would wish to go through challenges, adversity, or pain, themselves? None, you see. Those who would choose to attract beauty, pleasure, and abundance, do so; but understand that it is only a temporary attraction. For when they achieve what they have attempted to attract, it is a corporeal, materialistic thing; and then they will move on to the next thing.

Prophecy changes the world, and it is a point in which there is no return, no going back. Prophecy changes the world, and changes the people who are in and upon the world; those who live in this world have their lives changed by Earth-changing events. Think of it. When there was great change in the world, or the Earth as you know it, was there not an immediate change in how the world's people reacted? On September 11, 2001, often called "9/11," the world changed that day, did it not? Could this have been attracted by those who wish to advance themselves financially, or to wreak havoc against their enemies in the West? This had to be a collective mind change, and this event did change the world; to greater and lesser degrees in different places in the world, but it did change. Likewise on the day in America, when there was an explosion, and the Atomic age was born from that explosion, the world changed on that day! You can reference different points in time when you found that the world changed. Revolution in America, France, and Russia changed these places in one day. They are no longer the places they used to be.

By understanding this, therefore, you can comprehend the difference between prophecy, and attracting things that are of benefit to you that help you prosper. You cannot apply the Law of Attraction to prophecy, for prophecy has been "decreed," if you will, by the Divine. It represents those turning points, or pivotal points in this place you call the Earth, or the world you live upon. You cannot attract what you do not know, nor would you be willing to attract these things that are about to take place; for monumental changes are going to take place. This has happened before. This is not the first "destruction of the world," nor is it the second, or the third. We are on the verge of the fifth destruction or change in the world, and each time, the world has changed greatly. Humans, as you know humans, do not have the capability to attract such monumental changes! But there have been prayers for justice, and peace to come into the world. This is what is going to take place after this challenging time, this Earth-changing time. A monumental change in attitude will occur in all who exist in the world now. Think of this: when do people change? Usually when some disaster, difficulty, challenge, disappointment or failure occurs. When they are feeling in a pleasurable, blissful way, people do not really change too much. They just have a different outlook and they are at peace within. They experience the bliss of the soul while in the flesh. Pain wakes you up. Pleasure puts you to sleep.

As such, the Law of Attraction is that which is usually open to the individual. Prophecy is a collective consciousness that is ordained and decreed by the Divine so that there will be a collective change in this place, this dimension, this Earth, this world; so that all who live upon the planet may enjoy their future, spiritual sojourns, and acquire what is necessary for their spiritual evolution. It is sort of like changing neighborhoods, is it not? You move from one consciousness to another, one city to another, or one neighborhood to another, and you have a completely different environment in which to live; and as such, you must adjust to this new environment. So will it be for those who live through this time; they will adjust. But understand, this is the end result of all the decisions, all the actions, all the activities of those who have lived before! In the last five thousand years, there has been a path taken. The path leads to this point in the present, or now. That is why people can see the future, for they see the path. It is why many have foreseen what is about to take place. The only reprieve is that many people in the world would pray for peace and they would give up their pattern, way, or activities. For this is a consumer mentality, and the consumers are consuming the world, as you know it. They are imbalancing the planet by taking the stabilizing fluids out of the ground: oils and gases, salts, minerals, and metals. They are consuming the very planet they live upon! They are consuming the atmosphere around the planet, and they are putting into the air disruptive vibrational rates through all the frequencies of communications systems and other radiating sounds or frequencies from space, satellites and transmitters all around the planet. This is disrupting the vibration of the planet! And when you have harmonic interference, you have change! The delicate balance of this particular planet is now in jeopardy.

This can be changed, and if it would be changed, then there may be a softening of those events that are about to happen in which volcanic activity will be massive, there will be dust in the air, ash will fall to the ground, and there will be much in the way of innovation and changes that will affect society, as you know it, all over the world. This is the difference between attracting fortuitous things to the self, or even life lessons that might be considered challenging to the self, as opposed to those events that are the end result of activities that have taken place for generations, for which the world needs to be reset upon its course again. This fifth destruction, or new Renaissance, as you might call it, is leading to these changes for the betterment of the world itself, and for all who live upon the same.

HOW DOES DESTINY RELATE TO FREE WILL AND FREE CHOICE?

Destiny is simply the fulfillment of the purpose for which the self has entered into the world and has lived life. As you take on different experiences in different lifetimes, shall we call it, you fulfill the purpose for which you were born into the world. Realize that the privilege of taking on physical life by a soul is a precious thing, and there are many souls waiting for experiences but are unable to attend in the Earth.

As such, destiny is the fulfillment of their karmic or spiritual purpose in the world, as you know it. You come into the world for certain experiences, in order to give yourself the opportunity to advance, to become more enlightened, or to become self-aware, and to become, perhaps, realized and then fully realized, as a spiritual being in a physical form, you see. To understand fulfillment is to understand your evolution. Destiny is little more than fulfilling the course. You might liken it to taking a course in school. You start in one grade, and you go to the last grade, and you have fulfilled yourself and you graduate. Fulfilling your destiny is a graduation of the purpose, the course, or the ideal that you started out to take. You are now educated, both in theory and experience, in the world as a living soul, and now you have wisdom. Of course, you can fail at a certain grade, and repeat; and, perhaps, fail again, and repeat again. The destiny is ultimately that which will occur, for it must occur; it must be completed. It is a step. It is a fulfillment in the evolution of an individual, or a people in the world itself, you see.

Free will is how you go about this. You have the ability to

tenaciously succeed, or lethargically wait and fail. However, sooner or later, there is no getting out of this school, you see; you must complete the course and graduate. When you fail, you feel pain. When you succeed, you feel the bliss of the soul itself. And ultimately, you achieve your destiny and you graduate.

EDGAR CAYCE HAD PREDICTED EARTH CHANGES TO OCCUR IN THE 1990's. OBVIOUSLY, THOSE CHANGES HAVE NOT HAPPENED YET. WHY DO SOME PROPHECIES OCCUR AT A DIFFERENT TIME THAN THEY ARE PREDICTED?

People change! There is an influence, and the influence causes a delay. For instance, let us say there was a prediction about a certain catastrophe in which a bridge was going to collapse. If it is acted upon, an examination may find weakness in the bridge and repair it. This would seemingly negate the prediction. But sooner or later, the weakness in the bridge would maintain, and ultimately the bridge would, as predicted, succumb to its own internal weakness or pattern, and it would fail. However, if there are those who pray, and those who repair, and those who continue to examine, even though it is a weak bridge, it may maintain itself for decades, and generation after generation.

Nothing in the world, as you know it, is permanent. All things are temporal. But when a prediction is given, it is given more in a sense of looking forward in time to see the probability. If enough people change their mind (even two or three), then that probability may be avoided. It is a matter of how people think.

LONG AFTER EDGAR CAYCE DIED, MANY EXPERTS PICKED APART HIS READINGS AND ATTEMPTED TO DISCERN A SEQUENCE IN THE EARTHQUAKE PREDICTIONS. DOES SUCH A PREDICTIVE SEQUENCE EXIST WHICH WOULD BE USEFUL TO THE

INHABITANTS OF EARTH IN PREPARING FOR MAJOR CHANGE AND IF HEEDED, COULD SAVE LIVES?

There would be such a course, yes. First, you would find earthquake and volcanic activity in Mount Etna, Mount Vesuvius, and the Canary Islands. Then as you go across the planet, you would see activities in Japan, and then in the Hawaiian Islands. Then you would find activities sporadically around the European area of Spain. You will find volcanoes will take place where you would least expect them. For instance, in the Montreal, Canada region towards the Quebec south shore, dormant volcanoes will heat up. Earthquakes will begin, and they will be violent. Look to Turkey as a key that unlocks the sequence itself. Look to the Pacific rim and you would find the rim itself becoming extremely active. Great disturbances will occur up the west coast of America, and even into Alaska itself. However, look to Vesuvius, Etna and off the Canary Islands here, for the initiation, you see, and then see them moving forward around the world.

CHAPTER TWO

Future Earth Changes

NOTE THAT SEVERAL PREDICTIONS REPRODUCED BELOW IN THEIR ORIGINAL TIMEFRAME HAVE BEEN UPDATED WITH NEW INFORMATION IN APPENDIX I. THE OLDER PREDICTIONS ARE LEFT UNTOUCHED SO THAT READERS CAN SEE THE SUBTLE CHANGES IN THE NATURE OF PROPHECY OVER TIME.

THE MAYAN CALENDAR APPEARS TO END ON DECEMBER 21, 2012, WHICH HAS LED A NUMBER OF PEOPLE TO DRAW VARIOUS CONCLUSIONS ABOUT THE SIGNIFICANCE OF THAT DATE. WHAT IS THE REAL SIGNIFICANCE?

The obvious is that the first day of the last day will be the beginning day of the next day. You will find that this is a time in which there will be a shift from one consciousness to another, from one cosmic location to another. As you can see now in this time (a time that many will deem chaotic) it is a time that is ending.

Specifically, there will be an alignment in the heavens of certain planets in the solar system; the configuration will be such that the world you live upon will begin to feel gyrations and vibrations, and the disturbances will go through the crust itself. Leading up to this point, there are already circumstances taking place upon the planet. The core is spinning at a different speed than the crust. The poles are wobbling, and they are wandering. The equator is expanding and contracting. The stabilizing influences of the ice fields at the poles of the planet are now shrinking and reducing their stabilizing influence. The oceans are heating up, terribly so, and beneath the seas there are more volcanoes than there are above, and some of them are spewing lava at great rates, even now. The atmosphere of the planet is changing as well, and this hastens the heating up of the oceans.

As such, these contributing influences will arrive in conclusion, or what might be considered in a singular point on this date. Up to this point, there will be more cyclones and hurricanes. The oceans will continue to heat up, and the winds will change. The planet will begin the process of reversing its rotation, as well as a pole shift. This is the significance of this date. You will begin to see these worldly events coinciding with certain events as you look upon the planet itself, that they will seemingly be inexplicable, or they will be of such magnitude they would never have been thought possible. For this day in question, it is not apocalyptic, nor is it the end of the world, but it is a time in which you will find an accumulation of such events that will tip the scales. For the outcome of these events is that the world will wobble, the sun will be setting in the western sky and it will then rise in the same. The oceans will become blackened, and the planet will become hot.

Specifically speaking to this date, it is a calculated bottom of the cycle; as it would come to that arrival point, it will begin to turn, and the planet will turn to these new experiences. This reinvention of the planet will begin, you see. It will not be a single event, if you would expect one; nor will there will be a cessation in the world, as you know it. But it will be an accumulation of these things that will cause worldly changes *that are happening even at this moment!* Expect increased activity in volcanoes and earthquakes; more so at that point in time, than at any other.

This will be the fifth destruction of the world, as you know it. There is the probability that it will be far-reaching and devastating; much more devastating than can be imagined. That which will occur will occur, and it will not be similar to anything in recent memory, as of the human race mind. But there are groups of people, groups of minds now who are in the world, who are attempting to alter or change it, and prevent the world from going through such destruction. There is an opportunity for all members of the human race to cooperate with each other, to give that which is moral, as to justice. Through this, the world can alter or change its path. There need not be the loss of life that would be extensive.

As this continues, as the world turns, so to speak, you will find that the Law of One will return; the ancient comprehension that all things come from a creative source, all things are inter-related, and all things living in harmony live long, and they prosper. Those that do not, those that live in conflict, shorten their life span. This will take some education or some knowledge, and then these people who live in such environments will be able to save themselves. But it is not for anyone to say that this or that must take place. For those who have circumstances, they will work out and find a place, so that they will be content as they go through this time of uncertainty, for each has its role to play, you see.

This will be just prior to the greater collapse of those land-masses on the west coast of North America and those areas that would be on the eastern seaboard of China and Japan; even the coastlines of the islands of the Philippines, New Guinea, and Australia.

Look to Etna and Vesuvius, and you will see that when they are in harmony with each other, spewing ash and smoke, it would be like the key has been turned in the lock, the door has been opened, and the proverbial "Pandora's Box" has been released of those difficulties into the world itself. For those who have ears, let them hear. Move inland from the coastlines, or move up to higher land, so you are not suffering the intrusions when the oceans are rocked from their basins. See?

This would be the last, prior to the tipping, or bobbing and weaving of the planet itself. Then there will be a time in which it will settle, and the rotation would turn back to normal. There will be some scorching of the planet, from the rays of the sun, and there will be some freezing in places that will be furthest away from the sun. People will live in caves, in some areas. But this will be short-lived. Rather than fear, be prepared. Smoke, dust, and ash will cause breathing difficulties in some places in the Northern Hemisphere, and these would best be prepared for, as well.

It will take a long time to clean up, a long time to bury the bodies, a long time to regenerate food, and a long time to purify the water (which will be mostly adulterated with salt, excrement, or pollutants and sediments). Fresh water will be difficult to find, and in the future will be the most expensive commodity, you see.

APPROXIMATELY WHEN WILL THIS HAPPEN?

Understand this: that point that you would call pivotal has not been reached yet! There is an opportunity first for the world to maintain some equilibrium. The minds and hearts of those people upon the planet are basically what you would call the rudder on the ship. The wheel has not been turned yet. As long as there is the same course, then you would find that within the second to the fifth year from this point in time [2011], there would be these changes made. But these

would not come all at once, or simultaneous. Rather, look to Mount
Vesuvius and Etna. When simultaneously there are disturbances in
these two mountains, then you will see the quickening, or the beginning of quakes and shakes and disturbances.These will affect the
coastlines of North and South America. They will affect the Orient,
and Japan even more so. They will affect the European countries in
which there would be the rising up of certain levels of the ocean, and
the shorelines will be slowly, yet steadily inundated, irreparably, with
flooding; Africa, too, you see.

PLEASE EXPLAIN WHAT IS MEANT BY THE FIFTH DESTRUCTION?

This would be the ensuing circumstances in which the world would
find itself, you see. There have been (and there is a possibility of an
additional) experience you would call destruction. The fifth is now
at hand; the Hopi Indian have seen this, as have the aboriginals in
Australia in which the Great Rock has broken in two. You would find
there are many signs, such as the White Buffalo, and many other phenomena having been predicted; snow in Africa, for instance; and in
the Arabian lands, the blackness of the sky while in the daytime.
There is a shift in the planet, and from this point of view, it is the
heat in the oceans that is the cause. As in the last destruction, there
will be disturbances now, and there has been the manipulation of nature and the forces of nature, as in the time before. But it is the wobbling of the planet, based on the heating up of the world from the
oceans themselves, that are causing the stabilizing caps or ice caps
to melt, to dislodge, and to shrink. It is only a matter of time until
this place you call Earth would look like a top, and will flip, or spin,
or slip into a different rotation where the setting sun in the west will
rise from the west to the east (instead of what is now from the east

to the west).

You will find the floor of the Mediterranean will begin to rise. You will also find that there would be increased activity along the western regions of the European coast. This would extend in the south, from Spain, to the north, Finland, or even further to Iceland. This will be the first that would cause conditions to alter or change. The Earth will wobble as it is continuing to exceed its balance point. But last, of course, will bethe alteration to the mountain ranges in the Western hemisphere, and disturbances caused in the Pacific, in which there will be, again, the rising of land, as there will be the rising of land east of Bimini, in the Atlantic.

There will be continued volcanic activity which will cause the sea to be black and the sky to be filled with clouds of dust. This will come from the west and go towards the east. The end result will be a certain wobble, and the crust of the Earth will slip on its molten core. This will be a sign of the changes; the face of the Earth being altered and not recognizable as it would be seen in the present day.

Already, the disturbances are occurring. Look, therefore, to the western regions of the Pacific which are the precursors or the warnings that will happen, as there will be disturbances in Australia and Japan. The reciprocal aspects will be to these two points, Etna and Vesuvius; within a very short period of time, they will respond. For what happens on one side of the planet occurs directly opposite on the other. The Mediterranean and the south Pacific are somewhat linked, as you would understand it. Expect, therefore, the floor of the sea to rise. More violent activities which are occurring already in the Canary Islands will continue. In the sea shore near Gibraltar and Huelva, Spain, there will be a lever effect or a 'pulling up,' and the floor of the Mediterranean will rise. This will cause flooding along the coastlines of Spain and France.

This would be an indication of what you would call the first change, prior to what will be the onslaught or recognition of changes, moving very quickly. For there will be activities – earthquakes – that will be rapid thereafter. As the heating of the oceans continues, the quaking and shaking and disturbances on the planet will speed up. This is now occurring and will continue for the next few months and will ultimately be evidence of this condition in the area, as we have just given.

The subterranean worlds are active with flows of lava, steam, gas, and sulfur. Methane gas, and other poisonous gases will be released into the air. These will be conditions you would see as precursors to what will be the first of the disturbances that will be recognized in a major way, you see.

WHAT IS CAUSING THE OCEANS TO HEAT UP?

Destruction. We find that in the floor of the ocean there are destructive influences that are causing crevasses and separations in the crust of the Earth itself. Here, there have been caves and channels which have been depleted; the removal of gaseous substances associated with natural gas and oil fields, as you would call them. Although some of them have been filled with salt water or seawater or other aspects of filler, they have removed the integral influences of pressure; and, as such, there has been some collapse, or fissures have occurred. Certain shifting has happened in the world's crust.

As has been given previously, there was a change in the rotation. The speed of the crust is moving at a different speed than the core; and as such, one is slower, the other faster. Needless to say, this type of friction removes the integrity of the mantle from the crust, or the harder, cooler elements you would call the Earth. As such, this friction and this movement further weakens any already weakened areas. Pressure is unequal in certain places, and the natural occurrences of the folds in the Earth's crust, due to the velocity of the planet on its axis, being changed by the wobbling influence is causing, here, further loss of integrity in the crust itself. As you may know, the Earth wobbles on its axis. This is creating more fissures, more cracks, more quaking and disturbances in the landmasses above and below the surface of the ocean.

The cause of this is quite complex, but understand that if you had a crust around a liquid ball – a molten ball, at that – then you could see that as there would be the shaking, the wobbling, and the collapsing of pressures from the outside or surface downward, inward there would be considerable pressures built up between the molten, liquid center or core, and the harder, not-so-liquid surface. This pressure and this lava (or molten Earth, if you will) must escape, and it tends to do this through volcanic activity, through the cracks and fissures in the Earth, above and below the surface of the oceans or waterways. These volcanic disturbances are, indeed, vents that go from the surface directly to the center or core of the world, you know.

As such, this heats up the ocean, and as the oceans heat up, this has disastrous effects upon the delicate balance of all the creatures, the landmasses, and the atmospheres about the Earth itself. One degree is troublesome. Two degrees are frightening. Three degrees are disastrous. *Four degrees are terrible, terrible disasters!* We are past the first degree, and well on the way to the second degree of increased heat in the oceans, you see. This will speed up or be accelerated as the oceans percolate, so to speak, by that which is at the center, between the mantle and the crust.

HAVE THE CRUST AND THE CORE ALWAYS BEEN ROTATING AT DIFFERENT RATES,

OR IS THIS A NEW PHENOMENON?

Before this period in time, there has been a more constant, synchronized rotation between the core and the crust. Only at three other times have there been a disassociation or a disconnect, or what would be called an unequal rotation.

WHAT HAS CAUSED THIS DIFFERENTIAL IN ROTATIONS TO OCCUR?

As in all the other cases (and in this, the present time itself), humankind has studied the laws of nature, have harnessed the forces of nature, and they have used them. The consequence of this use has now caused circumstances to be set in motion. *Humankind does not know all the laws of nature!* And consequently when there is a disturbance in one area, there is the consequence or a disturbance in another. The balance between the activities in the world, you know – the consistency you might say – has been altered; yes, by certain uses of terrible weaponry [atomic weapons] to consume the planet itself, by digging mines in the Earth, and destroying the air or atmosphere above, by affecting the waterways.

But most importantly it is the attitude. It is the minds of all who live on the planet, their selfish aggrandizement, that might be considered the greatest cause of all, combined with all the others we have just given, you see. Bear in mind, this is not the first time the planet has wobbled and spun in space. During the Ice Age, it was much worse; the world had flipped three times, and was exaggerated in its orbit. This time, the planet will not shift too much in the orbit, but the rotation will be reversed, as there will be some change in the location of the poles, north and south.

IS THE WOBBLE THAT IS CURRENTLY TAKING PLACE HAPPENING BECAUSE OF
THIS SAME SET OF CIRCUMSTANCES, OR BECAUSE OF SOMETHING ELSE?

It is as of the same. You must understand there are certain pulls upon
the planet from without, as well. The planetary influences you would
call gravity are pulling the planet apart, like dough between fingers.
As you pull them apart, there is a certain stretching. The stretching
of the planet has also weakened the surface; and this, too, adds to
the complexity of fissures, and quaking, and disturbances that are
seen in the weaker points already. Has there not been the melting of
the ice caps? Yes. The caps act as stationary weights, holding the
planet in its axis so that the angle and the spin are constant. Because
of this melting, the stabilizing influences that hold the planet in its
orbit are loosening their grip, and they will wobble and slip because
there is no stabilizing influence or ice cap left, north or south, you
see. And for a while, equilibrium of the planet will be disturbed.

YOU HAVE DESCRIBED AN ALIGNMENT OF THE PLANETS IN THE SOLAR SYSTEM
WITH THE EARTH AT THE CENTER AND THE PLANETS FORMING A V. WILL THIS
ALSO CREATE A GRAVITATIONAL PULL ON THE EARTH THAT WILL HAVE CONSE-
QUENCES THAT YOU HAVE JUST BEEN DESCRIBING?

It will have the effect that the planet will be pulled in three directions, like the letter Y. The Earth will be at the apex or intersection.
Two arms will lead away from the planet at about a thirty degree
angle or split. The planets will be lined up, two larger on one side,
one larger on the other, and the rest of the planets will be dispersed
equally between the same. The sun will be behind the Earth, and
there will be a pull in three different ways. The effect of this alignment will be the shredding, shall we call it, of the seams that hold

the planet together.

WILL THE AVERAGE PERSON BE ABLE TO FEEL THE GRAVITATIONAL PULL AT THAT TIME?

Yes, there will be felt this, of course. Coming up to that point in time, even as we see NOW, there will be disturbances in the mind, and the heart, and the dark side of humans will come forth. We have given this previously; some time ago; decades ago. And as the dark side of humans come forth, as violence is shed upon the Earth, it is like lighting the wick on a bomb. Humans have the chance to avoid this time of despair, and great destruction, grief and difficulty, but it requires NOW the time for them to come together. Not to be concerned with what is beyond them too much, for they cannot help it, but to be preoccupied with how they can change or improve their own environment, their own backyard, so to speak. But if not, then, indeed, there will be the continuation of selfish aggrandizement, lack of compassion or caring. The planet is resilient; the planet responds to what it is fed. And in such a way, yes there will be difficulty.

COULD YOU BRIEFLY DESCRIBE THE PREVIOUS FOUR DESTRUCTIONS OF THE EARTH?

Prior to this one, it would be considered when there would be the change in what you would know as the Atlantean experience, which would be the ten thousand, five hundredth year prior to the entering in of the Master, or Jesus the Nazarene. This would be the five large landmasses that were submerged and became muddy fields or areas before sinking further into the abyss. This was caused by two groups being in warfare of civil conflict; those who were known as the Sons of Belgal and those who were the Sons of the Law of One. The Sons of Belgal were misusing the forces of nature, which they had, in those times, learned how to manipulate, or how to utilize. We speak of something similar to the atomic age as it was ushered in, and of the use of atomic energy or power, to give a reference point, you see. For at that point in time, there was the use of those forces that would allow ships to be lighter than air, and the maneuvering of those vehicles that would go through the air and the sea, through the use of the "terrible crystals," you see. And here, these forces were brought to bear upon the planet itself, through the selfishness and the arrogance, or the aggrandizement of the Sons of Belgal who were, through their selfish ends, causing the destruction, you see. As for the Sons of the Law of One, their attempt was to be united with all things and not to have selfish tendencies; but they were attempting to cooperate with all things, including nature, and to be communicative with God Almighty.

Prior to that, there was what is known as the Ice Age. Here, this would be a time in which the planet flipped or spun, and wobbled wildly in its orbit, and was exaggerated or tumbled slightly further out of its orbit. This was caused by certain explosions in the galaxy, in the solar system itself. The remnants can be seen as the rings around Saturn, the return of large comets on a regular basis, and the meteor shower "zone," as it might be called, between Mars and Jupiter. These would be the fragments of certain collisions that took place within the solar system, nearest to the Earth. If you would examine the moon, you would see projectiles had struck it in a specific array, as if a large shotgun blast would have taken place, and you would see evidence on the moon itself, that there would be such an array, as if a large force struck the moon, and smaller fragments radiated out around the center. This would be evidence of this time, which would be about the fifty thousandth year, extending a little further in time.

You would then go to that time that would be "in the beginning;" a time in which the planet itself was ravaged with fire. Here, there were volcanic explosions and eruptions. This would not be at the time of the great beasts, for this would be a later time, but it would be a time in which the planet itself was racked with explosions and volcanic activities; for, the planet itself was being formed and there was a cooling time. Large landmasses in the Pacific, as you would know the Pacific now, were above the surface of the water itself. There was migration of the great plates. South America and Africa were one country, or one place, as you would know it. Larger landmasses were in the Pacific, as given, and here, many of the isles or tthe ring in what would be the New Guinea area itself were a large plateau or landmass.

Prior to that, it would be the aspects of those beings that were inhabiting the planet itself. Here, this would be a destructive force, in which there was the invasion of certain influences into bodies or vehicles, as they might be seen. There was a development, and this would be considered a time in which the planet itself faced uncertainty, and there was a pillage, or the use of all things carnal and material, and those souls that entered into the world manipulated matter themselves, and caused the planet to react. This reaction caused the living in caves, and the variances of the climates, and the planet itself spun and rotated in different directions. This was at the will of those beings that were new, shall we call it, to incarnating into matter, and they enjoyed themselves at the destruction of matter. They were careless and caused destructions upon the planet itself!

IS IT POSSIBLE TO APPROXIMATE A TIME FOR THESE LAST TWO DESTRUCTIONS,

COUNTING BACKWARDS FROM THE TIME OF CHRIST?

The Atlantean experiences were ten thousand five hundred to eleven thousand years before the entering in of the Nazarene. Prior to that, it would be between sixty thousand and seventy thousand years. What would be previous to that would be almost one hundred to one hundred and fifty thousand years. And prior to that, it would be something in the neighborhood of close to five hundred thousand years, as you would know them. However, understand this is approximate, for the orbit of the planet was different! Humans, as you know humans, lived at different life spans, and we give this as reference of a time frame in the current measurement of time, you see.

WHAT WAS LIFE LIKE IN ATLANTIS?

Let us begin by saying that the time frame you refer to would be before the eleven thousand five hundredth year before the entering in of Jesus the Nazarene, you see. During that time, the world was quite similar to the world today, yet different. It was more of an agricultural-based society, but it was also combined with a high artistic development; and, indeed, this creative ability would be seen in certain artworks and construction of monuments and buildings. This form of agricultural society, so to speak, would be seen also in Egypt and in Brazil *at this point in time*: masses of people living together, moving about primarily by foot. In that time, they had devices that would move through the air and through the water with the same ability. They would float, but in fact would be motivated by electrical, magnetic and anti-magnetic means; gravity being the force that was manipulated. Disturbing the push/pull effect of gravity, the craft would move through just about any substance that was capable, like water or air, and as such, there would be a certain limitation only to the operator's ability. They would tend to go very quickly in any direction in a straight line. In the cockpit or cabin, if you will, anyone within the same would not feel the effects of gravity.

There were large parties or celebrations. There was the use of the forces of nature; the understanding of how to use them, you see. And, as such, there were supplies of all that is needed. These forces or these supplies would allow individuals to maintain themselves. There were no electric bills, or gas bills, you see, for there were certain devices that used vibration, both for the heating and maintaining of a building, as well as the cooling and the cleansing of the building.

However, a likely day would be seen much the same as an ordinary day in the present time. People would get up at a certain time and go through their routine; then, there would be a movement towards the left or the right, and people would move. Again, social activities would be the same, but there was a certain degree of hierarchy: those who would be at the higher realms were more like dictators or emperors, and those at the lower realms were more like those who would play artistic sounds, or music, and would discuss the world itself philosophically. Those who were workers or who were in law enforcement or security, would have what would be considered jobs. Those that were the Things or the slaves, as you would call them, had mundane, repetitious jobs and were schooled and bred for this position; a monotonous life, you see!

Food seems to be the same. Any multiple growth of food would be from that time. The banana, or banana tree as you might call it, would be from the time of Atlantis. Coconuts would be the same. Wherever you find multiples of the same food, such as grapes or clusters of berries would be from these ancient times. They were engineered or selected, that they would produce multiple offerings of the fruit (or the vegetable for that matter) from the single plant or host.

Beverages would include what would be seen now, such as alcohol, teas and herbal teas, as you would call it. Coffee and cocoa were not readily used in the same way as today.

Dance and the categories of dance were very important. Here, significant amount of social standing was evident on how well one could dance, and how well one could remember the dance steps, you see. Political natures were seen in groups, but primarily certain regions would have one person responsible as benevolent dictators. The person responsible would be furthered in his career not by how much wealth he alone materialized or acquired, but rather by how much good he would do for the society, you see. There was communication with the higher realms or dimensions above, and there would be a complete understanding of the clock in space itself; actually tracking the solar system's migration through space. There were many who were prophets, who would see the future. Seeing in part, they understood, but they did not comprehend.

There were world meetings; there was a congress coming together from various countries to discuss the tidal situations, the weather concerns, what to do with the large beasts that roamed the Earth, and also some mining capabilities, you see. Again, as we look over the place, it would not be too much different than what it is now, save for the ability to transport through mediums itself. There were certain elements that would attempt to advance themselves in the society; these would be more war-like; they would wish to have supreme dominance. They did have the availability to affect nature at the cell level, and there was experimentation in which there would be the use of the Things made into other things, you see. There was a certain availability to harness nature at the cell level, and crystalline influences, or forces that would be stimulated by crystal were often used. They would harness the great forces of nature, for they did understand the same, and it was quite prestigious for any who knew how to handle or manipulate the forces of nature.

WHAT SORT OF MANIPULATION OF NATURE WAS DONE?

This is somewhat similar in today's world in which you would find the breeders of dogs take the best dogs in their breed, and they breed them together to get a superior animal. And then superior animals are bred together to get an even more superior animal. In this way, there was the taking of the Things, and there was the development of those beings that would be allocated to repetitious, laborious positions. The Sons of Belgal were the ones responsible for this, for they cherished the wealth that the Things would produce for them. And as such, the Things were kept in low quarters. And experimentation was done at the cell level through the use of sound waves, vibrations, and the use of crystalline forces, you see.

WHAT WAS THE POPULATION OF ATLANTIS LIKE?

Prior to the dislocation or the breakup into the five sections, you would have similar to Brazil, or Tokyo; diverse but with more pure-race Atlanteans; but the social structure was diverse. Seven billion would be the total number, you see.

COULD YOU PLEASE EXPLAIN WHY THEIR TECHNOLOGY DID NOT PERSIST AMONGST THOSE WHO SURVIVED THE DESTRUCTION?

What makes you think it did not? If you would study Egypt, you would find that suddenly, almost overnight, it went from an agricultural nation, into a superpower in the world itself. Moses, and others used the force of gold, that was both beaten and crystalline; the Ark of the Covenant, you see. There was electricity, although its formation or development was different than the generator or the alternator. You would find that changes in Mexico and Arizona happened as well. There were degrees of light that were used, although it would be lower light. Walls would glow as they would be illuminated. And to some degree you would find toys and little things *in this time* that are remnant of that time. The use of rays or prisms was made even unto Roman times. Signals of light by reflection, either on mirrors or other surfaces would be memories of those substances that were used in the time in which the continent was still whole, you see. When you find societies that had water delivery or purification, or you find organizations that had a greater understanding of the chemical nature of things on the outside, you would see reflections or understandings of that which once was in the Atlantean era itself, you see.

There were many such implementations, but when the continent broke up into the five islands, there was a derailment of the flows of energy. If you would look in the Northern Hemisphere, you would find that a certain grid exists in holy places, pyramids and temples; in each of these places, there would be a level of mica and carbon at the bottom. You would see that this would be part of the anti-gravity/gravity transportation mechanism; a highway, so to speak. The terrible crystals themselves would be an exemplification of harnessing the forces of nature. It is still evident here, at this point in time. But when large gaps in the land cause certain temples to disappear under the sea's surface, and the crystals themselves to sink, then you would find that the generation of these influences that would cause the disruption of gravity, was at fault – and no one paid attention or knew how to retain it! See?

WHEN ATLANTIS WAS DESTROYED, WERE THE "TERRIBLE CRYSTALS" DESTROYED AS WELL, OR WERE THEY JUST SUBMERGED BENEATH THE WATER?

They appear to be evident as our perspective would be. They are still near Bimini itself.

DO THEY STILL HAVE SOME KIND OF CAPACITY TO AFFECT MATTER?

There is some disturbance, but we do not find any pulsing, or maser, or taser or laser effect, you see. They seem to be in darkness, which hibernates their power, you see.

DO YOU FORESEE THAT THEY WILL BE RE-USED IN THE FUTURE?

Should there be the discovery of the same, yes. The location is uncertain, and there will be some shifting or changes to the plates that may cause them to be submerged even further. However, when there is the opening of the Hall of Records near what you would call the paw of the Sphinx, there will be known to the peoples of the world at that point in time some of the technologies, some of the abilities, that nature provides; and, indeed, there will be an attempt to reinvent or to use these forces in nature. Depending how it is propagated, it would be either positive or it would be destructive.

RETURNING TO TODAY'S TIME, IT SEEMS MANY PEOPLE HAVE REPORTED HEARING STRANGE HUMMING OR BUZZING SOUNDS LATELY. COULD YOU PLEASE DE-

TERMINE THE SOURCE OF THESE?

Primarily this would be the electromagnetic influences in the atmosphere, as there are increased frequencies being broadcast. In the early days, there were radio waves and telegraphs, then the higher frequencies of the microwave, and now just about everyone on the planet has their own communication device. This increased electrical/magnetical energy is emanating from all sorts of spots artificially and we would find that the atmosphere is congested with all sorts of frequencies in the higher levels. This is causing skin and muscle of the human body (which is fragile) to deteriorate. And as such, there would be this hearing or this reverberation within the physical, human body itself and the sensation of a vibration or a shimmer. Now, also, there is a wobbling taking place upon the planet itself. This is disturbing the magnetic flux lines or the north/south magnetic poles. This, too, is reacting to the sound frequency, as you would call it, and it is being disturbed or disrupted. Whenever there is a certain twang or shift that is abrupt, it is largely the magnetic poles moving, you see, and they are moving a lot!

WHAT WILL BE THE NEW LOCATION OF THE NORTH AND SOUTH POLES?

They will tip to about the forty-five degree angle from which is presently seen. They may go a little further, you see. But the planet itself will wobble like the figure eight. The coming to rest will depend on certain gravitational pulls in the solar system. However, to the question, as we would perceive it, look to the Bering Strait, and you would have the north pole; look to off the coast of Australia and you would have the south pole, you see. One will move from its present location in a westerly direction towards the Bering Sea or Strait, towards Russia and Alaska, in that region or area, perhaps a little further towards the equator or southerly direction. The other will be directly on the other side of the planet. Here, close to what would be the Australian region or area. But the protrusion will be perhaps a little to the west of those areas you would call the islands in the Philippines, you see.

PLEASE GIVE MORE DETAIL WITH REGARD TO THE SLIPPING OF THE EARTH'S CRUST AND THE CHANGE TO THE AXIS OF ROTATION?

It is simply that the axis itself will spin or wobble, as if a top would be spun on a table, and as it starts to lose its velocity, it starts to wobble in the shape of a figure eight. Then, as it comes to rest, it tilts abruptly. The planet itself is spinning at twenty-four thousand miles an hour. As it starts to slip, it will decelerate. As it does so, the water will continue to move at the same velocity, and, as such, will spill out of the basins, and will go across the land. But as we see it, the axis will wobble magnetically, will wander while the poles themselves will change gradually, slipping over to what you have expected. The magnetic poles will wobble greatly. And like crossed swords, they seem to come to some rest, you see.

The planet is not actually a sphere; it is more like a cinder or rectangular shape (the planet without the water, we are speaking of). The water, being fluid, can migrate from place to place. If you look at the poles at this point in time, then see them being pulled down. The north now could be pulled towards Japan. The south now could be pulled up, towards Madagascar.

WHEN THE PHYSICAL POLE SHIFT OCCURS, HOW LONG WILL IT TAKE FROM THE BEGINNING OF THE TUMBLING ON ITS AXIS UNTIL THE PLANET SETTLES INTO A

NEW ROTATION?

Not too long. It may take forty-eight hours or it may take, with some pre-wobbling, and post-wobbling, about three to seven weeks. Not too long.

AFTER THE CHANGE IN ROTATION TAKES PLACE, WILL THE EARTH BE ROTATING AT THE SAME SPEED AS IT IS NOW?

It will rotate a little slower, and then it will accelerate. It will depend upon the inertia of the oceans, for they will wash out of their basins, but then they will subside again, and the Earth will wobble a little, while this is taking place. But as there will be a tumbling and spinning at the same time, they will counter-balance one another. You can watch the sun go to set in the west, hold stationary for a time, and then rise from the west to the east, you see. This crucial time may take a day or three.

AND DURING OR AFTER THIS EVENT WILL GRAVITY OR OTHER NATURAL LAWS BE AFFECTED?

To the stabilizing influences, yes. It would be like taking molten metal in a fifty-gallon drum, spinning it around while the metal would be super-hot in the middle. It will cling to the edges by centrifugal force, but as it would become more stable, it will accumulate or become of a more critical mass. Now, consider the drum spinning or rotating very quickly, and then also if you would see an up and down axis and the drum spinning on a vertical axis, for one reference point, then if you were to have a horizontal axis going through the barrel and you were to see the barrel tip over or spin on a horizontal axis, it would actually end up with a figure-eight so to speak, as a point of travel. This would be the accumulation of the metal as the molten metal would come to rest. It would take some time to unfix itself from the walls or the inside area of the planet. This is why it might take some time for stabilization to occur, you see. At the same time it would be a thrust upward, causing large disturbances in the crust, and the planet's weight will be altered in certain places, due to the sudden and fast movement of some ocean basins, you see.

When the Earth tumbles on its axis, and the oceans are rocked from their basins, how will people physically react?

They will be flattened to the ground a little, or they will be unaware, depending on where they are. The pivotal points will shift. Those along the coastlines, of course, will suffer an inundation of water, you see. For the water will come inland, but as it does it will surge and lessen in its surge. Its weight will shift on the landmass and the planet may stabilize as the water retreats. Those on the American coastlines should live two hundred miles inland, as a rule of thumb, if they wish to avoid this condition, you see.

However, it will be disorienting to those who are near the axis points and other certain areas. Because it feels as if the planet is rotating at a greater velocity in the areas of the equator, those who live in this area will suffer. Now there is not really a difference in velocity, but it will feel the same, for the sense of gravity will be different. These people will be flattened to the ground, dizzy, and disoriented, as if spinning in a circle for a time, and then letting themselves go. They cannot stand. Otherwise, they will be sick, they will be dizzy, they will be frightened. And others may be unscathed, you see. We are speaking from a perspective of looking at certain groups of people, from South America to North American, from Europe to Asia, Africa, and Australia to other points as we describe these experiences, you see.

HOW WILL THIS EVENT AFFECT PEOPLE EMOTIONALLY?

It is difficult to describe, you see. Understand there will be a flurry of activity. There will rise up new, powerful people who will have a certain sway with everyone on what to do. Emotionally, they will be willing to cooperate, willing to be used, while some will bury themselves in caves and holes, you see, and not wish to come out of the ground for some time! Different peoples, different reactions, as you might imagine!

WILL THERE BE MORE HOURS IN A DAY, OR WILL THERE BE MORE DAYS IN A YEAR, AFTER THE EARTH CHANGES?

Using the present calendar, as you would understand it, we would find that the day might be a little shorter – twenty-three hours for a short time (or it could be as low as twenty-two hours for a time as well). However, the orbit does not seem to change, and therefore there would be about the same amount of days; the year could be a little longer to three hundred and seventy days, but this would be only due to the centrifugal force or the elliptical orbit. There is a small possibility that it would be lesser in days, as the orbit might shrink a little, but this would be only for a short time.

WHAT STAR WILL WE LOOK TO AS THE GUIDING STAR OR "NORTH STAR" FOR NAVIGATION?

This appears to be the center star of Orion's belt. Sirius will also be close. This will be for the wobbling time we are looking at, you see. Look to Sirius Minor.

WILL THE GRAVITATIONAL PULL OF THE EARTH BE STRONGER OR LESSER AFTER THE DESTRUCTION HAS TAKEN PLACE?

At certain times, it will be lesser, but after the first four to five years it will be about the same as now, or just slightly more. Depending on the rotation and the movement of the mantle under the crust, and the speed of the two when they are synchronized, the gravitational pull will be about the same, but perhaps a little more. But, up until that time, it will be less.

DO YOU FORSEE ICEBERGS COLLIDING WITH ANY PARTICULAR LANDMASS?

There will continue to be the chunks of ice, but they will not be so extensive. We are observing brown ice and ice fields that are resident on top of landmasses or islands, and they are melting where they are. Understand the heat of the oceans may cause further breaking away of the ice fields or chunks, but because of the heat of the oceans and the atmosphere being heated, and the prevailing winds carrying hot, warm air or gases into the Arctic and Antarctic, the fields will melt right where they sit. Therefore, we do not find great sheets of ice breaking away, but there will be some of that that has occurred already. We have brown, dirty ice at the lower levels, for these have accumulated since the previous destruction. See?

WILL THERE BE ANY CHANGES IN SUNSPOT ACTIVITY TAKING PLACE IN THE COMING YEARS?

We would perceive that the sunspots in this particular time will, indeed, be more than flare-ups. There will be a series: a larger flare-up or sunspot itself, and then smaller, and then smaller, and then smaller and smaller. It appears to be four, if not five to seven of these tapering or smaller appearances, you see? The unusual aspect is that they will be in a horizontal or straight line, if you will, from a certain perspective. This will have the effect of disturbing electrical/magnetical services or storages. More importantly, it will have an effect upon the human body. It would be like a tuning fork being struck; certain vibrations or frequencies would be felt inside the nervous system of people. *This is now already taking place*, as there is certain resilience within the vibrational effects. It is called Harmonics, and this is somewhat known in the world at this point. However, the vibrational effect is such that as harmonic upon harmonic is built, and the vibration rate is maintained and intensified, it has the ability to crack or break steel or to affect any sentient being, or any object, as you would understand it. The effects will primarily be seen in the electrical storages of information; electrical/magnetic storage, you see. The influence will be subtle, the observances will be academically stimulating.

The real effect will be unseen, but it will be felt, as it will cause derogatory or negative feelings or sensations to manifest themselves within a physical body. There will be an influx of vibration that will be adverse to the human body (as well as to certain aspects in the Earth). There is a certain resilience and a certain reverberation that will be set up in the planet itself, for the vibrations will have derogatory effects and they will cause certain degrees of emotional waning and complaining and futility and sort of frightfulness that will come upon people, you see. For those who are already imbalanced emotionally and mentally, it would be like striking a drum. It will intensify the feelings within them. For those who have derogatory thoughts, or even murderous intentions, it will inflame them! For those who have virtuous intentions and aspirations to touch upon those forces on high, it will enlighten them and it will inspire them. But the overall effect will be to intensify whatever is taking place or emotionally felt within large groups of people. The ones who wish to have war will have a fearfulness of war and will be on guard; the ones who are pacifists who wish not to have war will have a certain sense of either accomplishment, or a sense of hopelessness and abandonment. For all others in between, the emotional characteristics of the ordinary people will be uncertain. However, some will be driven forward and inspired by this, and they will have insights into certain devices that would use electricity, magnetism, and gravity in such a way that they will be able to control the gravitational influx or gravitational pull as you would call it. To those in leadership positions, it will either make friends more friendly, or it will make enemies even more bitter. It is a harmonic. The harmonics will increase; for you do not need the large influence after, but you need it consistent, and in descending order. This will amplify the situation, for whatever cause or purpose it is directed.

WHAT TIME FRAME CAN WE EXPECT THIS TO OCCUR?

You will see these effects within a mere series of months, but the effects will be long-ranged you see; we are looking forward in the next ten years.

WORLD-WIDE, WHAT PERCENTAGE OF HUMANKIND IS NOT LIKELY TO SURVIVE THE COMING EARTH CHANGES?

From the perspective that nothing is going to change, and there will be the continued violence and the continued suspicion and hatred in the world, as you presently see – provided there is no change whatsoever – then approximately two-thirds of those who are on the planet at this point in time will not survive this time of travail, this time of change. For, here, there will be great upheavals. These are seen even now, as the planet is heating up. For those who have eyes, let them see; for those who have ears, let them hear. The planet is spiraling out of control in what would be the changes that are upon it. One would have to be blind and deaf not to pay attention! From the poles which are melting, to the Pacific Rim which is on fire, to the nations in Europe and Africa (and other places in the Pacific and Atlantic), there is, indeed, a heating up of the oceans, and the balance is quite crucial. One degree change in temperature is disastrous, troublesome. And there will be a change of at least four degrees of higher temperature! The sharks will seek the coolness of fresh water because the oceans will be so hot. There will be quaking and shaking, as heat expands things, does it not?

Places where you have no water will be flooded. Places that have plenty of water will dry up. This will happen in all the world. Think of this: if one continent that is submerged comes above the surface (or to the surface), where will the water that it displaces go? If everything west of the Rockies falls into the water, think of this: where will the water go, as the land goes into the sea and causes an even greater displacement of water? Where does the water go? It naturally floods the plains around all the continents on the planet. However, it is not the heat of the ocean that will kill; it is the inability to breathe, for dust in the air will be extensive! Mount Vesuvius and Etna are the key! And they are rattling and sputtering even now. After this, you can expect a rapid increase in volcanic activity! Woe be to those who look at the sea and at the ground and find the place shaking and quaking and do not see the mountaintops about to explode!

There is hope for the planet, from a wider perspective, as you have directed. The sons of peace, or those who would be of the Law of One will return, and perhaps counter those who are selfish and violent. Should this be done, then as the Hopi Indian prophecy has given, humankind may have the opportunity to avert these disasters, and the planet will be cooled. Should this happen, then perhaps not so much human life will be taken. Perhaps half of what we have seen would only be necessary. Perhaps less than that, if there was, again, the Prince of Peace stepping upon the planet, stepping upon the hearts of all who are alive at this point in time, this time of travail, that has been deemed chaotic by many. However, each of you has before you the choice of light and life, or darkness and death. Choose, but do not dally! NOW IS THE TIME!

There will be a speeding up of more and more earthquakes around the world. Like flashbulbs going off at random in an arena where a sporting event is taking place, these sparks will occur, and then they will speed up; so much so that it would be almost difficult to perceive when and where they are coming, have been, or where they are about to occur again. If you look at the arena as similar to the globe itself – round, three hundred and sixty degrees – you will understand that the planet itself will not be isolated or protected in any one area; these eruptions, quakes, shakes, and movements of water or tsunami will occur very quickly.

Expect a speeding up to the region or area of Japan. Yes, there will be crevasses, and there will be longer periods of shaking of the ground and earthquakes, you see. There will be the reciprocal influences to the North American and, to some degree, the Middle American regions, you see – not to exclude South America; for they will be affected as well. But we are giving this as reciprocal, back-and-forth to these two points, you see.

As such, there will be a resurrection of those old civilizations here and there upon the planet that have been submerged for more than ten thousand years; at least the remnants or the indications of these will occur as the planet readjusts its structure, its face, if you will; its very shape! And if you would view the world in a certain way as it is presently seen, in the forthcoming future, it will not be recognized as the same planet. It will change so much! What is above the waters will be below, and what is below the waters will return to whence it once was. See?

Expect large masses of seabed to be above; expect the planet to shift in its axis or rotation, and where there would be freezing lands now, there will be moss that will grow. The Japanese region will be in a higher latitude, but the spinning will be different. This may have a similar effect in causing these conditions or movements of the plates, as the planet will tip, you see; the north pole being about the Bering Strait region with the rest of the planet moving accordingly.

Look to Italy to be the master of the world, and it will be in a tropical or semi-tropical region, you see. The island of Japan may erode from what is now the easterly side; it may become smaller indeed and there will be a migration of people towards the greater landmasses that will be in the west.

A VOLCANO RECENTLY BECAME ACTIVE IN THE CANARY ISLANDS. DO YOU SEE THIS CAUSING A TSUNAMI?

Should there be disturbances as you are describing in the Canaries and other landmasses that would be in the upper west regions of the continent itself, shifting and quaking, the Mediterranean basin would rise a little, as there would be the throbbing or the separation of certain regions or areas that would now lie in a south/southwesterly region (the Canary Islands, you see). This will affect the North American coastline, yes, to some degree, as would other disturbances that will take place in the lower portion, west of the continent itself, as of Africa. There will be a shrinkage and the shoreline will not change the shape, but will certainly change the landmass, as it would be under the water and submerged for some time.

WILL ACTIVITY IN THE MEDITERRANEAN CAUSE FLOODING IN SPAIN?

To the contrary, we see some of this coastline rising again, for this would be the ancient foot beddings or foundations of Atlantis itself. You would find that this particular area will hinge upwards in all probability, and there will be reclaimed land, so to speak, especially those that would be the marshy or submerged areas; but not too far into the area of Huelva, and other regions here. More to the south-southwest, you see. And as we see, this particular coastline will be exaggerated or will rise. To what would be further east, that which would be on the other side of the mountains, there would be more of a flooding or a stationary coastline, in which the ocean itself will creep up. Into Barcelona, it would form two inland lakes where there are now rivers. To that of San Sebastian, there would be an increase and the waters will come up the shore to a great distance, to the foothills or those hills or small rises that are now evident as dunes, you see. The entire city that is now close to this will be somewhat underwater; a few meters. To that which would be towards Portugal, you would find this, too, will be in the south rising, but in the north there would be inundations of water into certain inlets or bays. To that of the extreme east, that which would be bordering the Pyrenees, or into France itself, you would find a modest rise in the ocean, and here the waters themselves will reach inland.

The floor of the Mediterranean will come up in one place, and down in another. Look towards the gateway of the Gibraltar and you would find that these particular areas may rise a little further. To the Canary Islands themselves, possessions of Spain, we would find that these would rise up out of the water and the islands themselves may form a single mass of land, you see. To Huelva, we do not find it devastated, but we find there would be windstorms and there would be some disturbances or shaking, but the place itself seems to be on coral and rock that is rather ancient, and we do not find this submerged, but rather slightly above any rising waters, you see; as if it had been levered up. This corner of Spain would be like a turned-up corner of a mat.

EARTH CHANGES AFFECTING EUROPE

HOW WILL EARTH CHANGES AFFECT THE MEDITERRANEAN REGION?

There will be an increase in the level of the Mediterranean Sea, as well as what would ultimately be the surrounding areas of the ocean outside of the same. The floor of the Mediterranean will rise somewhat, and there will be volcanic activity that will raise and create new landmasses here, especially to the south/southwest of Spain. There will be tsunami that will go northward, and will strike the islands of the United Kingdom. This will be done by the floor of the ocean itself rocking with earthquakes. The quake will go east-and-west and the tsunami will go north-and-south. There will be the surrounding of Barcelona with water that will capture like two hands cupping the city; these will be two inland lakes. In Cordova and other places that are desert, there will be water but then there will be more heat.

To the African coastlines and to Turkey there will be much in the way of activity or disturbances, quaking and shaking. Kazakhstan, which is silent, will be suffering shaking and quaking. In the northern regions of Europe, there will be a flooding, or the ocean coming in-land, with the rising of the ocean.

In San Sebastian in Spain, you will see water coming up grad-ually, rising inland to the hills which would be in the southern area of the city itself. That which is on the shoreline now, or the beach areas of San Sebastian, will all be under water by this slow, gradual, yet steady increase of the surface of the ocean itself. This will be largely done by landmasses appearing off the coast of the Canary Is-lands, and of certain rising of a land bridge between France and the British Isles, you see. And, to some degree, the water will flow higher and faster than expected. There will be continued flooding or melting of the ice caps that will add to this condition of difficulty.

To the Red Sea, and to those areas in Africa, to the Nile itself, there will be flooding, and, indeed when there is a certain altering or changing of direction, the Nile will flow east and west again, like it used to, rather than north and south. Therefore there will be pen-etration of water inland from the Mediterranean to the delta in the Nile, and it will flood, you see.

In Greece and Italy, these will suffer volcanic activities and they will once again, spew flames, lava, and dust into the air. The prevailing winds will take it away from the country in particular, but there will be a shattering of the lifestyle of the peoples here, due to these poisonous gases and ash that will derail their economic and geographical situations, you see. There will be increased shaking and quaking activity in Malta and also in Tunis and the Gibraltar regions, as they will be affected by volcanic activity as well. But look to Vesuvius and Etna as being the instigation of this shadowy existence in Italy, you see.

WILL THERE BE FLOODING IN NORTHERN EUROPE AND ASIA?

There will not be so much of a flooding, as there will be inundations of water from above, and there will be washing over the land large waves, you see. When the planet stops in its rotation one way and begins rotating in another way, it is not a sudden stop. It is more like a twisting action, and the waves that are going east and west, when the planet begin to wobble or shift to go northeast to southwest, you can see that the oceans will rock out of their basins and sweep across large areas of landmass, as they have before, you know! This will occur in this region or area.

COULD YOU DESCRIBE THE EARTH CHANGES PERTAINING TO THE COUNTRIES OF AUSTRIA, SWITZERLAND, AND NORTHERN ITALY?

Switzerland may disappear "in the twinkle of an eye." This will be largely due to their generational separation from the rest of the world. Often they have said, "We are not our brother's keeper. We are his banker!" And as such, that which is within the ring of the Alps, Switzerland itself, we find that it would simply vanish, as it would plunge into and around what would be these disturbances, or areas of fault lines, you see.

To the remaining areas on the outside of the Alps, these seem to be basically intact, although with great destruction, disturbances, or shaking. If you would understand Switzerland and the mountains that surround it, see it as if looking in a volcano; you would look into the crater, and Switzerland would be at the base of the crater. The sides of the mountain, or volcano, would be sloping upwards. What if the sides simply collapsed flat? The crater would be filled in, would it not? And as such, it would be a flat mass or area. What once was above in the base of the crater is now buried greatly under large sheets of Earth. This is given to give some understanding of what will take place, in a very crude or rough fashion; that the country itself will evaporate.

To the other countries, those that would be towards the North Sea or close to the ocean itself, they will have water rising up and coming in the low-lying areas, and, to some degree, there will be much in the way of small lakes and rivers. From Belgium, and Germany, and, here, extending further north, you would find there will be some disturbances, although not too extensive, along the coast-lines, you see, until you find Poland where there would be more, in the flat lands, or what would be within a meter or two height of the North Sea or ocean; this will be inundated by water.

To the area of Austria, Liechtenstein, and northern Italy, and somewhat to France, there will be disturbances here. But along the coastline in the English Channel, this will tend to be more active, or more fluctuations will take place, you see, and there may be the English Channel rising up so there, once again, will be the islands conjoined with the mainland, as once was.

But here, the countries that are further around the Switzerland region will not be modified to misshape their present appearance on the map, but they may have severe quaking that will flatten many of the buildings, especially the old ones, for they will not be able to stand the up-and-down motion.

You will find that the Mediterranean, and the English Channel will be affected simultaneously almost, and they will rise up. To the British Islands, they will be either risen up with the same, or there will be a tilting; but we see that there will not be too much in the way of inundation of water. Expect them to be not flat, but more on the side of a hill, if you would call it that, in that there would be a rising up towards the Channel. But, as such, it might appear to be on a severe angle, rather than a flat, rough angle of buoyancy. Now, this is contingent on the fault lines that run through and under the Channel itself. There is a possibility that the U.K. itself will be somewhat swamped with water for a time, but if it is, it will rise again. If not, it will simply slope more on the eastern seaboard side, or eastern side of the U.K., and the Triple Crown will remain as it is; somewhat intact, and somewhat in authority financially. Otherwise, expect what would be seen currently.

SPECIFICALLY HOW WILL LONDON, ENGLAND FARE IN THE FUTURE?

First there will be some shifting of the oceans, and there will be seen some tsunami effects off the coast of Spain and Africa. This will be somewhat towards lands' end in the south/southwest regions. This will cause difficulties in the ocean currents, especially through the Channel itself, and there will be some concern about underground activities, mining and transportation. However, the country itself will seem to do quite well, and as much as there will be influences in the Spanish regions, we would find that anywhere north of the Netherlands, there will be some difficulty or some apprehension in doing business, but the crossroads will be towards Spain itself and the U.K. in an east/west direction, you see. We cannot see that it will be difficult; rather, we would see there would be varied interested parties for a variety of reasons. We see the Monarch here with many jewels upon her chest, indicating there will be wealth at the highest levels, and this seems to spill over to the lower levels as well. Therefore, the country should do well, but there will come times in which transportation difficulties will occur, and this would seemingly be frightening to those who cannot move about in rapid transit or through aeronautical vehicles. As we observe it, the country seems to be maintaining its position in its alliances with Germany, and the Western countries, both in manufacturing and in investments, you see. It will form – and it has formed – close alliances with Israel itself, and this has been a wise decision. As such, you will find they will receive benefits from this country and others when there is time or need to expand. However, there will be ocean surges to the coastlines in the south, in the southeast, and perhaps to the western areas, but to the city itself, yes there will be flooding here.

HOW WILL POLAND BE AFFECTED BY THE EARTH CHANGES?

To the northern regions, you would find some inundation of water itself. To the south, from the mountains that would be the Pyrenees, through to the south of Poland, these would be high above the waters. Expect not extensive flooding, but some flooding to the northern regions. If you would take a straight line and draw it across northern Europe, you would have an idea in general where there would be flooding, and where there would not be, you see. Expect more wind storms and quaking or shaking than inundation of water, but it will take place. And to France also on the southern side, there will be submergence of the coastline that would make it look very finger-like. And to that of the north side, there will be some rising up, or higher cliff in what would be lowland now, you see; a rocking or a shifting of this region. The Pyrenees in the middle will somewhat be influenced as to receding in their size, you see (as to these mountains or hills). We find the country France will be maintained without too much difficulty; the leadership seems to be solvent, and the people seem to be cooperative one with the other.

PLEASE COMMENT ON EARTH CHANGES THAT WILL AFFECT THE AREAS OF NORTHERN EUROPE AND IN PARTICULAR, SCANDINAVIA, THE NETHERLANDS, AND ICELAND?

As we would observe various activities within this region, the Scandinavian, the ground will shake and quake, like a vibrating bed. To that of the Netherlands, also there will be some waves going through the ground with a movement that would be reminiscent of being on top of a teeter-totter, at the pivotal point. To the Icelandic conditions, you would find the cauldron bubbling and boiling over with molten lava; for, you see, this has always been the same, as to geysers, mountains and lava (even before there would be ice on top of Iceland or Greenland, you see).

You would find conditions here are quite extraordinary in this region of the world, for there will be a corridor (as there already is) through the straits in which there would be currents that would rush very quickly. This would be from the southwest to the northeast, you might say, through the areas between the Scandinavian, Netherlands and Iceland areas. See? There will be a rising up of the sea from the Arctic towards the Russian region or coastline. This will be quite extensive, and will run almost in a straight line from the west towards the east (as you would now understand directions). This particular region will suffer mostly from the disturbances of the land shaking and quaking, but it will suffer inundations of water mostly from the northern regions where the water rises, and rises towards the south, and flows inland itself, you see?

There will be activities of spewing forth the volcanic ash out of the Icelandic region itself. The waterway will become quite warm and the ice in the region will melt quite quickly. It will relieve some of the pressures that would be considered downward, you see, on the plates, and as this downward pressure is released, the plates that are under pressure will be relieved, and they will spring upward, you see, causing somewhat of a reflex action in the Netherlands. Those that would be in the area of Finland and other small countries will see themselves almost gobbled up, you see, as they will be inundated. Care should be taken. There can be some engineering that will keep the southernmost coastlines somewhat protected with a degree of retaining wall and/or flood damage control, you see. However, it would be more of a shaking and quaking, and the disturbances will lead to large sections of land being inundated with water. As we have given, there will be a leveling, or an almost straight line from the west due eastward you see, across mother Russia itself.

PLEASE DESCRIBE THE ENVIRONMENTAL CHANGES IN THE REPUBLIC OF BULGARIA IN THE NEXT FEW YEARS?

The country will move further into chaos into the next year or two, or eighteen months. There will be continued difficulties with the weather. There will be inundations, or too much water, or rain, and this will cause severe flooding, and conditions will deteriorate. Some of the farming areas will be unaffected, while in others, the topsoil will be taken right down to bare rock! And, therefore, you can expect that the prices in the grocery stores will continue to increase. The situation throughout the general region itself is such that there will be increased inflation and, indeed, shortages of supplies. There will be arguments over lands and the use of lands, as we see it. The economic situation will be inflationary; there will be shortages of products, including food, and there will be arguments in the street, as different factions or groups side opposite each other, and more discontent due to the lack of leadership and the lack of association, shall we call it, with other nations.

The country itself is on an economic decline; there may be a change of currencies, or the devaluation of the currency. The social activities in the government will cause a furthering or separating themselves from each other, causing more chaotic understanding or thinking, or leadership in the hands of those who would be authorities, you see. To the people, you will find there will be a resurgence towards religion; they will attempt to understand what is taking place, and the Virgin Mary may appear in this country. There will be sorrow on one hand, relief on the other, and there will be contests or contention here throughout the lower areas. This would be in the south/southeast areas. We find the landmasses being somewhat a place of uncertainty.

Within the third to fourth year, there will be an increase in knowledge as to what is taking place within the economic fronts. There will, however, be difficulties in dealing with the disturbances: the shaking and quaking of landmasses, and too much water coming down from the heavens above. See? Severe flooding will cause work projects to be put into place that will help the economic downturn, shall we call it, and there will be employment and jobs; attempting to amend what would be disastrous conditions.

This would be within the third to fourth year. It could be a little sooner, depending on activities of volcanic ash that would be erupting or spewing forth in various places, you see; not from this country, *per se*, but from the adjoining area or region itself. There will be an insurgence or an intention for invention, and there will be economic common sense that will come from this time of uncertainty. It is a time of chaos, and many will view it as such. Complicated by weather extremes, the country will suffer, but it will survive as the people are most hardy! Learning cooperation and not to be selfish is, indeed, the lesson here.

Earth Changes Affecting North America

How will Earth changes affect North America?

Specifically, you will find that towards the eastern seaboard, there will be continued quaking, and this will go north/northeasterly. In the Mississippi region, there will be further disturbances. You will find in the Great Lakes there will be more earthquakes in Ontario, along the escarpment, northwest, and also towards Montreal in the Kingston/Ottawa region that would be severe. These would be preparations for the St. Lawrence River to widen, or for the inundation of seawater to come into the Great Lakes. On the western seaboard, you would find that there will be disturbances from California, west of the Rockies, all the way up to the "Jewel of the North," or Alaska itself, in which there will be separation and great disturbances, and there will be activities that will expose lava to the ground itself; not like volcanic activity, but a certain surge from under the crust. You will find quaking and shaking in Wyoming in what would be the geyser valley itself, and there will be plumes of ash that will come to the surface. Likewise, in the Montreal region, or Saint-Hilaire, there will be the same. To the west coast, all that you would see now in those regions that would lie in a low-lying region – San Fernando valley, San Francisco region – they will be flooded, and there will be a large inland sea.

In Florida, you will find there will be sinking holes in the southern regions, as there already have appeared in the past. There will be rising in the ocean's surface that will come inland, and there will be tsunami or waves that will come along the east coast, and they will go up to the Potomac, and they will flood the capital!

Understand that as the oceans heat up, the weather will be more erratic and severe. It will cause the planet to wobble, and as this wobbling occurs, the oceans will slosh in their basins, and that is why they will come inland with their sloshing or spilling out of their basins, several miles (if not hundreds of miles). This would be in the North America area as you would know it.

To the south, again, there will be inundations of water and there will be further sinking of the Louisiana area or region. The entire Caribbean will be expanded, and there will be some shaking and quaking, and rising and falling in Central America, or what you would call Mexico and Latin America. There will be disturbances in the islands, and much in the way of shaking in Cuba and the surrounding areas or islands of the Caribbean. The Bahamas, too, may have great difficulty. East of Bimini, there will be large rises of land off the surface of the floor of the ocean. This will also increase the level of water on the ocean's surface, as we have given, making it somewhat higher. And in the area of New York, you would find that there will be flooding, and there will be a cavernous structure that might collapse, and the island itself will have certain depressions, or flooding occur here in this region.

In the regions that expand out into the ocean, Long Island and Rhode Island, they will be flooded, and into the Carolinas, there will be great storms, rain and flooding. The Maritime provinces a little further to the north will suffer some inundation of water as well, but more of disturbances than shrinkage, you see. They will be levered out into the ocean a little further, and there will be some changing of the coastline here. In that area of Labrador, there will be islands seen, or the water may be drained from some rocky structures as there is a protrusion or a thrust upward here.

In Greenland and those areas that would be in the north, they truly would start to grow moss and become green again, as they once were prior to the fourth destruction. In the northern shores of Canada, there will be flooding and protrusions into mining centers. Generally speaking, the temperature in the tundra will increase, and there will be more muddy plains for a long time, until there is a redirection and a drying of the same, but you can expect moss, and then small plants and trees to grow in this area that would be north of the tree line (as presently seen). Larger rivers flowing towards the north will occur. The Mackenzie River would be greatly enhanced.

To the mountain range of the Rockies: everything west of the same will disappear, including that which would be in the northern realms or reaches as well, as to the landmass you would call Alaska or the Jewel of the North. There may be a shrinkage of about the middle and western areas, which would tend to be in transit at this point.

To the eastern regions or the northeastern regions, you would find there will be somewhat of a loss of some of the islands that would extend from the Canadian north to the continent or country Greenland itself. There will be more visitations from Greenland into the west, you see.

To that which is in the east, you would find that the channel which is not appearing yet will be from the St. Lawrence mouth, towards the Ohio valley you see, in a straight, roughly diagonal line. Hudson's Bay will be larger. The line of the lakes from Great Slave and the Yukon downwards towards Winnipeg will be more of an open underlying region of water.

Expect more of the fault lines that are obvious in Canada to be disturbed, not that there would be great loss of life or destruction of property, but, indeed, there would be an opening up in the eastern side of the Lakes that are Great, and that would extend to the St. Lawrence seaway as well. Look to smoldering volcanoes here. This, too, will be an indication of disturbances under the crust. For, here, as measurements would be taken, the core itself is spinning at a different rate or speed than the crust, and this will be more obvious as there is the advancement, or the differential between the two is exaggerated or increased.

You would have between that of the second, possibly as late as the fourth year from this time [2011] for these major alterations to take place. But best to look to the mountain regions in Europe, and Switzerland, as it would shudder and, perhaps, disappear in the twinkle of an eye. However, the disturbances will begin as a door unlocks when Vesuvius and Etna are in harmony with their eruptions, you see. Even now, it is drawing closer and closer.

WILL VANCOUVER, BRITISH COLUMBIA SUBMERGE COMPLETELY, OR WILL THERE BE REMNANTS OF SURVIVAL?

It will slip under the surface; everything west of the Rockies will be submerged, you see. You will find that the land will not collapse, but there will be, rather, a pulling apart. Envision in the early days, the crust was pushed together. The forces had upwards or downwards to move. The resistance was least in the upward thrust, and they became mountains. Now, as there would be a reduction or a pulling apart of these same two places, what will happen will be a collapse and then a submergence, you see. All of the Rockies, everything west on the Canadian coast, including Alaska itself, all will be susceptible to the various degrees of being submerged, you see.

What other parts of the United States will be submerged?

The lower portion of Florida will be rounded. The Carolinas southward will be inundated with water within two hundred miles of the coastline. The capital of Washington will be inundated with water; not really submerged, but soaked with inundations of water, repetitively.

The eastern regions, Maine and Vermont, will be roughly the same, but extending to Virginia Beach where you now find sand, you will then find white rock, and the buildings that are near the beach will be devastated or disappear, save for their remnants.

To the western coast, in Seattle there will be exaggeration of the water inward, and most of those lake areas or bays that have contributions out to the ocean themselves will be widened or submerged. The west coast up to the Rockies will indeed be submerged or gone. There will be water into Nebraska. To the Baja, there will be a removal of the same; not fast-acting, you see, a sort of slipping into the sea very slowly; mostly the Catalina islands, you see, and to the Baja coast of Mexico. The Caribbean will be enlarged as well. You will find that the Heartland of America will be submerged, for there will be a large waterway that will run from Michigan southward. Not like a sea or a lake, but a very, very wide river!

Can you please explain how water will reach Nebraska?

The Rocky Mountains will not be mountains. The coastline will be submerged, and the water will naturally flow eastward, and it will come into those areas that will be considered the cliffs along the Nebraska region. It would be seen somewhat as a line with a large bump in it towards the Nebraska area. This will be inland from Washington state, through Montana, perhaps not so far, down towards Nebraska, then it will take a large turn towards the coast of Mexico itself - to give you some idea of the probability of what will happen here. For they will be called "the cliffs" or "the Palisades east," in a black-humorous way, you see.

DOES THIS MEAN THERE WILL BE AN INLAND LAKE, OR A RIVER?

We do not see it as a lake; we see it more as a line with submerged Earth on one side, and a very well-established side on the other, you see.

WHEN WILL PERMANENT COASTAL FLOODING IN FLORIDA TAKE PLACE?

This would depend on certain aspects in the area to the northwest of Africa, or to the southwest of Spain itself, you see? There would be volcanic activity here, which is currently appearing. And then there will be some volcanic eruptions of Vesuvius and Etna together, and that of Pelee, also, in the Canary Islands. When these three erupt, either together or one shortly after the other, it would be the time to look towards coastal flooding or tsunami, or storms that will batter the eastern seaboard, from the Carolinas southward, you see. Look to the Carolinas, North and South, or to Virginia Beach taking some severe weather. This would be an indication of that which is in the northeast that will migrate to the southeast, you see.

You will see a series of hurricanes or storms that will come in on the east side of the Florida peninsula; looks to be about three, and there might be two on the western side of the Gulf coast that will strike Texas or Louisiana. They will seemingly come together or converge at the same time, or one after the other. This may be within the next twelve to twenty-four months as we see the buildup of activity taking place, you see. Look to the explosions in Europe of Vesuvius and Etna, and you would see the commencement of this, as to the period in time, within the next few months. For what occurs on one side of the world occurs on the other side of the world. What is occurring in the European, Mediterranean region will be resident within the Americas itself. See?

WHICH NORTH AMERICAN CITIES WILL BE MOST AFFECTED BY THE COMING EARTH CHANGES?

Look to any of those cities that would lie on the eastern seaboard, within two hundred miles of the shore. The western seaboard would be the same, or perhaps a little further inland. As we have given, all the way to the Rocky Mountains themselves, from the Baja, or even further south to the Jewel of the North (Alaska itself) will be influenced adversely. Again, two hundred miles inland, predominantly on the east coast, but also on the west coast, you see, Those cities that lie within this realm would be mostly affected. Those that are inland further would tend to be safe, you see, save for those along the St. Lawrence area, as this will tend to be disturbed as well.

The four corners, in Arizona, for instance, would be safe. The area east of the Rockies would be safe. Larger cities like Chicago, Winnipeg, Toronto, Cleveland, Atlanta and Amarillo will be relatively unaffected. But Washington, D.C. will be overrun with water, as would the Carolinas, and everything along the eastern seaboard, you see. Higher up, into the Appalachians' higher altitude, these areas would tend to be not as affected, or as disturbed as those places that would be in a low-lying area.

YOU HAVE MENTIONED DISTURBANCES IN THE GREAT LAKES. HOW WILL THESE AFFECT NIAGARA FALLS?

In the first place, there will be a migration or a stepping back of "The Falls" (as you know it) rather rapidly. This would be almost to the bridges on the American side of the river. You will find that there will be a sinking of this region. Although it will not be too devastating quickly, it would be more of a push or migration upward, here. The Falls will be somewhat level and then there would be a flowing backward from the region of the seaway. For as there would be an opening up in the volcanic regions in that area of St. Hilaire, Quebec to the south shore, there will be a separation and there will be a vast but shallow one. And as such, the salty water will migrate almost like a tidal surge, towards the Great Lakes, which, because of the rise in the area of the escarpment, there will be a reversal, so to speak, of the flow of water that will primarily drain through Lake Michigan southward, as there will be no pressure, no water pushing the sea out. But instead, as there would be a rising up of the levels or the height of the ocean, the forces of the sea will migrate inward, you see, and the region you would call the Falls would be somewhat more like a riverbed, although it may protrude from the left to the right, or a reversal of the Falls may occur. But first, expect the stepping back of the shale and these large sections that are now the top of the Falls, you see.

IS IT POSSIBLE THAT LAKE SUPERIOR OR LAKE MICHIGAN WILL MAKE THE MIS-

sissippi the largest river ever?

We do not see the lakes making a huge river, if this is the question. Rather, there will be a drainage of the lakes that will be quite severe, through the Michigan valley or through Lake Michigan and what would be south. See?

As you see it, will this over-run the city of Chicago?

It would appear so, for this would be the natural flow of water in the southerly directions, as there would be Michigan flooding its banks and there will be some disturbances in the states just south of Chicago. Yes to the question.

Given that, at present, Lake Erie is higher in elevation to Lake Ontario, how will Lake Ontario drain into Lake Erie?

It would, of course, be a lower elevation; there will be a rising up of what you would call Lower Canada, and there would be somewhat of a submerging of what you would call Upper Canada now. However it would be more to the rising up of those areas or regions that would be on the north shore of the St. Lawrence River, and those that would be already there. They would tend to fall down into the south shore, into the lake itself, you see. Look to certain repercussions or ripple effects that will cause the landmasses to move in waves. The Niagara escarpment and the country nearby, as to the landmasses that are at least flat, they will roll like waves on an ocean and will come to rest in such a similar way! They will not move, of course, but it would be in this position they would be found.

WHAT WILL BE THE NEW ELEVATION ABOVE SEA LEVEL FOR BOTH LAKES ON-
TARIO AND ERIE?

Depending on certain activities that would be from the Ohio valley,
towards that of the St. Lawrence mouth of the river, we would find
this as not very high; maybe fourteen or sixteen meters, if that, you
see.

IT WAS MENTIONED THAT CANADA WILL BE DIVIDED INTO THREE REGIONS.
COULD YOU PLEASE CLARIFY THIS?

The south shore of Canada in the Quebec region will be vastly separated. The western regions or the mountains will be separated and
the center of the land will not be divided, but the lakes will drain
through the center of the continent in the Mississippi valley which
will be somewhat of a separation, but not too much, although there
may be the drainage or the sea expanded in Hudson's Bay, you see.

HOW WIDE WILL THE MISSISSIPPI BECOME?

If you were to draw a straight line from Michigan due south, to the
headwaters of what would be perceived as the Mississippi valley, you
would have an approximation of the waterway that will exist in this
regard. There will be changes to the geographical region; there will
be some diagonal movement of the river, but otherwise it would be
fairly straight, as to a line. This would be also in the area of the
Michigan basin, for it would swell its banks and, indeed, there will
be the emptying out of Lake Superior and Lake Huron to Lake Michigan. They will empty southward, not so much eastward where Lakes
Sinclair, Erie and Ontario will somewhat flow backwards in their di-

rection. They might deviate southward here, past Detroit in the southerly-most regions. This will depend on certain buckling of the plates that run diagonally from Oklahoma towards the Montreal region. See?

It should be a fairly wide river, as you would expect. The lake itself will drain at about the same rate you would see the waters moving eastward now. They would move southward and you would find this would be not a "teardrop situation" of one large body or lake draining into another, but we find there would be something similar to this. Mostly it would be a straightforward channel or river. This could be considered the same drainage as what is now moving eastward in Lake Ontario or Erie.

CAN YOU EXPLAIN HOW WIDE THE ST. LAWRENCE SEAWAY WILL EXPAND, AND ITS EFFECTS ON THE ISLAND OF MONTREAL?

If you take the narrower part of the St. Lawrence, and you make it as wide as the mouth of the St. Lawrence, towards the ocean side, you would see it as a considerable corridor. This corridor could continue under the lake, through Lake Ontario, through Lake Erie, and continue in a southwesterly direction towards the drainage of the Mississippi. We do not see that the lakes will separate as wide as the river, but the river will be considerable. It will be remembered in the future that the south shore *used to be* attached to the mainland, or the continent, in the north shore.

The gap would, perhaps, be as wide as Lake Ontario. Certainly it has the probability to take place. But the key here is in Kingston, Brockville, and those areas between Brockville and Montreal. The effect on Montreal will be that the island itself will be under severe disturbance; but after all the shaking and movement, it seems to be built on solid stone, and therefore will not move too much into the water, nor be affected adversely. That which would lie in an easterly direction, will be affected, you see.

HOW WOULD THE OPENING OF THE ST. LAWRENCE RIVER AFFECT THE OTTAWA RIVER?

It appears to drain dry, you see. We do not see it extending too much further past the capital itself [Ottawa]; rather, it appears to be a muddy bog, you see. This will be the result of that which would be further west (as you would understand west from this point) in which there will be reduction.

WILL THERE BE A GREAT DELUGE OF SALT WATER IN THE ST. LAWRENCE?

To the St. Lawrence River and the Great Lakes, it would be seen that there would be some inundation, some broadening of the lakes, some flattening out of certain areas. To the narrowness or the bottleneck towards the eastern seaboard, as to the St. Lawrence, there will be some widening of this to the degree that there will be, indeed, a separation that would be rather great from what would be the south shore. This particular area will allow the salt water to reverse and come forward. That which is fresh water now in Ontario, perhaps Erie, would be salt water that would be not as a tidal wave, not as any pressure wave, but as a wave that would come from one end to the other, perhaps instigated by the separation where there are the volcanic mountains, through to what would be the plains leading to Ontario. This is a general region as we see a corridor between Cornwall and Kingston, you see. Expect therefore the challenges to be fresh water and fresh air, so to speak, and how to maintain a cooperative nature between each other during times in which there will be difficulties, but they will be temporal.

WILL THE WATER SUPPLY FROM LAKE ONTARIO BE UNDRINKABLE?

Ultimately there will be an opening up as to the St. Lawrence River, in which there will be a separation of the south shore of Canada, much greater and broader than it is presently seen. This will be more like a channel, rather than a river. Instead, there will be a channel and as such, this will allow the flooding of seawater as it would come towards Ontario. Yes to the question, there will be saltwater in the lake itself. As there would be further disturbances, sea creatures that live in the salt water even now are appearing in the fresh water and these, too, will continue. For here, it is quite violent in the fishing bands, in the Atlantic areas themselves, you see. Expect this to continue.

To the question: the water supply in the area of Toronto will shift towards the east, to those lakes and streams that would be towards Campbellford or the Trent River, you see. But you can be certain there will be saltwater in Lake Ontario itself, you see. This will cause disturbances to the power plants that require cooling of water, circulating in and around the reactors and pipes, you see.

For the larger population of Toronto, you can expect some disruptions here, in this region. This will not be too extensive, as we see it. But, here, there may be some disruptions in power for short periods of time, and there will be more droughts or heat, as this will be a place of some considerable temperature change, you see, especially in the summer months.

WILL THE NORTHERN PARTS OF CANADA, CLOSE TO THE ARCTIC CIRCLE BE

COVERED IN WATER OR WILL SOME ISLANDS STILL BE VISIBLE?

This would be to the affirmative; those lands you now perceive as islands will shrink. They will be somewhat in a temporary situation, however; what is quite possible will be the rising up of certain masses. Remember, as we have given, tundra - that which is under snow - these will freshen up, and they will spring upward. Where you will have barren land, rock and snow now, in the future you will have fern and moss growing, you see. Yes this would be an area or region in which there would be somewhat of an extension, and then there will be a joining together of these smaller separations. Then eventually the tundra will be somewhat of a fascinating and fundamentally inspirational place, you see. To further south, you would find that Hudson's Bay will be exaggerated out, and for the same calculation inward, some one hundred kilometers (or miles depending on the two extremes), this same height can be extrapolated and you will see the islands themselves will be inundated. Those that are higher at this point in time will tend to convert, as we have given, and they will not be submerged.

EARTH CHANGES AFFECTING SOUTH AMERICA

HOW WILL SOUTH AMERICA BE AFFECTED BY EARTH CHANGES?

There will be disturbances to the west coast, and there will be disturbances up the middle of this continent itself. There will be prevailing disturbances that would go from the west, as to Peru and the Argentina areas, outward into the ocean itself. While there may be some submergence of thin areas of land, there will come up not too far away from Peru those areas or landmasses that have been submerged for some time! To the east/southeast, there will be land-masses that will rise up and attempt to join with Antarctica; you would find that the sea bottom will rise up here, you see. There will be a connecting in the northern part of the Americas as well. This will be done by arbitrary means, shall we call it. However the planet will shake and this part will be altered or the latitude in the lower end will be different. There will be plenty of rain that will come across from the east to the west, rather than the west to the east now, you see.

WHAT WILL BE THE APPROXIMATE SIZE OF THE NEW LANDMASS OFF PERU?

There first will be a slushy, muddy landmass; it will be from the Straits of Magellan; this will be a rounding of the horn as it is called that would make it more the shape of a football.

APPROXIMATELY HOW FAR INTO THE WEST COAST WILL THE WATERS INUNDATE SOUTH AMERICA?

Rule of thumb would be somewhat of fifty miles, you see.

WITH REGARDS TO LANDMASSES RISING FROM THE PACIFIC, YOU DESCRIBED A LANDMASS RISING WEST OF PERU, AND ONE THAT WOULD ATTACH ITSELF TO AUSTRALIA. ARE THESE TWO SEPARATE LANDMASSES?

As of the same; it would be the shape of a hand or glove, you might say, reaching out with the hand one way and the fingers the other. Yes to the question.

IS THE LANDMASS RISING WEST OF HAWAII A THIRD LANDMASS?

This would be the building of that which is already seen; the mountaintops that are now above the surface of the ocean. They will tend to rise up and take their place as they once were: gigantic mountains on a continent, you see.

APPROXIMATELY HOW LARGE WILL THIS LANDMASS BE?

It will rise over time; if you would have it as a certain area, let us give a general proximity of about one thousand square miles.

HOW MUCH LARGER WILL THE CARIBBEAN SEA BECOME?

As there has been evidence that Mexico and Central America have been both below and above the surface of the oceans, you would find that, once again, there will be the inundation towards South America, towards the coastline; but here, it would be largely to the buckling of the Latin America/Central America regions, you see. There will be a rise in the oceans on both sides of this strip of land. But you would find it would be somewhat expanding. If you were to take inland the rise of the ocean, it would be a narrow range across the region itself, as to Mexico. But here, further south it may be more; considerably more as we see it!

EARTH CHANGES AFFECTING ASIA

HOW WILL EARTH CHANGES AFFECT THE REGION OF SOUTHERN ASIA; IN PARTICULAR INDIA, CHINA, AND THE FAR EAST?

Primarily, from the Pacific, you would find there will be inundations of water; this would be several waves, one after the other – at least five, perhaps as many as seven. These will push inland, and they will flood the rivers that are presently seen. There will be tidal activity that will raise the rivers in China in an ongoing and long duration upstream. It will take a long time before they are receded, if they recede at all. This will have flooding throughout the general regions or the low-lying lands themselves. We see disturbances along the coastline, but not too much internally, save for disturbances of shaking and quaking. The mass of land of China itself, or the eastern regions of Asia, would presently be similar in appearance, but it would feel the same effect of the Pacific. For there will come rising out of this, in the area west of Hawaii, larger areas of undersea masses of land, you see; a rising up, so to speak. Shocks and volcanic activity will cause these tsunami, or waves to come inland. Now, they will be broadband as well. They will be an arc that will stretch out; if you would draw a compass, with one leg close to the mountaintop in Hawaii, and draw an arc that would come close to the coastline, you would find that this would be similar to the arc we are observing. That region would be inundated with these influences of water.

Now, the plates that would affect the Indian continent itself, its migration northward will continue. The continent will shrink, so to speak, as it moves north. There will be considerable activity and disturbances along the Himalayan mountain range, to the north. This also will be affecting the Asian regions easterly from this point, as there will be a separation, or like grooves cut in the continent itself. This would be somewhat of a separating influence in which there will appear to be inland lakes, you see, where there are somewhat none now.

We would find in the Asia regions that the steppes in the Tibetan region will continue as they are presently seen, but they will be more subjected to ice and snow, and covered for longer periods of time. The mountains themselves will shake, and there will be some submergence, or some of the mountain ranges will be parted, as if cut in half. What would be the easterly, northerly regions will subside or will withdraw. Large flatlands will appear where mountain ranges are now. The entire region in the area will be pushed or thrust northward, from the Pacific towards the mountain ranges that run east and west now through this area.

There will be a basking or a period of intense sunlight, through India, but it will tend to cool over a period of time, as the rotation of the planet would alter or shift. You will see the continent of Africa flooded, and you may see the same along the coastlines of India, as well, where there will be a large margin along the coastline that will be submerged, you see. Some of the islands in the general region will be affected. Sri Lanka will be not so different in its appearance, save that it would become very warm or hot to live in this region! There is underneath this sliver of land – Ceylon – molten lava close to the surface. This may spew out here and there, as if small vent-holes have occurred, but the underlying continental region will be hot. Thermal heating, you see, will be seen here for some time. This may cause the population to move away from this location, you see.

HOW FAR INLAND WILL THE WATERS INUNDATE THE COASTLINES OF INDIA?

What is seen now, in the shelf or the plateau itself; in some places, this will be a matter of ten kilometers, and in other places it will be about one hundred, for the coastline is irregular, you see. But, here, look to the flatlands where there is little more than a few meters above sea level at this point. These will be submerged, you see.

How far will the waters inundate the eastern coast of China?

Somewhere between fifty and seventy-five meters, you see, in places. Otherwise where there is presently a delta or wide-mouth – Yellow River, you see – this will have a greater intrusion, shall we call it.

Will Japan experience more earthquakes in the near future?

As we would examine the region itself, the answer would be to the affirmative. There would be continued shaking and quaking. We can see the ground shaking rather violently for a long period of time. There will be about four aftershocks, and the ground will split. As we will find here, the Pacific Rim is but the ring of fire. You will find that there will be, as there is in North America, more shaking and quaking. There will be more violence and there will be more volcanic action or spewing of fire, fragments, and ash into the air. In particular, this region that would lie more in a southerly direction from the center portion of the island downward, you see. There will be a reciprocal effect on the other side of the planet. See the Pacific as a bowl, and as you would push down on one side of the bowl, the opposite side would go up. In the North American region, as there would be a pushing down and the mountains will collapse, there would be a pushing up on the opposite side into the Asia/Japanese region, you see.

Therefore you can expect a lifting up of the sea bottom in some areas, while there would be a shrinkage along the coastline in the Japanese region. Although we do not find it extensive, we can find the effects being quite shocking, shall we call it. Be prepared; there will be continued movements of the land. The plates will quake and shake, and this will be devastating in that it will cause waves in the ocean, tsunami but also it will be a precursor to the fire and the rain of ash which will be devastating to the North America region (as it would be also an indication of those aspects that will come into the southern regions of the Japanese country, you see).

There will be seen disturbances under the surface of the ocean, and there will be sightings of cities or what look like submerged structures. These will come closer to the surface, and we can see individuals looking from ships down through the water at not too great a depth, and seeing structures that have long submerged into this area, belonging to those areas of Lemuria: Mu and Og in different places in the Pacific. The mountaintops will rise up a little, and there will be plains or areas that will be irregular in their shape but they will be somewhat geometrical, and these will be sighted from ships passing above, you see, indicating that the floor of the ocean is rising. This will take place within the next very few months or a year. It could extend a little further, but as we see it, this is already taking place.

WHAT ADDITIONAL EFFECTS ARE TAKING PLACE DUE TO THE RADIATION LEAK IN FUKUSHIMA, JAPAN?

At the higher atmospheres, there are clouds of radiation or active particles, you see. These are somewhat floating and are moving towards the high Arctic. They have circumnavigated the middle and northern hemisphere, a little more. But the peoples who have suffered this inundation seemingly will survive, but they will not be able to curtail the leakage of these reactors too much. It does seem to be shutting down, and over the next five to ten years, there will be recovery or cessation. However, there will be further shaking and quaking of this place, and there will be further leakages, so to speak, although they do not seem to be too extensive. This is already occurring. The influence about the world is at hand. Large populations will be listless or sleepy. The radiation will seep into water tables and it will bring about difficulties in respiratory disorders. Some birth defects as well, as we see it. There will be more influenza, colds and grippe or viral/bacterial diseases of the lungs, throat, and nose, as there will be a weakening of the immune systems of those who have been affected; and in particular those who drink the water.

The island of Japan itself, which is a remnant of that that was once before (the land of Lemuria, and encompassing Mu and Og), it, too, will erode slowly from the east towards the west. This will place difficulties in Osaka and other places within the country itself, you see.

HOW WILL EARTH CHANGES AFFECT CENTRAL AND NORTHERN ASIA, INCLUDING RUSSIA AND MONGOLIA?

To the upper portion of Russia, take a straight line and cut it across from the Netherlands, and this part will disappear; not too suddenly, but rather aggressively. Kazakhstan will be more predominant in its military, social, and philosophical/intellectual circles, and this will tend to be a haven for people who would be fleeing southward from this point, from the shores of the North Sea or Arctic. They will move to Kazakhstan, and it would be a place of refuge.

To what would be further east, again the line being drawn, there will be a flooding, rather steady, and it will come westward through the prevailing areas, through these regions along the coastline. Mongolia will be not flooded, but certainly disturbances will happen. We see large caverns underneath this place, opening up to what appear to be canyons or fissures, as if someone would take their hands and claw across the continent, across this region, and country. There will be discoveries of metal and minerals that will be utilized here in the future, found in Mongolia itself.

To the areas of Russia in the western regions, they will be somewhat maintaining themselves, and more inventions will come out of Mother Russia. But in those areas near Moscow - Chernobyl and other places where there is energy developed by nuclear or atomic power – these, unfortunately, will not be too safe, and their intact preservation will be questionable. You would expect large plumes of poisonous gas to be emanated from here, and to travel in what appears to be in a northerly direction, towards the sea, you see.

EARTH CHANGES AFFECTING AFRICA AND THE MIDDLE EAST

HOW WILL EARTH CHANGES AFFECT SYRIA AND THE MIDDLE EAST?

You would find that there will be upheavals here, and there will be somewhat of an opening of the Red Sea itself. To Syria and to those areas that would be of the Arabian influences, we see that there will be changes in their weather patterns, and their lands will be soaked with water, and there will be some flooding of the lands with sea water. The salt will affect the landmass in an adverse way. Syria itself will seemingly be suffering many disturbances, and, as such, there will be leakages of the "black gold" from these regions or areas that will leak into the sea; and, as such, there will be difficulties for a large region in the Middle East. This is provided there is not the atomic blast that may take place here. For this would be somewhat seen as a hotbed of disturbances, and in Syria, you may see this somewhat being, in the very near future, a place of assassination and adulteration of authority; and there will be conflict from time to time with those who would be considered their arch-enemies throughout history.

But to the changes that would be seen in the world here, we would expect these to be not geographical changes, but environmental ones, you see, with some soon-to-be experienced political chaos. For it will continue here, even unto the lands of those who wear turbans, you see. They will come together, and they will be brother against brother. This will lead to environmental disasters, as we see it. Already has, and these will continue.

WHAT IMPACT WOULD A WAR IN THE MIDDLE EAST HAVE ON THE CHAIN OF EVENTS THAT YOU HAVE BEEN DESCRIBING?

If there is a bomb exploded in the Middle East, you would find this, indeed, would be a trigger, for this will send out influences underground for miles and miles and miles. It is foolish to think that you can start a fire on top of the ground and have volatile, combustible substances under the ground in caverns that are half-full of liquid ignition substance, and fumes that are instantly combustible, and to think that they will not merge, or that the self is isolated. This is the height of stupidity and vanity in the heart and minds of men! For here, would one sit on a gasoline can, light a match, poke it into the hole in the can, and expect nothing to happen, save, that it will burn on the surface of the can? As we see, there will be those minds, those hearts, that are black; they have no forethought, they are corrupted in their evil ways, and they are thoughtless. Yes, to the question; there will be those instruments or those areas affected rather severely because no one is looking, or appear to be watching, or appear to be concerned.

As such, you would find in this particular region, there may be certain activities of combat or conflict. This will place ash in the air, and it will cause certain quaking and shaking in these regions. There will be black skies, and there will be ash everywhere. In those areas in Dubai and other regions, there will be shaking and quaking, and there will be a rise in the ocean floor by several meters, you see. Within Syria, Iran and Iraq, there will be great difficulties of earthquake, and there will be a rising up of Iran, but Iraq will not rise as much (we talk about altitude, you see). And there will be various and continuous activities which would make it difficult to walk, due to the frequency of earthquakes, you see. Great disturbances in this region! Almost all buildings will suffer damage, or will not stand one block upon another. Those who would be kind in the world and cooperate with the West will have a tendency to save themselves with more aid or help from the West. Those who are not will find themselves suffering. But look for the ground to be shaking and quaking, and even for underground eruptions and explosions to take place, due to the igniting of gaseous substance or fumes, you see. This particular region can expect to have severe and prolonged earthquake activity or shaking and quaking, and ash will fall, as will there be the possibility of atomic explosions or "dirty bombs" going off.

WITH REGARD TO THE CONTINENT OF AFRICA, YOU HAVE SAID THAT IT WILL SHRINK. HOW MUCH OF THE COASTLINE WILL BE SUBMERGED?

All the plains that surround Africa up to the plateau and the rising of the same will be underwater, you see. This will circumnavigate around the continent itself. It would be as if you took the continent itself and shrunk it, as if you were taking a font size down from twelve to eleven or ten. The continent will remain in roughly the same shape, but it will be smaller, due to the island it might become, you see; water all the way around, except in the northeast, you see.

DOES THIS MEAN THAT EGYPT WILL BE SUBMERGED?

To the flatter areas, yes, there will be some inundations, you see, but not completely.

EARTH CHANGES AFFECTING AUSTRALIA

WHAT WILL BECOME OF AUSTRALIA DURING THE EARTH CHANGES?

To the continent Australia and the surrounding islands and New Zealand, we find very little will change in this general region, although there might be some land surfacing nearby, extending the continent itself. It has survived two destructions, you see, and in all likelihood it will remain intact. However, there will be a shifting in its location, and this shift will affect the atmosphere or the prevailing winds. And what you now see as lush areas extending to the coastline may suffer to be dry, while the interior remains moist because of the prevailing winds shifting and coming across the northeast to the northwest, and then perhaps extending a little from the southwest to the northeast.

IN WHICH DIRECTION WILL THIS LANDMASS BE, IN RELATION TO AUSTRALIA?

NORTHEAST.

IN COMPARISON TO THE CURRENT SIZE OF AUSTRALIA, APPROXIMATELY HOW

LARGE OF A LANDMASS WILL THIS BE?

It could be the same size, you see. It will be an amalgamation of those islands that are now present, you see.

THE RETURN OF ATLANTIS

IS THERE A POSSIBILITY THAT THE LOST WORLD OF ATLANTIS WILL EVER RESURFACE IN OUR LIFETIME?

Understand the world is not of Atlantis. You speak of the island Atlan, Semino, and those that would be in the north Atlantic. Understand the landmass itself was quite extensive, from the sub-regions, as to Antarctica, to what would be the north Atlantic. This was not a small place. It was rather a large plain that would stretch from Bimini to Huelva, Spain. As such, you would find these particular areas rising again, as there would be the slipping off in the Western Hemisphere of all the land west of the Rockies, including the Jewel of the North. These would submerge like a plastic soda bottle; as you push down on one part, the other depressed area pops up. The crinks and the crevices in the Atlantic and the Pacific will now shift or rise, and you will see landmasses rise off the Canary Islands, and you will see that there will be a shallow place east of Bimini, and you will see the floor of the Mediterranean rise, perhaps breaking the surface. And you will see the north shores of Europe gobbled up by the rising flood; whereas the landmasses rise, the ocean must creep along the shorelines, from San Sebastian in Spain, to the surrounding of Barcelona, to the flooding of the St. Lawrence and the lower lakes in Canada. These would be evidences of these things taking place, of the old continent rising again. But it will rise, first in islands, then a large mass will appear in an easterly direction from Bimini. It will be muddy, slimy, as was the original slipping into the water; filthy or salty or muddy. But it will be the same place! Expect to see signs of this in the near future, VERY NEAR FUTURE. And look to the older remnants of Atlantis from the eastern seaboard of Japan to the western coast of Spain, making themselves known, you see!

WILL LEMURIA RISE AS WELL AS ATLANTIS?

The answer would be affirmative. There will be some breaking of the surface in the Pacific, west of what would be Peru: the coastline of Peru will be changed again. On the western coast of North America, everything west of the Rockies will disappear, and this will be submerged. This will cause areas further out into the ocean (Hawaii, for instance) to rise or to ascend; some mountains may break the surface, and some may not. But this large landmass will be seen as muddy or soggy, unless it has high altitude or mountain range. For the most part, it will not.

We do have the area east of Bimini, and west of the Canaries; this will come arising again, you see. Expect some rising or floor level in the Caribbean to be raised up or seen as rising; Cancun may alter its present situation due to disturbances, as it has in the past (been below and above waters many times, you see).

THIS SOURCE, AS WELL AS EDGAR CAYCE AND OTHERS, HAVE REFERRED TO THE TIME WE ARE CURRENTLY IN AS A "TEACHING OR TESTING TIME." PLEASE EXPLAIN IN DETAIL WHAT THIS MEANS.

To the finite mind, or to the human mind, there is a constant circling, like an animal going in circles and chasing its tail. Humans, as you know humans, only learn by example. In this time, those things that are given would be seen as education or knowledge; theory, you might say. As people go through these times of great difficulty, their theories, knowledge, expertise or beliefs are challenged. If they are correct, they are supported. If they are incorrect, then they are abandoned.

This teaching time is a time to understand that only through pain, seemingly, do humans grow. Through mistake, or suffering, or difficulty, they seem to realize the error of their ways. It is not to say they cannot learn in a pleasurable and comfortable atmosphere, for they can! But this teaching or testing time will be a time to teach the world to cooperate, to come together, rather than to be indifferent to each other, and not to cooperate. This time will test those who profess their closeness to the spiritual aspects, or to the Divine. It will also test the goodness and the generosity of those who are upon the world itself. It is a teaching time. For humans, as you know humans, learn by their mistakes; they learn by the examples of others, and they will not be afraid to apply what they have learned, for it will be the right thing to do.

The testing time is to test those who are belligerent, who are ignorant, who are indifferent, and who are selfish. The test will be for them to give up what they hold dear in the material world. The accumulation of things would make them larger or smaller, depending on if they win or lose, for they believe in *things*. They will be disappointed always! The testing time will show how wonderful the soul within the body can be, and people will touch upon the Divine within, you see? Their test will be to give up those things that lead them into darkness. These tests will be the hardships that will come into the world, and how humans will respond to each other, all over the world! Usually they support one another; usually they do the right thing, perhaps for the wrong reasons. This testing time will allow them to know when and what to do, and why it is the correct thing to do. For they may profess many things, but those things they know to be the truth, they do automatically and repetitively.

This is a time of chaos, a time in which there will be great uncertainty. Be prepared to give direction to those who would wish to understand why this is happening! To those who cannot understand the difference between hate and love, or night and day, or darkness and light, be prepared to furnish them with reasons as to why this is taking place.

This is a time of travail; it has been long predicted, and it has waited five thousand years or more. In the beginnings of twenty-five thousand years ago, this time was spoken of. There was preparation of this time between ten thousand five hundred and eleven thousand five hundred years ago! There were preservations made in different places – deposits of information – and these will be unearthed in times coming. When the Nile flows back around the Sphinx, you will find the trap door, so to speak, of the Hall of Records of Atlantis. When there is the movement through the disturbances of South America, you will find the meaning of those giant metal balls and the temples that have been covered up for millennium. You will find the reasons that the temples are full of mica, and how they caused the passageways or the highways in the air for those devices that ran by antigravity means, you see.

There is much yet that will be exciting that is ahead, once this fossil fuel generation or system, seemingly, is subdued! The planet itself is the source of all energy! Contemplate the possibility of cold fusion rather than fission, and you will have an understanding of the promise that is coming at the end of this time. But, humans, as you know humans, usually do the right thing but for the wrong reason. Be part of that which does the right thing, *for the right reason*, at the right time.

Many will want to know why. Many will want to know what to do. Many will need to know who to look towards. Furnish them with what to do, what to know, and who to look towards. For the Divine is the Divine. No one else need challenge it, nor comprehend it, nor understand it, save for you. For those who wish to choose to do so, may they have ears to hear.

CHAPTER THREE

Economic Outlook

YOU HAVE SAID THAT THE INDUSTRIAL REVOLUTION IS ONE OF THE FACTORS
CONTRIBUTING TO THE IMBALANCE WE NOW FIND OURSELVES IN, AND A REA-
SON WHY CHANGE IS TAKING PLACE. COULD YOU PLEASE COMMENT ON THE
DANGERS INHERENT IN THE ECONOMIC PROCEDURES IN THE WORLD TODAY?

Indeed; there is artificial growth. There are people who keep changing the rules to fill their own pockets at the expense of their clients
or customers. This has been continuing now for some time, and there
are individuals who do not care about the outcome. As such, yes,
there is the migration towards the artificial economy; that is to say,
making money by selling other people's stock short, buying back at
the lower price, and then returning the stock that belonged to the
owners previously, at a much deflated price. The ones who would be
doing this would be the gatekeepers or those who would be in charge
to maintain the value of the stock in the first place! Politicians have
learned how to line their pockets. Venturing off is not for the protection of others, but for themselves and their personal gain. Others still
have developed schemes and ways on how to live off the poor. They
know, to the penny, how much a person can afford on a payment,
and they know that within a few weeks, or months, any car or vehicle
they are allowed to buy will have to be returned, for they will not be
able to maintain the extra costs of fuel and maintenance.

This type of calculation, as we see it, is the artificial economy. The courts, municipal governments, and other individuals are now seeking ways and means to glean money from the citizens of the country. Yes, it is dangerous! Because now those who are supposed to be civil servants are not; they are attempting to squeeze the people. Their incompetence or their callous thinking has left their budgets lower, and the income, through taxes or tax sharing, is also affected to the negative aspect. You will see a continuation of fines as the courts, police, and politicians think up new ways to fine people for infractions in traffic or civil law. You will find there will be a more harsh climate in this regard, and there will be a callous or uncaring attitude towards the people who these services are supposed to protect and guard.

To the bankers, they will not be their brother's keeper. As they often say in Switzerland, "We are not our brother's keeper- we are his banker!" And this attitude (that the banks are not friendly) is permeating around the world and is becoming prominent. And, indeed, they are not, as they attempt to increase the artificial economy and learn to live off the poor. This will continue, as we see it, and there are ways and schemes and individuals who are now in the world who are able to function on the shadier sides of the law without much risk of penalty.

However, these particular situations can only exist when there is the changing of money and there is no integrity; there is only the self-serving accumulation, through greed, of funds for individuals. This does seem to permeate all levels of society. Expect, therefore, more disruptions in government, less service, and more charges; even fines and user fees. As the saying goes, "they will nickel and dime the citizens to death," because they are not watching their expenditures. They are only paying attention to how much they can gain, and if the people remain asleep, then indeed they will deserve what they get (as some other politicians would say).

This will awaken the general public and, indeed, this would occur soon. Tensions will rise and there might be violence in the street. To the question, yes it is dangerous. You will find assassinations of politicians will be on the rise soon because of this, you see. And even those who are judges in courts may suffer some disruption in this regard. But it is a matter of isolation and it is a matter of callous feelings or thinking that is propagating this increase in taxation, and an increase in obliteration of savings for those who might save their wealth for their old age. They will have to relinquish this. Those who now pay reverse mortgages are, in fact, falling into the trap of, once again, ending up to be poor at the end of their life.

There is no caring, and when there is no caring, then those who are mischievous can function and danger is, indeed, prevalent. There does not seem to be any end to this, or any will to stop this. As such, they will continue through the inflationary aspects, as we have given, to the thirty or more percentage points. This will cause great havoc and, indeed, it is dangerous. It will take many economists and the will of the people for this habit of taking advantage to be curtailed. Unfortunate!

WHAT WILL BE THE CONSEQUENCES TO THOSE WHO HAVE MANIPULATED THE WORLD'S ECONOMIES AND HURT OTHERS FOR THEIR OWN ENRICHMENT?

Short-term gain, of course. Then there will be some isolation, as they will need to protect their gains. Then, there will be a certain degree of fear and mistrust, and this will bring, indeed, opportunities for those who would steal from them, or would make inroads into their family situations, to overcome them, you see.

DO YOU SEE ANY DOWNTURN IN THE ECONOMY IN THE COMING YEARS?

Yes, this would be continuing through what we see now. As the Arabs continue to separate themselves from the American dollar and the dollar continues to wash out, inflationary influences are afoot, although they are not recognized in the traditional sense. You can expect some disclosures from some European countries that they are a little worse off economically than what most would think. And you would see that the particular region or the economic circumstances will worsen or weaken there. Yes there will be some disclosure that the Americans are not doing business with each other and therefore there is widespread idleness within the American countryside.

THE STANDARDS AND POOR INDEX (S&P) IS AN INDEX OF STOCK MARKET PERFORMANCE IN THE U.S. CURRENTLY [IN 2011] IT IS AT ONE THOUSAND, TWO HUNDRED AND NINETY-TWO POINTS. WHAT WILL IT DO IN THE COMING MONTHS?

As we would examine the conditions involving this, we would find it vacillating or bubbling along here for a period. There will be some economic circumstances that will be somewhat devastating in that of the Far East itself. The index itself should have some good rises here, from the one thousand, two hundred and ninety-two mark approaching one thousand, four hundred. As there would be vacillation, the volatility will be quite high. There will be, after that point in time, somewhat of a lull or even a downturn, as there would be some economic news that would be a little more difficult in the Western region. As such, this will tend to be derogatory to the marketplace itself. We see this as conditions of labor unrest being the cause. If this is maintained, then there could be a reversal from this higher point towards one thousand, one hundred or even as low as nine hundred and eighty points, you see. There will be inflation this year, and these inflationary influences will tend to be productive in some factors or regions, and this will moderate the index itself, for the remaining portion of the summer and into the fall of 2012. In the fall, you can expect some uncertainty, and we find great movements in volatility here, up and down one hundred points at a time, you see.

However, there will be war, and there will be economic influences that will look favorable in the first and second quarters (more in the second quarter), and there will be an optimistic outlook for the early part of the year. Should there be an assassination, then there would be a downward movement, as we have given. Should the assassination not take place, or be avoided, then we find that the markets will not be in arrears or depressed too much in the spring 2012 time-frame, you see. The marketplaces are very difficult at this point in time, as there are inflationary influences on one side, and uncertainty due to indications of warfare in the Middle East. There will be disruptions in the airline industries, more hijacking of planes in the Mediterranean regions, and as such, this will be somewhat derogatory for the aircraft industry, which will be a spillover and could be dampening to the S&P itself, you see.

However these are uncertain times and this uncertainty would exist into our observations of what will take place in the marketplace. However, expect a volatile year; but for the main thrust, it will be inflationary influences that will run the market in an artificial way. Manufacturing and mining will also be somewhat supported or beneficial, until there would be some degree of labor unrest, and then the manufacturing arm of the index will be lower itself, or will be derogatory. This will be compensated by the mining faculties and certain demands for the precious metals. This will also be an indication of inflationary influences.

These would be our observations in the marketplace, giving the probability of some highs and lows during this most volatile year.

PLEASE COMMENT OVERALL ON HOW THE ECONOMY OF THE WORLD WILL CHANGE OVER THE NEXT FEW YEARS?

In various aspects in history, when there were inflationary influences, and governments or banking-type individuals tinkering with the system, greed would allow that they would take a little in the giving, and a little in the taking. As such, you would find that usury of money, and the gambling of money, and the money-changers, are all dreaded, because they do not add prosperity to any country. They complicate the prosperity, and like leeches, they feed off the wealth of the land. These "Middlemen" themselves will be eliminated in the future.

As you would look back in history, you would find what is called the Gold Standard. Societies who printed money or had different implementation of items for money, when they got to a certain point, there had to be enough promissory wealth in the chamber, or coffers, or treasure-chest in order to cover the outstanding debts or the implied value of such an implement (whether it was paper or something else). In the past, the Middlemen were executed, or banished, or taken away, and then the true economy was basically one in which no one could overspend what was already in the public treasury. Now, of course, it is of little concern, or at least seemingly so.

You will find that the use of gems, precious metal coins, or things of value will, once again, surface. Then eventually there will be an entire change to real property rather than promissory notes you see. Stones, precious and semi-precious, including diamonds, will be used right alongside gold, silver, palladium, and platinum as portable property. The barter system will be well-advanced by that point in time. Bullion or bars of gold and silver may be traded more on the open market, but there will still be a considerable amount of skepticism and fear that the metals are being supplied; for the metals in supply will mean there will be real money, and real money means portable property. The problem is that the values of the money and the negotiating aspect will be somewhat difficult. But already there seems to be extensive bartering. Already there seem to be certain houses open to the use of precious metals and other precious items that could be taken for security.

DO YOU FORSEE THE SOCIAL ORDER COLLAPSING?

In the larger centers, this would more than likely be as you suspect, for there will be panic and there will be shortages, and there will be those who would reach for the club or the gun. Yes, you can expect the social environment to disintegrate, but not so much in Canada, as in others. In the larger centers, look for some of this to take place. Look for military rule to be prepared, so that there are not looters and rioters. But, yes, there will be disruption, especially when there is ash in the streets, the temperatures are high and water is short, and there will be the forces to drive people to madness and into a state of chaos! And this is a very real possibility in large centers, you see.

There will be mobs or groups of people that will be quite upset, and you have already seen the beginnings of these. There will be, in certain regions or areas, mob rule for periods of time. They will be difficult for the police to handle, for there will be a swarming effect or large groups of people who will engage in this desperate act. For there are many who will be unemployed, many who will maintain their lifestyle as it is, which is one of desperation, and there will be preparation or harsh treatment of the citizens in large cities by the governments; for they have learned that one way to increase their taxation is to increase their activities of the police, to increase fines to higher amounts, to be strictly callous and indifferent to people, so the fined amounts can be enhanced or they can be influenced, or taken advantage of, shall we call it. And as such, this will spread a degree of resentment, anger and even hatred between certain groups in the society and the protective forces or the police forces themselves. This form of taxation will be cruel and will be excessive and there will be brutality; this will escalate into this mob rule or rampages by large groups of people, you see. Not excessively, but it will be evident, as it always is when there are taxations and burdens placed upon people who are already in difficulty. And as there is a certain expectation, there is a certain depression that follows with this mindset, and this will be the cause or the reason, shall we call it, for these difficulties.

But already there is preparation for the same. In the higher levels of individuals within the government, there are self-preservation techniques taking place. And as such, this is obvious even to the people who are even now walking the beat on the sidewalk or working in some truly laborious fashion, you see. Unfortunately it will be a matter of indifference that will cause these difficulties, you see.

THIS SOURCE WAS ONE OF THE VERY FEW TO PREDICT SEVERAL YEARS AGO THAT A TIME WAS COMING WHERE THERE WOULD BE PROTESTS AND RIOTS IN THE STREETS. THESE PREDICTIONS WERE GIVEN AT A TIME OF RELATIVE QUIET AND WERE LOOKED UPON UNUSUALLY AT THE TIME, BUT IN FACT THEY ARE

It goes to the gun and the club and the knife. It goes to extreme behavior in some quarters. It goes to others who will act appropriately, and they will be providing peace and calm. It goes to the time in which there is a decision. Those who would act in the animalistic way and react violently are those who will retreat and move away in isolation. As always there are two diametrically opposed forces. There is a third option, and this would be cooperation, that there would be compassion and the willingness to cooperate rather than what might be perceived as indifference, that there might be a perception between the classes being distinct – one higher, one lower, with no middle class at all, you see.

The problem is not difficult to solve; the problem is implementation, you see. Usually when there is a sufficient amount of violence, humans, as you know humans, usually do the right thing, but for the wrong reasons. In this time frame, action and reaction will be expedited because of the lightning-fast communication ability! But you can expect more violence in the world, unless there is that which would change the same; unless there would be seen as a more profitable way why there should not be brother against brother, neighbor against neighbor. Cooperation is the most important aspect; being fair and equitable and looking out for one another. This would be the Law of One in effect; all inter-related, all connected as one, you see.

Understand there is a thread that flows through all things; an energy or force that causes the smallest particles you could see, perceive, or understand to move. This force is what you would appeal to as God itself, at its most fragile or suggestive level. There is one

God and that all are one in the eyes of God. This thread reaches out through every heart and mind on the planet as you know it, in all its varied ways, shapes, and forms, and it reaches out through all living things, including the planet itself, and from there to the solar system, to the galaxy, and to the Universe beyond! It is an ambient, coherent force, for thoughts are motivating, thoughts are real, and they are the influence of these smaller particles, these small essences of things. What is seen within them, this force, is God itself (if you would understand it from a certain perspective).

The microcosm and the macrocosm are the same; take steps down and steps up, and at each step you would find similarity. Some would call this fractal understanding, but it better understood as, "As above, so below."

However, it is not to say that the degree would be to the animal action/reaction. In some places where there is frustration, where there are felt inadequacies and unequal behavior and the unequal sharing of resources, this would cause certain minds to act in such a way, to be violent and destructive. But there will not be the violence as there has been in the world before, more than likely. There will not be the attempt to conquer one region by another. Instead, it will be simply social and economic warfare, violence, combat, for short durations, you see, between gangs of undisciplined individuals. There is the option that if they all cooperate, one looking out for the other, this period of violence need not be experienced in the world, as you know it. See?

WILL THERE BE ANY WARS BETWEEN COUNTRIES IN THE NEAR FUTURE?

If you would find any, it would be in the Middle East itself. The Chinese will come westward, and there will be the tinderbox in the Middle East between the Jews and the Israelis.This does not seem to settle between the Arab brothers and the Jewish population, you see.

In Africa, there will be some subduing of tribal warfare, but in the Congo regions, deep in the jungle, there may be some conflict. In Argentina and eastward towards Brazil, deep in the jungle, there will be tribal warfare. There will be some combative forces here that would be in the Latin areas, should they persist.

These would be considered origins of warfare. To the far eastern regions of Kazakhstan, there may be some conflicts with that of ancient Russia, and Japan, you see. This is not yet established, but if there would be conflicts that can be for certain, it would be in the Middle East between the Israeli and the Arab brothers, you see; old, ancient Persia and what would be the Chinese coming westward.

We would find some activities in northern Europe in which there would not be warfare, but certainly there would be some opposition to cooperation. But here, the economic front would be Italy, which would be destined to rule the world, and Spain being the crossroads for commerce to the West. These will not be in conflict, but they will have some security forces or armies. In ancient Egypt, you may see conflicts here, within that of the nomadic tribes and that of the city dwellers, you see. Skirmishes along the eastern seaboard of Africa as well; these will be maintained, you see.

PLEASE COMMENT ON THE ECONOMIC CONDITIONS COMING INTO THE UNITED STATES IN THE NEXT FEW YEARS?

The American economy is failing, and it will continue to slide into a lower realm of existence. The living conditions or status are in decline, at this point in time. Expect this to continue, but also expect that Louisiana and that coast may prove to be the salvation of the country itself, in the production of food, you see. At this point in time, the economy is weak, the currency is getting weaker, and, indeed, there will come a washout of the currency and other expectations of the States that are United, you see.

DO YOU FORESEE MULTIPLE AMERICAN PRESIDENTS IN THAT TIME PERIOD?

We do not see multiple presidents, though we do see multiple military leaders here. Only seems to be one or two, but there will be some suspension of the diplomatic practices, as you would know them now; more martial law than democracy. If you are looking over this period of time in which there will be a time of chaos, then you can expect more military intervention and policing, so to speak. In some countries, it will be brutal; in others, a little more humane. The larger democracies will be challenged in keeping to their fundamental beliefs, however.

There will be (and is expected to be) blood in the streets, as they say. In the larger centers of Chicago, the Ohio region, and that of the New York/Manhattan region, and extending to Georgia, Texas, and then to California, yes you would find labor unrests, especially in the areas in Georgia and Atlanta. There will be some great difficulties here that may extend into Florida and the panhandle itself, you see. Yes, there will be, without question, strict rules of procedure, and, indeed, look towards curfews, then the curfews will lead into segregation of individuals with weapons, and with certain forces to keep the peoples separate.

Again, if there is an assassination, there will be an increase in this activity, especially among those peoples that would be of the darker-skinned race, you see. If not, or if this is delayed, then you would find there would be a general removal of freedoms, as is already taking place, you see. And soon, there will be no ability to transfer monies from one state to another, or one place to another, for that matter. Look to the influence of the Virginia regions and extending of the police forces inland somewhat, as their controls - Langley, Norfolk, and other places like this – for they will go inland, as there will be seen some threat to the general regions in these areas, as we have indicated.

Yes, to the question, there will be protests, there will be weapons in the street, and there will be difficulties; but not, at first, in an explosive way. This conflict energy will creep into the society as it already is, with domestic violence, leading to mayhem and murder. There is already an indication of family members that will be exasperated into unions and other groups, as they continue to oppose military and governmental influences. Unfortunate!

PLEASE COMMENT ON THE STATUS OF THE UNITED STATES IN TERMS OF POLITICAL, ECONOMIC OR MILITARY INFLUENCE IN THE FUTURE?

All the world's forces will be taxed, and more than likely the influences of the Americans would be lesser and lesser as there would be a shift towards the eastern directions, or the Orient itself. Major trade routes will be through southern Europe, terminating, if you will, in Spain (termination meaning a gateway to trade in the Western hemisphere). The Americans will seemingly fade in their prominence in the world; their military might will be felt for some time, but as there would be a division of the country, then the paramilitary or military forces will, indeed, become less, and less, and less. Their political influence will fade as their money is shifted from paper to the demand for gold, as all countries in the world will deal only with gold: gold ingots, or coins, you see.

Their political influence in the world will become less, but not nonexistent, you see; just less. More prominent will be the Eastern worlds themselves; then next will come the prominence of the races from the continent of Africa. There will be some competition between the Orient and Africa, but if there is some determination, then you will find that the shift of power – political, economic, and military - will go to the East, you see. When the four Arab brothers unite, and there is a rejection of the American currency (as there has already been some indication), this is the beginning of the end for the Americans having dominance in the world, you see.

WHAT IS THE BEST OPPORTUNITY IN THE NORTH AMERICAN STOCK MARKETS?

It is a matter of looking at what sectors in the stock market would be best. The markets themselves will seemingly do well in Canada, for they are based on resources. If there is stock held in mining or energy supply, or real estate holdings, or oil, they would tend to do rather well, you see. As to food stocks and those of the agricultural worlds, these, too, would do well and maintain as time would go by. To the question, the stock markets would need to be looked at on an item by item basis, and how they would respond to inflation. This can be predictable by the sector they are in, you see, as we have given. Some are perfectly predictable. However, moving the monies to certain sectors that would be safe havens would be an investor's best opinion. The metals, especially, would prove to be supportive of stock prices, you see.

The Americans are in difficulty with their dollar and it will be under attack for some time, for as the American currency withers and is washed out, other currencies would tend to do a little better, would they not? As there would be more of the inflationary influences coming into America because of the high debt load, the dollar would seemingly do worse; and so goes the dollar, so goes the stock market. Those in the Canadian resource industries or sectors which are based on wealth in the ground will tend to suffice and do well. We would encourage any to do this, you see. In the future, Canada will be a communicative area, a place of negotiation, and there will be a large surplus of resources that would keep it interested in the financial aspects, you see. It would not be an extensive or large contingency, for it will be divided into three great regions. But in understanding this, it would be to say that there is some cooperation with this place, for it seems to have safe harbors and safe lodging, you see. As now, as then!

HOW WILL THE AMERICAN AND CANADIAN DOLLARS COMPARE IN THE FUTURE?

The currency in the Canadian region, based on its resources and economic strength, should do quite well, as there will be continued water damage or flooding in the mid-U.S. Look to this as severe disruption in their farming regions, due to excess amounts of water, and there will be great disasters requiring much in the way of money, which will tend to erode any strength between the Canadian and American balance, where the Americans will have the lion's share; in fact they will have less. It will be difficult for them to remove the water, or to save the land, or in that area to strengthen the currency against the Canadian resource-based currency itself, you see.

HOW WILL THE EURO COMPARE WITH THE AMERICAN DOLLAR?

We see the currency in the Americas being somewhat stronger at this time, and if we have a mark at 1.29 for the euro, it will vacillate a little, given some difficulties in Greece, and we find the low could be 1.10, perhaps even 0.99 for a brief time. Then there will be a retracement, and the currency will be quite strong, as Germany, and France, to some degree, have some acquisition plans for their own currencies. There will be economic structures taking place in the countries affecting the working individuals that will strengthen the euro against the dollar. But we would see this as a possible high during this year or the next eighteen months as 1.57 and then a further increase to 1.67 to 1.72 as a high, within the next eighteen to twenty-four months, you see.

It will depend on whether there is an assassination or not, and if there are some activities or increased warfare in the Middle East, you see (and it appears that there will be). Look to the Israelis; they will be somewhat passive, but when they become provoked, they will be extremely aggressive in this time, and the Americans will not hold them back! This will be an indication that the weakness of the U.S. dollar is at hand, and it appears to be self-evident that the value would be greatly lesser than it is now.

WHAT COUNTRY WILL ISRAEL GO TO WAR AGAINST?

This is the traditional tinderbox in the Middle East, you see. The Iranians will advance and will fire upon the Israeli. There will be difficulties in Turkey, for there will be some activities or explosions, you see, and there are smaller islands that are more Muslim, for they are related to Turkey itself and connected to Iran. The Iraqi/Iran brotherhood seems to be busted; they do not seem to be in synch or in harmony with each other. There does seem to be a branching out towards Turkey.

THOSE WHO CONTROL THE WORLD ECONOMIES, WILL THEIR CONTROL CEASE
IN THE FUTURE?

There will be continued influence in the countries' economies in Europe as well as what would be in the Western hemisphere. There will be an attempt to dismantle the economies in the countries they are now affecting. There will be more political assassinations in the East and in the West in order to divert attention away from their internal activities. Inflation will be afoot in the world. As we have given before, there will be those disturbances, economically, that will find difficulties in the street, and unemployment will continue to provoke crisis in some of the European countries. The Chinese themselves are reinforcing their position even now and are secretly improving and increasing their military might, for they fully expect an onslaught towards themselves as the world's banker, and as the world's manufacturer.

The shift in power away from the West and the European,towards the East and the Chinese is evident. When there is need for more oil, there will be an increase in their westerly direction or influence. To those who are already in control of the world itself, why change? To those in a lesser degree, the younger generation, you might say, they are playing a chess game with countries of the world. Why? Because they can! This is the danger that we perceive as to certain amalgamations of individuals, that there would not be ten against one another, but that there might be three or four that will band together and would be against the others individually. This would be dangerous indeed!

We see, in the next few months, that there will be disharmony, there will be increased assassination, and there will be increased inflation, all at the expense of the common person, you see!

Look to those in the East for more difficulty than those who would be the bankers in Switzerland, or Norway, or in the European Union itself. For here, as the world goes through another series of revolution, there is in the minds of those who have and control power the real expectation that there will be civil unrest; and to minds who profit by this, it would be procured, if possible.

COMPARED TO THE ECONOMY THAT WE NOW EXPERIENCE, COULD YOU PLEASE DESCRIBE WHAT THE GLOBAL ECONOMY WILL BE LIKE IN THE FUTURE?

Those in the East will seemingly do well. Those in South America will seemingly be moderate in doing well. Those particular influences in Europe, the Economic Council, will somewhat survive. They will be bruised, but they will survive. The American dollar is fading from the world markets as something important or being a world leader; in fact, those who wish harm to the Americans seem to be manipulating it to the lower side. Too much inventory, too much supply will drive the prices down. Even though there will be some crisis in the world that will require these types of items, they will not be readily delivered. There will be bribes, there will be holdups, there will be demands for monies, you see, and it will be allowed or tolerated because it is expedient to get the items from one place to another, unfortunately, you see. However, to the question, we would expect to see the economic situation in Canada holding its own. Spain will do likewise after a time of grief. China will maintain its position of aloofness, and may come westward, you see, looking for sources of power. This will be the difficulty that, under the ground, others will come to claim what is not theirs, you see.

SHOULD ATTEMPTS BE MADE TO CLEAR ALL DEBT?

It would be a good idea, for debt is basically slavery, is it not? This type of debt is dangerous, for the property that is secured against the debt, usually, is much greater than the debt, yet the whole amount of property can be taken! The time of extremes is a chaotic time, and those things in the extreme will take place. Inflationary influences will be extreme! Unfortunate!

Be prepared. Own a few silver coins, and perhaps a gold coin or two. Keep the seeds, the stones and semi-precious stones that might be used for barter or trade, as there will be disruptions in the currencies. Be debt-free! For then you will own your property and not be subject to schemes and devices that would cheat and remove yourself from your property. Best if you would have five acres to be self-sufficient. But be prepared! Times are afoot! These serious times are changing and they are changing faster than most suspect. Be prepared!

AS YOU SEE IT, WHAT WILL BE THE HIGHEST PRICE OF GOLD AND SILVER?

Looking forward, the price of gold could be about two thousand eight hundred dollars. Looking forward, the price of silver would be about one hundred and five dollars, if not a little more. There will be some vacillation in the value of gold, but given the time frame of the next three years, easily this will be in the mid two thousand five hundred dollar to two thousand eight hundred dollar range, based on the U.S. dollar. There will be some disenfranchising from different countries in the world in which the U.S. dollar is losing its benchmark valuation, even now, and, therefore, this will play some fluctuation in the price as well. However the price will be onward and upward; and as there would be volcanic activity, earthquake activity, there will be a suppression of mining, drilling and oil production, especially in those areas that are offshore. This will tend to drive the price of the precious metals even higher, as they will be used as legal tender, or will be demanded as money from the various countries that would lie in an easterly direction beyond Persia (into that of the Chinese, you see). Likewise, the silver market will follow. There would be a rise from the thirty dollar point, which will foreshadow or move in advance of the price of gold itself, towards one hundred and fifty dollars, or possibly as high as two hundred dollars. It will be used more in the production of weaponry; in particular, batteries and other laser-light equipment, you see. This will be extending to the next four or five years, or as many as seven years, as we are looking forward. Again, this will be used as legal exchange or tender, and there will be a demand from those countries that would not want the paper money, but would look towards inflationary influences for real property, or real value.

These prices we are observing are the probabilities of those influences that will thrust them forward, in the next two to five or seven years. But make no mistake. This particular demand for metals is because of the confidence lost in the paper monies, and, indeed, the inflationary or arbitrary printing of more monies to cover debt (especially in the Americas). Those countries that would be well-founded, or will not suffer will be those that produce metal, and those that are enriched with resources: South Africa, Canada, and those areas or regions in Russia itself. See? But those in China, India, and Africa will be reluctant at exchanging the metals. The world will find that they will keep even the copper, nickel and base metals to themselves, and this will tend to drive the price higher, as you would expect.

WHAT TIME FRAME CAN YOU PREDICT THAT THIS CHANGE WILL TAKE PLACE

FROM PAPER MONEY TO THE GOLD STANDARD?

It appears already to be taking place in certain aspects of the world itself. You would find that the monies are being changed rapidly, due to a variety of reasons, including counterfeiting. However, the next will be the refusal of people to accept government notes. They will rather have real monies or things that are of real value. This should take place in the economic resurgence or the adjustment period, within the next three years.

WILL WE SEE A GREATER RETURN TO THE BARTER SYSTEM?

Indeed, it will continue, as it would be the underground economic market or economy. The people who are in charge of governments now come from other, foreign countries, and, as such, it is their way of doing business not to pay taxes, to avoid calculations by paying cash, and indeed manipulating with their cash (their expenditures, as well as their profit). You can expect this to continue as these ethnic groups cooperate one with another, and you would find that sooner or later, it would be required that gratuities must be paid in order for simple functions in government to be carried out. But this increase in barter is already taking place and is growing rapidly!

WHAT SKILLS OR COMMODITIES WILL BE THE MOST SOUGHT-AFTER?

We would say water across the board will be sought as there would be droughts and dryness and ash in the air. We would then find other forms of foods, bartering for labor, seeds, semi-precious and precious stones. Then there would be the metal coins of course: gold, silver, palladium/platinum that would be available in other forms you see.

~ 142 ~

However, it would be the simple staples of life: these would be food, water, and power, along with some forms of transportation.

YOU HAVE SAID THAT IN THE FUTURE, THE MOST VALUABLE COMMODITY WILL BE FRESH DRINKING WATER. PLEASE INDICATE WHAT THE VALUE OF WATER WILL BE IN COMPARISON TO THE VALUE OF GOLD IN THE COMING YEARS?

It could be almost as much, you see. But it is clear, clean water that will be the most valuable. It will be expensive. That which comes from the tap will be suspect, as it may be loaded up with runoff ingredients. Bottled water, spring water, and other forms of water that are tested will seem to do better. If you would look at it from a dollar perspective, it would seem that it would be about three hundred dollars for a five-gallon jug. But this would be even more, as time would progress. When you find droughts, when you have dust in the air, the price will go up ten times!

YOU MENTIONED THAT SPAIN WILL BECOME A CENTER FOR WORLD TRADE. COULD YOU PLEASE PROVIDE MORE DETAIL ON HOW THE ECONOMY OF SPAIN WILL CHANGE IN THE COMING YEARS?

As we would examine the economy of this country, you would find that, indeed, as we have given previously, there are inflationary influences and these are being imported from other countries. There is, indeed, labor discontent. This, too, we have given. You will find that this will continue; for those in authority are lacking direction and they are looking towards the bankers of the neighboring countries and the European Union itself, and the bankers themselves are not in accord with sharing! These bankers are more in accord with surviving themselves, you see, and you will find that this particular country will, indeed, continue on a downward slide in its economy. There will be increased unemployment, increased labor unrest and there will be riots in the streets! This, too, we have given previously. You would find that the economic stability will be in solid assets; those who would be debt-free will do much better and fare better in this economy. Those who are debt-laden will find themselves losing and giving up their property, their wealth, as they will be beholden to those who would be the money-lenders.

Expect, therefore, some disruptions still within the economy, but Spain itself is not as poor as the other sisters: Ireland, Portugal, to name a few. The German economy will be somewhat beneficial to Spain, as would France, you see. However, out of this will come more of a stability and there will be more regulations that will not allow the bankers to be involved in so many different ventures! There will be, once again, a return to some segregation of institutions, and how they perceive to make their monies from the people. However, we do find angry people, we do find weapons in their hands, and we find that in the street they will continue to be disruptive and there will be damage!

The economy itself, in different parts of the country, will, seemingly, be unaffected, but the larger, more financial centers will be affected in an academic or a paper way. Those on the high end of the scale will not suffer as great a loss as those who would be on the other end; those who are poor will suffer greatly, and those who are infirm and handicapped will suffer even more so!

As we see it, inflationary forces are now afoot, and they will continue for some time, for the next two to three years, as we see it. There will be more reliance on gold and the institution of gold-backed currency, as there is supposed to be now. It will be deemed more of a necessity. See? And, indeed, Spain, sleepy as it might seem, will once again wake up to the economic pressures, and the whole country itself will change. There will be more observation and moderation of the economic situation by the people themselves. They will be angry, but change will come of this. And out of this, Spain may lead the way, along with one or two other countries in the Council, in establishing some form of stability. As we have given before, it would appear that Spain itself will be the crossroads for future economic trading. And like all trails that cross at a certain place, the place will prosper, for there will be economic sharing and trading, and the country itself, in the future, will do quite well, and it would be one of the most prestigious places to be, economically speaking.

Italy will rule the world, but Spain will be its partner. For the short term, for the next five to seven years, the economy will not be so good, but it would recover rather quickly. When it is put more to the gold standard, you would find that there would be some stability.

There would also be some crisis that should be paid attention to; there will be the shrinkage of the coastlines and this will affect the economic situation. People who live in the north will have to migrate south towards the hills and people who live in the west and in the west-southwest region will have to take some precautions for flooding. But as we see it, the country itself will maintain its shape, save for the loss of the coastline that is somewhat at or slightly above sea level. This would be because of the rise in the ocean surface, you see.

The economy then will do much better. But expect the next two to three years to be somewhat merging more towards the crisis level, and as inflationary influences come into the world and rise to the thirty to thirty-three per cent level, Spain will not do well, but it will not do poorly either. But it will survive.

As to the housing market, it will continue; those without debt will seem to prosper, and those with currency to spare will be on a buying spree to buy whatever property they can get. The country should do well in some sectors, but in others, especially where there is the financial or "Middleman" trading (bonds and paper vehicles), these will not do so well, you see. The currency will alter or be changed, as it will be in comparison to inflationary influences. The people themselves will survive. A little rocky at this point in time, but for some, they will not even notice the change, you see. However, for the most part, those who are working (or working-poor) will suffer the most, and there will be migrations to France, to Greece, to Africa; something that was never done in the country before.

The property values will continue to increase, especially those that are not embedded in debt. Those that are will have a tendency to suffer, as there will be increased interest charges, to the point that they might forfeit or lose their property. The interest rates will go higher, and the value of the property will do likewise; as we see it in Spain and in other places that would be desirable for those who would wish to get away from the chaos and turmoil of their own home country, you see. However, there will be an exodus in Spain. There will be the same in the northern part of India. These two countries will suffice to have the population itself moved, in part or in whole, from one place to another, with the intention that the peoples would be taking care of one another, with the intention that there would be the good minds and hearts that would be behind this initiative or intention. We do not find the country itself destitute, but we do find much anger and, indeed, shortages and willful disturbances are coming. The property values will not dissipate; indeed they will grow stronger.

PLEASE COMMENT ON THE GREATER EUROPEAN ECONOMY DURING THIS TIME.

There will be further inflationary influences in the world itself. The European countries that are borderline in their solvency will, in all likelihood, have great difficulties. Spain is now in such turmoil; although Spain would seemingly be a stronger economy than Ireland, or Portugal, or Greece, it will be part of the same, with the difficulties in labor unrest and the shortcomings of the treasuries of these countries being almost empty! They will be clever in how they will regain monies through taxes, through social restrictions and fines for breaches of certain laws. The taxation will increase as well. Make no mistake; the inflationary influences in the world are great. The precious metals, as we have given before, have risen considerably, because of the lack of confidence in currencies or paper money, and because those countries may default on their debt or even the backing up of their own currency. Caution is warranted indeed! If you would expect thirty percent or more inflation, and be able to prosper by this, then it would be a good time. But as we see it, those who are ill in their administration of their governmental responsibilities, and are not prepared for such inflation – or perhaps they are denying the existence of the same – these are heading down a short path to greater and greater difficulty.

WILL SENIORS' AND DISABILITY PENSIONS CONTINUE TO BE PAID?

The monies will be paid, but the inflationary rates will tend to eat up the value of the monies. Again, those who have debts will suffer the most. Those who are debt-free will tend to survive the most, you see. Pensions will be paid, but inflationary influences, governmental tweaking of the economy and interferences in Europe especially will seemingly cause a barrage of nickel-and-diming it, taking monies away from those who have worked for life and are entitled to it, you see. This would be the outcome of the strategy of those who would be in the business, so to speak.

WITH LARGE NUMBERS OF PEOPLE IMMIGRATING BETWEEN COUNTRIES FOR SAFETY, DO YOU FORESEE ANY PROBLEMS AMONG PEOPLE OF DIFFERENT RELIGIOUS, SOCIAL, OR CULTURAL BACKGROUNDS?

As we have given, in the future, there will be more of a tendency for the peoples of the world to come together and cooperate. For you see, the power sources will shift or change. There will be the use of the planet's natural forces of power. The same electricity that runs through crystals will be used to illuminate walls and assist in power supply. This will lessen the burden upon those races that are ignorant of the comforts that are shared by many. Prior to this point of euphoric cooperation, there will be destructive influences that will be shed one upon the other, or nation against nation. But at that point in time, you will find that there will be a reluctance for any group to profess that they must, by force, overcome their enemies, and, as such, there will be a lesser and lesser effect of those influences of hatred.

As we look forward in time, we would see that, yes, there will be improvements, and there will not be those peoples who would arbitrarily cause disturbance and chaos in the name of God, or for peace, or for righteousness' sake. For, as we have given, the planet, and certain groups of people are coming to a point of justice rather than injustice, you see. The answer is simply: there will be huge improvements in the social and political activities between various groups now that seem to be at variance with each other, or who are fighting. For, here, they will need to come together, and work shoulder to shoulder, to move earth and stones, for plenty of good, constructive reasons, and they will come together to understand that God really is not blind, deaf, or indifferent; that God's all-seeing eye will see them even in their darkest time or place.

In essence, there will be more of a unifying religion that will be based on understanding the principles of nature, and there will be many who will come to this understanding, for their self-preservation, their self-maintenance, or their life. There will be the recognition that the planet is alive, has a consciousness unto its own, and has rebelled, due to all the infractions that have been shed upon it over the last several whiles, you see. This consciousness or understanding will be known, and, therefore, violence, transgression, evil, and destructive influences will be lessened, for it will be seen that they are counter-productive to the advancement of anyone! There will be social balance. Out of necessity, those who criticize one another now will work shoulder to shoulder, moving earth, sand, and stones, for mutual protection, and benefit, as well as rescue. The pivotal point of power will come from Italy. There will not be influence from the Arab world or from those who would profess to use force and terror to get their ways, for this will be found to be a great sin or a mistake, for any group of people who would use, in the name of God, murder, chaos, destructive forces or weapons, you see.

COULD YOU PLEASE EXPAND ON WHAT CHINA'S ACTIONS MAY BE?

They will move to Persia where they will attempt to control the resources there, you see. There will be an expansion of their territory, for there will be a shrinkage in some places, and they will attempt to move westward so there can be more accommodation for commerce;

business itself, you see.

Will China go to war with India?

We do not see the Chinese and the Indians fighting; we see more the Chinese coming into the Arabic lands. There are spaces in Africa, especially in the Tanzania region, and these Chinese-owned mines will be somewhat swarming with military advisors or protectors. For these raw materials are sent directly to China from these places; and as such, there will be some subordinate activity that may cause disruptions or difficulty by the Chinese in the African regions. We do not find it intruding into the Indian regions.

Will Israel be attacked with nuclear weapons in the near future?

The answer would be affirmative. We are observing, in a way, activities that would be subversive. It would be economical, you see. There will be hostility, gang warfare, you might say, various factions. Yes to the question.

Please clarify a statement you made. "Italy will rule the world"?

As you would look in history, you would see that certain countries - the Ottoman empire, the Roman empire, the British empire, the American empire – all have taken their time at the helm of ruling the world. China now seems to be ruling the world as the world's banker, as the world's economic giant and supplier of goods. Italy will be, in the future, the same. Like Rome, once the pinnacle of power, it will be, once again; and it will dictate – DICTATE – its power and rules to the world, and the world will follow suit. It will not be the same climate and procedure as you now understand, as countries communicating with countries. Not an east/west hemisphere communication at all, but more of a north-to-south (north of the equator to south of the equator) economic flow.

But through Spain, there will be the trade routes that will lead east and west, north and south; and through Spain, Italy (and its political, willful minds) will oversee this, you see. Therefore, they will control the economy and the flows of the economy through other neighboring countries. They will rule the world. They will not have to conquer it as they did before!

PART FOUR

☙ ❧

Being Prepared

ARE THERE SAFE PLACES TO LIVE, TO MINIMIZE OUR EXPOSURE TO ALL THESE EARTH CHANGES?

"Safe" is a relative term, you see! Canada will be relatively safe, for the peoples of this place are the peacemakers of the world, therefore they will not need to suffer as extensively as others who might suffer, who are seeking power over each other and the world itself. To the question, you can expect that this would be a time of uncertainty. The safe places will largely be somewhere about two hundred feet above sea level, two hundred miles away from the sea coast, on both the east and west sides of the country. And indeed, not to have separation of assets, but keeping things together so there is a control over what is (and has been) spent.

GIVEN THE CHANGES IN THE EARTH THAT ARE COMING TO US, WHAT CAN WE DO TO PREPARE OURSELVES?

First, it is to be willing to prepare yourself! Not to wait, not to suspect, not to vacillate. Water will be in great need. Also there will be a need to prepare, store, and collect food items; not that one should be frightened, but that one should be prepared, in all ways to sustain oneself for six months or longer. Eighteen months would be the best.

There are groups already who know how to survive and how to have food items ahead of time. Some foods need to be made from scratch, of course. Take a lesson from these people and be prepared for a few months at least. It would be examined that most people have seven or ten days' food in advance, if they are prepared in the normal fashion. However, by extending this period into months, then you would be better prepared.

Monies will continue to inflate, and therefore protecting money from inflation will sustain your wealth in the future. Coins of value would be gold and silver. Precious stones, and semiprecious stones may be collected or held as money. Have no debt! Own your own home and have access to a plot of land where you might grow food. But have storage of food that would be several months in advance, and include water and any devices that would be necessary to prepare food, or to store food. Most importantly, band together through friendship or through common values and desire. The tribal mentality would be the best; ten families coming together to sustain themselves under all circumstances. This is possible. To have alliances and associations with others who can be trusted.

Extend yourself, but not overly so. Attempt to have no debts, and have storage of food or a food supply for several months, including water supply, and then take onto the self those things that might be bartered with: toilet paper, for instance, propane tanks, or other such items that might be usable during times of shortage. Remember, the transportation of food from one corner of the country to the other may be disrupted. Electricity and the supply of electricity may be disrupted. You can see there may be difficulty, perhaps not for an extended period, but at least for a period that may last from five to ten days (or the same number of weeks) depending on the ash that will come from the air and disrupt transportation. Suddenly, food supplies could become difficult! To be prepared for this is the best way. The best would be to have supportive friends who could look out for each other and cooperate and share during times of uncertainty. Through these numbers, there would be less chance of robbery, or food and water being taken away from one another.

However, the best is to come together, to be prepared with an abundance of supplies. Not to fear, but be prepared in case there is a shortage, or in case there is ash from the sky, or in case there is water flooding inland, you see. To be prepared is to have comfort; to have comfort is to have faith; and to have faith is to be able to deal with the circumstances at hand, you see.

WHAT WILL BE THE BIGGEST CHANGES AND CHALLENGES DURING THIS TIME?

Look for shortages and food disruptions. When the clouds in the sky are grey with soot or ash, this will be a challenge for people. There will be difficulties in mobility or transportation; there will be difficulties in the quality of air. However, it would be disruption in the supply of fresh water that would be a concern. Food will be somewhat seen as an issue or a concern. As those who have prepared for this time of change – some might deem it a time of chaos – there would be opportunities to unite the people within this time. Those who would be of the selfish mentality will be ostracized and maybe would be rebuked and even banished.

Those who would be of one mind and would take care, helping one another would be accepted and would start the challenge that you speak of: one of cooperation.

The duration for this particular time may be a matter of years, perhaps as much as a generation; but, indeed, there will be the learning not to be selfish, not to be frightened, not to seek power over others; but rather to be compassionate, and to take care of what happens to others. This will be a challenge that will be quite difficult, for there will be a tendency for those who would be frightened, attempting to feed themselves, and to take provisions for those who would be meaningful to them at the expense (or even the termination) of others who are not meaningful to them. There may come a time in which there would be a coveting of food, a coveting of shelter, and there may be a time of lawlessness. This would be temporary, if it is allowed to manifest. This would be one of the challenges, you see.

For a rule of thumb, it would be to understand that in times of crisis, when people come together, they can, through their togetherness, overcome any shortage, any difficulty. Look for power outages, look for water to rise here and there, and look for disturbances where there will be shaking and quaking. Air quality, fresh water, and, indeed, the ability to have a cooperative, so to speak, of caring for one another, will be the answer to this question.

WHAT CAN WE DO TO PROTECT OURSELVES FROM LOOTING OR LAWLESSNESS?

What communities *will do* is enforce their military strength to keep the peace; there will be law and order, and there will be certain civilian groups also that would be involved in this. Generally speaking, throughout the world itself, the military, paramilitary, and police forces will combine and will be utilized in keeping the peace, rescuing, and transporting goods to peoples who are stranded or to communities that are isolated. They will also be used in altering certain conditions.

There will be fires, there will be lava flows, and there will be the burden of volcanic ash that would need to be removed. They seemingly would be the opportune group to do this, you see. And, indeed, there will be a severity of bands or gangs, should there be such (and in all likelihood there will be), and they will pay *capitally* for their mischief, shall we call it. There will be orders brought into the society which, for a time, would seem to be tyrannical or harsh. And, as such, the communities themselves will invoke some sort of martial law, but it will be a paramilitary style, with civilian support, you see.

WOULD YOU RECOMMEND THE AVERAGE PERSON ARM HIM OR HERSELF?

Of course. The type of weapon is the problem! Weapons that would kill instantly, like guns, or bows and arrows, or explosive devices, would tend to be not so good to have inasmuch as they will cause more domestic difficulty by accident or by will, than any other. Long guns might be a solution here, and certainly there is preparation in certain governments to allow the permission of long guns to be held within the general population. This would be a matter of course. We would not recommend that there would be the use of the same, for the taking of life wantonly. But indeed, in certain regions, in certain outlying areas where there is not police enforcement, then, perhaps, as it is already evident, it would be necessary, to protect the family, or the self. Long guns may be necessary for defense, rather than of-fense, you see.

However, when there are marauding gangs or groups of peo-ple, then it would be better to band together as a tribal community or mentality and this would chase away those who may have destruc-tive, murderous thoughts, and a lack of caring for human life and liberty. Certain areas may require this, and they seem already to be prepared in different aspects in North America, and in other countries beyond; they would be prepared, you see, for a certain on-slaught of invaders. It is a fact of life. It is evident that many already are prepared, and many have such weapons as you would inquire about.

Our recommendation would not be to arm yourself in order to take the life of thy neighbor! But rather it would be to band to-gether so there would be a constructive use of acceptance and of co-operation. Through numbers, there would be less intimidation or the use of firearms by those who are desperate. Weapons that are less offensive, like staffs, or canes, or even bars, and sharp implements could be kept handy for use in certain circumstances. But, again, we are not recommending or advocating that any would arm themselves. If they do, then it would be better to have some sort of self-protective implement or weapon, as you might call it. However, there is nothing more fierce, nothing more aggressive, no weapon that is better than the human mind. Using the mind, the self can, indeed, abate an in-vasion, by simply altering the circumstances of the confrontation. And, therefore, it is acceptable to be compassionately rejecting of those forces, intrusions, or invasions upon the welfare of the self, the family, or the neighborhood which the self holds meaningful. How-ever, believe in what is unseen!

Be prepared for any invasion-type influences, but be prepared to help those who are without. Those who are starving can be turned into friends in a certain way. But those who are armed themselves and are marauding and careless about people may suffer at the hands of weapons and of circumstance, you see. Remember always: it is the choice of each and everyone whether they take a life or not. Training in prevention of such circumstances goes with the responsibility of handling any weapon. It may be necessary to have weapons in the household in certain communities. In others, it would certainly not be necessary. It depends on where the self resides, the mentality of the community, and the availability of protection provided by paid and trained police persons or security forces. If there are none, then by all means, protecting the self would be a logical and natural conclusion.

How may we talk to our friends and family who may not believe that Earth changes are happening?

By showing, rather than telling. By simply being logical and speaking of the benefits of having a stockpile of food very handy, or that money can be saved by having large quantities of things stored, you see. Be a little mysterious and a little teasing at the same time.

However, you cannot *convince* anyone that something is going to happen if they have in their mind or heart that it is not going to happen. In fact, the rule is that, usually, the more you try to convince them, the more they are entrenched and will not believe or even attempt to observe or consider what is being put in front of them! Humans, as you know humans, have a problem. They cannot believe the obvious, they cannot hear the truth, and they will not do what is good for them. They seem always to do the right thing for the wrong reasons. Therefore, do not attempt to "Bible-thump," convince, coerce or otherwise shame them into belief. But, rather, simply and merrily go about your own way, and if there is someone who asks a question, then you might say, "Yes! This is how you do that." And, indeed, by showing them, they will learn how, you see.

When should we begin to store food and water?

Today would be good. The time would be for a few months in duration. And yes, food and water, but water in particular; for there will be shortages, and problems with the transportation and delivery of the same.

WHAT TYPES OF FOOD SHOULD WE STORE, AND HOW MUCH?

The volume would be simply calculated from the amount of intake per person as they would consume food even now. The idea is to have sufficient amount, so there are not stoppages or shortages that would necessitate having no food, which will occur for those who shop week-to-week and might be caught unawares of difficulties in transportation of foods, especially fresh foods. And as such, there might be delay, and this might be of an entire growing season or two.

As to the staples themselves: canned goods, of course, would be sufficient; the basic grains that would supply basic food to the peoples themselves, as has been done in the past you see. Food that would be made into porridge has always been a good staple! Water, of course, is most important. But here, the staples would be salt, flours, and canned goods or dry goods, as you would know them. Now, depending on how meat is stored, whether it is hung and dried and stored in a traditional sense, or whether it would be in cans, or foil packages, or containers that would be engineered to keep food available, fresh, or good for long periods of time, these may be used as ways and means to keep the staples, that the self would endure. Spices would be important. Honey would be *very* important.

Medicines might be also kept, but those foods that would be grown from seeds would also be beneficial, so a certain amount of seeds (which would be extremely valuable in the future) should also be hoarded or kept in jars, moisture-free. Tuberous food that can be grown, like carrots, and also foods that would be green and leafy, like cabbages and foods that can be planted and would multiply, like potatoes, should be considered part of the staples. Lentils, and dried beans and other foods that would be kept over long periods of time in such way or shape should also be considered.

Now, frozen foods would be possible, as long as there is no interruption in power, but there might be! Therefore frozen foods would not be considered priority, or should be counted on. Look to the Mormon, the Hittite, or to those who would have natural purposes in procuring food and storing it for a long time, and you would find that they could provide a long list of foods that would be available and how to store them, whether they would be in the ground, in a sand pile, in plastic bags and containers, in foil envelopes, or jars and cans. This information is readily available.

To have the wherewithal to plant seeds and to keep the body whole, one would need a little more property than the balcony of an apartment or a condominium which supports grass and flowers. Rather, a little larger chunk of land – five acres, for instance – would be sufficient to sustain a family of four. Animals may be kept in such a place; chickens, ducks, even lambs, you see.

Any food that can be sustained in a can would be good; whatever your preference. But, here, look to the beans and the lentils, to corn, and to the squashes, to the carrots, and to the thick, dark green leafy variety of the vegetable. Fruits that are dried would be good. Nuts of all sorts would be good. A little common sense here, you see, and this would be sufficient to sustain an individual, a couple, or a family. Frozen berries and jams might be good for awhile, and they should be considered, but it would be better to have preservatives "the way Grandma used to make," and there you can preserve most anything, you see. Rice and wheat make good meals and can be turned into many dishes, and are easily stored. Build on that, you see. Salt and sugar make good contributors to this as well.

Remember, it is not that it might be needed for a length of time. It is that there might be disruptions in transportation and power supply; and there will be, as the world goes through what would be termed the fifth destruction. Should this conclude, it would be a matter of survival in a common sense way; not to be fearful, not to be panicked, but in order to cooperate with others. For there is no need to build a bomb shelter in the basement any longer. What is needed is the convenience and the security of having food so that you might stay indoors, and not risk the life to go gathering food here and there, you see.

COULD YOU SUGGEST A LOCATION WHERE WE COULD FIND PURE SEEDS THAT HAVE NOT BEEN MANIPULATED OR GENETICALLY MODIFIED?

In Norway! In many countries, there are many seeds that have not been modified. This is not a standard process of modifying seeds, which have the atomic structure. But if you were looking for ones from antiquity, they would exist in museums and other places. Also you would find there are certain cooperatives of those individuals in the regions you would call Hittite, Mormon, or Mennonite. They would have seeds that have not been modified, but have been consecutively grown on the land they now re-seed every year, for some of the plants have been left to go to seed. There are many caches or hoarding of seeds, here, in various countries that would indeed stem backward in time one hundred or two hundred or three hundred years. Look to those who travel in horse and buggy for ancestral seeds, you see.

IF WE WERE TO STORE WATER FOR OURSELVES, WHAT WOULD BE THE MINIMUM

QUANTITY PER PERSON, PER DAY APPROXIMATELY?

As to rations per day, it would be, perhaps, a liter. For sustenance and cooking, it might be a little more. However, between two and five liters would be sufficient; even more than you would require.

ARE THERE ANY SPECIAL PRECAUTIONS FOR PEOPLE TO TAKE, WITH REGARD TO ANTICIPATED CLIMATE CHANGES?

We would suggest there be some form of breathing apparatus or mask available, for there will be ash in the air, there will be sulfur in the air, and there will be great waves, as there would be an increase in water temperature (as we have given previously) which is now occurring worldwide; the oceans are hot! Fishes may be taken as food, but we suggest precaution, for they may be poisonous or may have substances that have risen up from the bottoms of the ocean which humankind has deposited there in the first place. And these garbage dumps will be toxic, and therefore this toxic influence may come from the water and be spread. As such, there will be, in the air and in the water, these substances that may cause difficulty to breathing, you see. Those who are old and those who are very young may have great difficulty in breathing, for there will be gases in the air or pollutants, as we have given, from sulfur, to ash that is volcanic; it will be fine and difficult to breathe. But, here, the precaution will be to have a breathing apparatus, or mask, or filtration devices that could be used in some areas that are affected.

Otherwise, methane gas and other fumes (natural gas) will also be escaping from the ground, especially near areas of oil springs, you see. There might be black clouds and soot in the air coming from these poisonous substances from the ground. Best to be prepared with filtration devices, or a mask, or breathing apparatus. Even a simple handkerchief may be sufficient when there is dust in the air! This may be one thing to consider, you see? Heat, dust, and ash from the sky. Pay attention to this.

HOW LONG SHOULD WE BE PREPARED THAT DUST WILL BE IN THE SKY?

It will be a considerable time. Depending upon the wobble of the planet and certain prevailing winds, you can expect this to be three months.

CAN COLLOIDAL SILVER (OR COLLOIDAL GOLD) BE USED IN GREATER DOSES TO PURIFY WATER?

It would not hurt, but we find that the value of silver would be so high it would be done sparingly and would not be seen as medicinal, but rather more as a commodity! Yes, to the question, it would be functional.

WE ARE TOLD THAT WATER SHOULD NOT BE STORED IN PLASTIC BOTTLES. COULD YOU PLEASE COMMENT ON THE SAFEST WAY TO STORE WATER?

Depending on the size and thickness of the bottle, or jar, or container, those that are made in a thicker plastic would seem to be acceptable. For those that are made in a thinner, disposable sense, their construction and compounds seem not to be as dense, and therefore you would find that there may be some leaching of chemical reaction; but it also depends on the water itself. As we see it, the controversy over the disposable, thin polyurethane or polystyrene extruded plastic - these would be in the process where there would be some contamination; the machinery, the spraying on the inside, the heat used to extrude the bottle or container. This is where some contamination or derogatory effect can occur. But those that are made in a larger mould in which there is more heat rather than stretching, so to speak, the walls would not be holding so much contaminant, or more exactly, they would be formed in a more solid space. The stretchy, disposable plastic bottles seem to be aerated and have gaps that would have these chemicals entrapped, if this is helpful to the question. Then, a larger more durable or thicker container seems to be a better choice, you see.

In order to maintain a safe drinking water level, would it be beneficial to purchase a distiller?

In comparing distilling with boiling water, or purification filters, it is of the same; equally, you see, one no better than the other. There are advantages and disadvantages. The distiller leaches minerals and nutrients out of the water. Boiling tends to remove any bacteria, or even virus, you see. Steaming water and recapturing it seems to use up plenty of energy. Putting chemicals to purify the water or adding something to the water that removes one thing but adds itself seems to be an encumbrance, you see. It depends on the choice. But to the question, distilling the water does not seem to be any further advantage to boiling.

Would chlorine tablets be useful to purify the water?

It would put chlorine into the water and would help kill some bacteria, but the chlorine would still be in the water, would it not? Chlorine softens the enamel and softens bone. What would be necessary would be for fountains, or sprays, in which the water would spray into the air or run over courses of rocks that would babble and break up the atomic structure, so to speak. This would release the irritants and the pollutants. There are processes of simply running water down a trough filled with rocks and pebbles; as the water would babble over these rocks, it would purify itself in a natural way. This form of natural purification occurs over rocks, through waterfalls primarily, wherever the water can be taken and made into a small mist or spray, or where the water itself is bashed against rocks, this is the healing process and it releases the potential irritants from the water. To the question, this would not suffice too much in the way of preventing bacteria on one hand, and adding chlorine to the water on the other. It does not seem to be a viable balance in this formula.

COULD YOU OFFER A SUGGESTION TO PURIFY AND DESALINATE WATER FOR DRINKING WHICH MAY BE IMPLEMENTED BY THE AVERAGE PERSON?

There are several available mechanisms that basically already accomplish this. We would find these in small units in which there would be some sort of distillation taking place, or some removal of salt using filters from the water itself. We have these as cylinders. They appear to be bright yellow in color with black sealing rings or adaptation for the water to be removed from this package. We see these being evident at this point in time.

IS IT POSSIBLE TO PURIFY WATER WITH THOUGHT OR INTENTION?

Your intention of using Reiki, or spiritual energy, or other forces of biological energy would tend to reinforce the water, but it would not necessarily purify it, you see! But water that is purified, or at least drinkable, would be energized and would be beneficial to the body, where no harm would come to it, you see. Yes the water may be blessed and it may be increased in its vitality. But best to purify the water first by some way or some means that would remove any feces, or *e-coli*, or bacterial influences.

ARE THERE ANY SPECIAL PRECAUTIONS TO TAKE REGARDING INSECT INVASIONS OR INVASIONS BY BIRDS OR ANIMALS?

There will be some diseases from certain stagnant pools of water. Yes, there will be need for some sanitation or some cleanup in this regard, and animals that would be exposed to this form of decay or death may truly be contaminated themselves with some disease. There seem to be patrols coming, or people responsible for capturing animals that may be sick and injured, and they seem to be taking care of them, you see. Therefore, we would expect some effort to repatriate those animals that are ill, and to control some diseases, you see, that would be spread through stagnant pools of water. This would affect mosquites, and would affect other, smaller amounts of insects that would seem to be quite prevalent. We find some burning of swampland and some chemical sprays will be used to keep down any outbreak of bacteria in this regard. These will be crews on boats, as we see them.

WHY ARE SOME OF THE LARGER COUNTRIES – SUCH AS RUSSIA AND THE UNITED STATES – PREPARING FOR EARTH CHANGES?

Why not? They are intelligent; they have been aware from their intelligence sources. There are intellectuals at universities, engineers; there are geologists, vulcanists, those who would understand much in the way of the world and what is taking place. There is preparation always, and there are individuals who are taught to think conversely. Military leaders, for instance, do not plan peace. They constantly plan war. They are paid to do so. There are those within the farming and agricultural regions who are far-reaching in their assessments and those who would be involved in weather and the movement of weather (meteorologists). These have been preparing, and have shown and have forecasted huge alterations or traumatic events taking place in the world.

For years there has been seen, if you would recount, that the planet is warming. In particular, the oceans are raising their temperatures at an alarming rate. It will have surpassed the one degree crucial temperature mark; it will surpass the second degree devastation mark; it will pass the third degree catastrophe mark, and it will touch upon the fourth degree which would be the global destruction mark! This is already known, and there are those forces within the government that are preparing for the same. They are not idle, although it would be seen as a collective form of communication. Discussions at the United Nations have taken place, discussions within the European Council and discussions within certain governmental, commercial, or corporate influences have already taken place as well. The evidence has been forthcoming for a decade. Publication of such preparations has not been forthcoming, but it does not mean that preparations have not taken place. There are always preparations for disaster. When such a disaster takes place anywhere in the world, resources are taken out of places of storage and delivered. Someone had to put them in storage in the first place! Those who would be anticipating disaster and would require supplies and resources in the first place, these individuals are the sources of information for governments. They are not covert operations, but they are not publically broadcast either.

However, in certain circles, those who would look far into the future have already reported such to their various governments, and as we have given, there has been some subsidy, some preparation in those countries that are wise and not selfish. To some that have, indeed, served the master of the land itself, these are not so readily prepared; North Korea, you see, and some dictatorships and monarchies that still exist. The question being: who would have such knowledge?

Information-gathering forces within the governments have, for at least the last two decades, foreseen that this is taking place, you see. Preparations for the same have commenced, but not too extensively in various countries; for they do not have the money on one hand, and they do not wish to lock up their funds in regard to their populations on the other. These would be more to the families and individuals that would be selfish in their dictatorships, you see.

CAN YOU OFFER ANY ADDITIONAL INFORMATION ON BEING PREPARED?

This particular activity is to prepare the body, the mind, and the soul so that when there are those times that will be deemed chaotic, there can be the entering in and going through these times, which will be short, and the planet itself will be changed forever. This particular time is at hand.

Some might say that people who survive are lucky; some might say that people who survive are fortunate. But in reality, to be lucky and fortunate is to be prepared! The world itself is shaking and quaking; it is getting ready to expand and there will be lava flows, there will be dust or ash in the air, and there will be an increase in the temperatures of the oceans that will bring about a myriad of disasters.

The planet is wobbling in its orbit and the axis is shaking both magnetically and geographically; and as such, it is a time that will be deemed chaotic by some (and is being deemed chaotic even now!). Being prepared means being practical. Living in an apartment, expecting food to grow on the balcony to sustain you may not be practical! But by having influence and associations with others who live in the countryside, this would be practical.

Take the steps not in fear, but with love. Be prudent and practical so that any disaster that comes can be lessened or even avoided. But it takes one thing (and it is the purpose of this time) and that is: cooperation between peoples. When you have a sisterhood or brotherhood rising up out of need for mutual survival, there you will have God Almighty and the plan unfolding to bring souls together, that they might experience the love of cooperation.

Indeed, there will be upheavals, and, indeed, the world will survive. The question is, will you survive? Are you prepared? What are you willing to do to help? Do you have it in your heart to cooperate? Then, prudently, directly, and immediately, steps can be taken to soften the blow, to avert the damage. Coming together is the first thing. Having an extended family and having resources from many individuals makes it easier for any group to continue. It is a time of travail, a time of testing. Humans, as you know humans, as they go through these times, will not see them as moving, as crisis, as devastation. They will, of course, recognize the same, but more than likely they will endure. For going through a disaster is not as bad as looking back upon it and wondering how was this averted, shortened, or lessened.

The human willpower is the greatest force in the Universe. Let your will be in accord with the Divine. If God is with you, who can be against you? But do prepare. Do form alliances or associations. Pray to God Almighty. Meditate upon what you need to do next, and the guidance from above will help you avoid whatever falls upon those who are lesser.

The comment is said: read the past. Look to those who know how to store food and to survive on less. Copy their method! For they live peaceful lives already! Any impending difficulty will simply be a challenge, not a disaster.

Humans, as you know humans, are resilient. They are brilliant. They are, when they are thinking of good things, quite capable of moving a mountain, if they care to, if they put their minds towards it. Humans, as you know humans, should be guided, directed, assisted, but they will find their way out of the circumstances they now see themselves being plagued with, you see. The leaders in the world are somewhat incompetent or frightened at the decisions, or they have no idea whatsoever. Others simply endure, thinking their families will be all right and it will be the other peoples of the world who will suffer. Unfortunately, *everyone will suffer*. Those who are in politics, or parliaments, or courts will be called upon to do things and to make decisions they have never had to make before! The society should be prepared to have the best, or if this one is not the best, then to have contact with all the others so there can be a use of the same when necessary.

This is a time when people will come together because it will suit them. It will be a time of necessity, but the world will not change all that much. Business will keep trading, product for product. The technologies that are at hand will not disappear, but they may be limited. Humans, as you know humans, provoke a Divine being of light; this provocation is evident in each and every one of them; yourself included! Pay attention to the guiding light within. Thy God, thy soul, will lead thee to wherever is a safe haven. All you have to do is listen and cooperate.

PART TWO

THE NEW
EARTH

CHAPTER FIVE

The Golden Age

CAN EVERYONE IN THE WORLD COME TOGETHER TO MINIMIZE OR NEGATE THE EARTH CHANGES?

"Everyone?" Impossible! It is impossible for *all humans* to compre-hend, or to cooperate, or to do so, at any time. This particular time will be a time of adversity, a time of panic, a time of crisis; it is not going to be a time of cool heads, warm hearts, and companionship. It will be a time of destruction and despair, and there will be those who will cry out in the night, who would see themselves entering into horrible places or dimensions.

However, prior to this, there are those individuals who would wish not to cry out in the night, those who would wish to come to-gether, united in the compassion of the Christ consciousness. For those who have chosen to be on the spiritual path, there need not be any fear. Prior to this time that you speak of, there will be many sober thoughts, clarity of actions, softening and weakening of the ego and the nature of the human beast, and a bringing forth of the refinery of the soul, so that there can be the sense of compassion and love sent forward. Even this will be adulterated by the minds and hearts of those who attempt to do the same, but at least they will be at-tempting! As they come together, it would be by choice, and it would be those who are worthy, or who are similar; not those who come together to save their lives, but those who come together to save their *souls*, you see.

IF EVERY PERSON ON THE PLANET WOULD DROP THEIR NEGATIVITY AND COME FROM A LOVE VIBRATION, WOULD THAT CHANGE THESE PREDICTIONS IN THESE EARTH CHANGES?

What would aid the planet considerably would be the compassion from within; if each individual would consider that when they do something, it affects another person in some way. In other words, to remember that there are consequences to actions. If they care about these consequences, they will be on the right track. If they are indifferent to the consequences, then they are not! As there was the loss of the great landmass Atlantis, in the last destruction of the world, there were the warlike Sons of Belgal, and there were the Sons of the Law of One. At that time, the world was going through a similar extreme behavior as what would be upon the planet now. Those who are compassionate have consideration for others who would be at their hands, or those who would suffer or benefit from their actions. As we have given, there is action and reaction, or consequences. If individuals, in taking action, take into consideration the consequences of others, and avoid harmful consequences, then they would be on the right track. If they know that the consequences are going to be harmful, or painful, or difficult, and they do them anyway, then humankind is slipping into the darkness of the abyss.

This is what is taking place now. There are warlike minds and hearts that do not care, save for their own benefit. There are individuals who are taking countries apart and destroying them as if they were companies or corporations (which they have done to in the past, and have prospered by). There is always the will, the intent, and therefore the consequence. If any who choose to be on the spiritual path choose not to harm as a consequence of their action, then they would be on the path to enlightenment, for they would be governing themselves and they would not be selfish, nor would they be seeking their own aggrandizement, their own pleasure, and their own hoarding over the hearts and minds of others.

Humans, as you know humans, only learn by example. If each in a single city would consider the consequences of their actions always, and avoid causing harm to anyone, the entire planet would change its temperature, and would change its rhythm or vibration; for in fact, you would have love in the making, would you not? The absence of love is evil. Evil breeds darkness, decay, and death. Those who wish to be on the path of enlightenment do the opposite. Love, indeed, is the way. Love, indeed, always finds a way. But make no mistake: the world is in for a change. It is the destiny that the planet's face will change. But think of it as this: as there is change, as there is hardship, those who are of the Law of One, do they not reach out? Do they not bring aid to those who are suffering? They do so with the intention to save life and reduce human suffering, without judgment, without demand for compensation, and certainly without demand to rule the land of those who are misfortunate!

There are some who would do the opposite; they would demand great sums of money even from their own people, to give aid that would be important to sustain life. They would demand their own political position to be sustained, and they would demand to be in authority and to benefit personally from the disaster. Therein lies the difficulty, the indifference between humans; those who may help and those who are suffering. The choice is for each to make. But to answer the question: yes, certainly, love is the way, for love is God, and God is love. But acting upon it, holding back the restraints so that you are not selfish, allowing others to go first so that you may, indeed, enjoy the relief, and to see the benefit that is being caused by the self, these cause the soul to grow. To love and be loving is the way, yes. To consider the consequences of your actions and then to have the discipline not to take action that causes adverse consequences, this, indeed, is enlightenment! This, indeed, is love. This, indeed, is the holding back so that others may gain. This is the way.

WILL THERE BE ANY TYPE OF GUIDANCE FROM ABOVE, THROUGH THIS TRANSITIONAL PHASE?

There already have been visitations by certain observing entities. There has already been the intervention of Divine beings. There has already been influence from certain levels of consciousness, and it will continue. There is no reason for the assertions of the wise to be wasted or forgotten. But it is understandably wise that there is no interference from those who have interest. For there is certain ability to act in secret or quietly; and this is being done. But to the question itself, what makes you think it is not happening already?

IS THAT FOR THE PURPOSE OF HELPING US THROUGH THIS EVOLUTION?

Yes, it is of the same, for humankind, as you know humankind, always does the right thing, but for the wrong reasons. The intention is to do the right thing for the right reasons, and this requires compassion and a sense of being unselfish; it requires unconditional love. This can be generated first towards the self, then from the self towards a neighbor, and then between the self and those who are loved. Even those who have caused difficulty can receive a blessing from those towards whom they have caused a difficulty! This is the

Divine spark that is within each. The problem is that humans, as you know humans, have very short memories. A miracle, a blessing, a contribution, an altering of their destiny so that there is some peace in their heart and mind, this is invaluable to them, and because it was given to them through the spiritual aspects, there is a sense that they do not owe anything. How wrong are they, you see!

IT SEEMS THAT MANY PEOPLE HAVE HAD PREVIOUS LIFETIMES IN WHICH THEY PRAYED TO BE A PART OF THIS TIME. WHY IS THAT?

This is the time in which there will be the advancement to the Divine. At this point in time, many have come into the world to be of service. They wish to be here to see this birthing process. Remember, this is a time like a birth: great difficulty, great travail, great pain. But as soon as the delivery is concluded, there is relief, and those things that are painful are forgotten, and those things that are beautiful are embraced. Understand, those who have prayed in the past have prayed to be here at the beginning, that they might be able to direct, keep on course, or put on track those philosophies, those understandings, those behaviors that will lead all in the world to be in accord with what is right or correct.

Those who have foreseen this time want to be here in the beginning. They want to help the human race back to the point where there would be compassion, understanding, and care for all. But they have returned here also for their own development, so that they might enjoy this testing time, to see if they can be tested to overcome their inadequacies, to avoid temptations, to accumulate their basic understanding so that they are, indeed, more aware; to be fully aware, to become realized, then to become self-realized, then to be fully awakened or realized.

This time will give them the opportunities to accomplish this, for at no other time in history will there be such availability for nations to help nations, for countries to rescue countries, for communications to be instantly about the planet that will divert resources or assets from one place to another - not because it is for the funds that will be raised, but because it is the right thing to do. This is the realization that many have come to. They wish to be here at this time in which the world will wobble and shake its way back to what it once was: a time in which there was communion between those in the world with those things in nature and those aspects of the Divine, as well as the heavens or dimensions above.

COULD YOU PLEASE EXPLAIN WHAT YOU MEAN BY "NEW RENAISSANCE"?

The Renaissance is the Renaissance is the Renaissance! There are changes taking place at all levels of society in the world, as you know it, from education, to medical advancements, to political changes, to weather alterations, to religious and spiritual changes or understandings. It is a time in which there is an ending of one age, and the beginning of another. Our reference, here, is that the world itself will also change as the people on the planet themselves change. And the reference here is that in all strata or areas of society, there will be a new beginning. A review of what is taking place in some of these aspects is already underway. But we do not find that the planet, or the cities themselves, will be without change; rather, the changes will be common sense, and will be beneficial to all who would be involved in these decision-making organizations.

To answer the question in a simple way, it is that every level of the society you live in is being changed, modified, or altered at this point in time. The planet itself is changing its face, and this, too will be changing even as it is changing now. Out of this will come a time of peace, a time of prosperity and trade, but it will take some organization and some distribution of food items, and other objects in a controlled way, you see. To the question, it would be to see that all levels of the society you live in are changing, from the medical sciences, to the philosophies, to the theologies, to the social status of individuals, to the supply and demand of goods and services; all are changing.

How long will this next age last?

This will last for approximately five thousand years.

You have said that this is not an end of the world, but an end to certain activities in the world. Specifically, what activities are coming to an end?

Warfare will be coming to an end (for a time). Those souls that have been released upon the planet who have caused disturbances for the last five millennia will be corralled, and there will be a cessation of their disturbances.

The heavens will open and there will be further visitations by the Divine. This will cause changes in the structures which you would call religion or belief, for there will be apparitions and appearances of saintly beings. For those who are on the spiritual path, they will be enlightened and enlivened. As such, there will be a moving towards a single, world religion or belief system; not because it will overpower or take away from others, but it will be in accord, amalgamating the world's great religions.

The cessation of hunger, and the cessation of greed will be

on the way. There will, of course, be reductions of the population, and there will be disturbances in communications and transportation – and transportation may be established in a new way – and you will not see transportation as it now occurs, ever again!

You will find that the peoples of the world will truly reach out to one another and, therefore, you will see some cessation of indifference and prejudice; this will take a little longer than a year or two, as you might imagine. There will be a cessation to the inhumanity that humans plague upon one another. There will be an attempt, not in a utopian or euphoric way, but in a realistic and logical way, for those upon the planet to express themselves and to live their lives fully; but in a new essence of art, education and knowledge and a new appreciation, one for another.

Politics will change greatly as well, for those who are now entering the field of politics to line their own pockets or to find ways and means that they can be selfishly rewarded, their time is at an end. Those who are capable and able will come to the forefront, and they will assist in an organized and intellectual, practical way of ruling the people; by the cooperation of the people and the various groups. There will be a variety of individuals who will have authority. They will be like governors over certain regions and areas. They will, themselves, be personally responsible for the implementation of their ideas and authority. Therefore, political leaders who no longer are responsible, or accountable, these will end as well!

More social injustices will be overcome. You will find different countries coming to the aid and assistance of other countries, as there will be a need to reach out. Through the generosity of certain groups of people reaching out over great distances, this will bring a spirit of gratitude into the world, and therefore indifference and ignorance will be lowered.

There will be cooperation between people that has not been seen before. Rather than keeping secret inventions, ideas, or technology, it will be shared openly! Monies, in the way you understand them, will change greatly as well, and the monetary systems upon the planet will be greatly changed; not that it will be a barter system, not that it will be trading hard goods for hard goods, but there would be an accountability – an honesty perhaps – and the "Middleman" (who usually causes inflation and usury on the monies) will come to an end! This will take some time, but as there is a movement towards real property or the gold standard, or jewels and diamonds used for currencies, it will allow this to take place. No longer will there be an adulteration to the use of printed money, you see. Again, it will take some time, but it should happen abruptly when it does.

We are looking forward far in time, you see; this is not within the next twelve months. All in all, however, you will find the world will be a better place, for the people upon the planet will be relieved and grateful that they have come together to support one another, through rather unusual, unexpected, and turbulent times; but they will survive. And the survival will lead to a greater consciousness, for the reasons the world will survive remain with the people who live upon the world at this time. See? As they check their hearts, as they come to understand their well-being, as they learn that they need each other, so shall it be: a new world; a world without limits, that is in contact with the heavens above. The Universe will open up, and there will be communications with the higher beings above, and beyond.

WHAT WILL THE NEW SOCIETY BE LIKE, COMPARED TO TODAY?

It will be based more on the development of the human being or the individual, than it would be on the acquisition of products or wealth. It will be based upon the improvements of a person, and it will be seen that those who are elder are not less greater than those who are coming into the world after them (which would be naturally more evolved). You will find that the brain will function much faster, and more parts of the brain will be in harmony and under the conscious mind's control. You will have thinking that will be deep, concise, expansive, and more worldly in younger and younger minds, you see, indicating the advancement of the ability of mind power, so to speak. However it will be done more for the accumulation of minds (and the calculation in these minds will be quite swift), but it will be also combined with their subconscious or super-conscious or that part of the rational mind communicating openly and easily with the contemplative mind. You will see that they will be able to use both hands equally, as an indication of both hemispheres working correctly, or in tandem, you see.

However, you will see that the cooperation of these minds will be: confidence in themselves, compassion for others, and a desire to work together! There will be less and less resentment of authority, for those who rise to levels of authority will have earned the right, and they will have established themselves, as to their capability. In other words, there will be more truth in the societies, as you understand them. Each level, each segment of society will look for truth; the truth within, of course, is the greatest journey! This will happen naturally. But as you would understand the stars, you would understand the inner self, and just how similar they are.

CAYCE HAD PREDICTED THAT A SIXTH ROOT RACE WILL EMERGE. IS THIS TRUE?

Indeed. They will deal with the difficulties and shortages and the atmospheric changes that are taking place, for it will be difficult to breathe, you see. As such, it will cause the changing of the color in the skin, especially those who are sensitive, even now. The water they will ingest will change the pigmentation in their skin as well. They will be very industrial, very quick, and very agile. They may have dark features and hair in the lower latitudes, and they may be blonde or light-haired – more like white hair – in the higher latitudes. They will be firmly built, square-built, and look more like Aztec in their body shapes, you see. They will be firm and strong, and there may be many who would be very tall indeed, like the Titans returning, you see. They will be very, very large, or they will tend to be square-built and stocky. Very strong and smart. Their eyes will be a little more slanted or Egyptian-looking, you see. They will be very abrupt, and they will gather information quite easily. Therefore they will accumulate practical and pertinent information that will allow them to be quite logical and aggressive in their pursuits. They will have a single-mindedness; not that they would be of one mind, but that they would be of one accord. They will work together cooperatively and will be very industrious, indeed. They may be exclusionary of some of the other races, but they seem to welcome the dark-skinned races, you see, almost like equals or partners.

DO YOU FORESEE OUR PRESENT-DAY LIFESTYLE, WHICH RELIES ON ELECTRICAL TECHNOLOGIES SUCH AS MOBILE PHONES AND COMPUTERS BEING DISRUPTED, CHANGED, OR EVEN DISCONTINUED IN THE COMING YEARS?

There will be difficulty in electrical supply, there will be difficulty in transportation, and there will be difficulty in the staples of life. In different parts of the worldm that may be permanent; in others, there will be a recovery. Certain areas (those in particular that would be on the coastlines themselves) will suffer the curtailment of these communications. There will, however, be a re-establishment of communications in a similar way, in the very near future thereafter. But it will be done in a different way! It will be done in a way that is caring, so there is not a monthly bill, so there is not a termination of services because one cannot pay. It is an opportunity to be seen that these particular influences, these conveniences themselves will be with humankind for a long time thereafter, but there will be disruptions. Those that run by battery alone will be negated for long periods of time. Those that run by electrical cable into the wall and have electrical power from outside the wall will tend to be recovered or would be utilized rather quickly. And those in some areas of the world will not be bothered or affected at all!

These will be the seed-points to bring forth the communication and the application of power from an artificial means, so to speak, as you would know it. Yes to the question, there will be shortages, there will be curtailment of power and memory, for there will be certain magnetic blasts or bombs, so to speak, that will, indeed, wipe out many memories and many computer services. These are not actual bombs, as you would understand dynamite, but they will be pulses, you see, that will seemingly have an explosive nature, and will curtail electrical input and will wipe out memories, you see. Best to have the hard book handy with all that would be needed within it. Just as preparations are being made now for disruption or interruption of food, to some degree (storages of seeds, for instance), it is also happening for different fossil fuels, and even energy, or power itself, you see.

ARE THERE ANY PRECAUTIONS WE COULD TAKE TO PROTECT OUR EQUIPMENT FROM THESE DISTURBANCES?

Surge protectors would be good, and certain shielding of any external drives or magnetic storage devices could be done. This would be any that would prevent magnetic disturbances, you see. There are many cloths, blankets, shields that could be used. They are commonplace even now.

COULD YOU DESCRIBE WHAT CHANGES WILL TAKE PLACE, WITH RESPECT TO THE ARTS AND CULTURE, IN THE FUTURE?

There will be a flourish of art and creativity. This will spill over into the world of machines, the worlds of metallurgy and invention, and the worlds of understanding the small worlds (or the microcosm). But, here, it will be a burst of appreciation, especially of sound, frequency, light, or vibration, as you would understand it. There will be seen more in the way of light, sound, and vibration therapies, music and stimulation, appealing to the inner core of a human. In other words, not only will you see something beautiful and be impressed, or hear something wonderful and sweet and be moved, or touch upon that and wonder at the arrangement of colors, there will be a *feeling*, a sense that you will feel within, for all of these things will be stimulated at the same time, like a light show, only more so. And out of this will come advances in understanding structures. You will find there will be crystals grown rapidly, and stones will be shaped as if by a hot knife cutting through butter. There will be an array of understanding of the rays of light that enter this world. There will be a burst of creativity and grand masters will come back again to display their works of art, using light, sound, and material of different colors and those materials that have yet to be discovered (such as the use of clear stone).

WHAT CHANGES WILL TAKE PLACE TO EDUCATION IN THE FUTURE?

Education would not be seen as it is by present standards. It will not be by rote, or one teacher with many children. Rather, the computer and individual teaching will take place. There will be a greater number of small groups who will confer or discuss the overall tone of the lesson. This will be carried on into the higher levels of learning as well, where it will be left up to a child to seek its preference on what he or she likes to do, not what would be considered by the family for the individual to do. You will have that teaching will be done through different stimulations: visual, audio, and touch, you see. There will be certain understandings of memory pegs. Scents or fragrances will be used to enhance the mind so that it remembers better. This would be to the olfactory area close to the pineal gland itself, you see. This will be used in hotels, education facilities, and different places where there are people. It will be found that certain types of air can be used with fragrances that will induce mood swings or keep people alert. Negative ion generators and technologies that would keep people alert will also be used.

There will come an understanding that the way people think is different, and therefore the presentation of what is being taught will be done in different modes or ways to the different groups who would respond to the different aspects. For instance, one who needs more information in detail will be given all sorts of detail on a new project. Others need to see the project as somewhat bold and easy, just the big steps to take. For instance, some will use charts, some will use music, some will use repetition in memory. But all will have their own way of learning, and it will be discovered that some people can look as if they are disinterested, but they are intently understanding. Others who are intently understanding are focused so much that they cannot perceive the larger overtone of the lesson itself. And therefore, there will be adjustment to the individual ways in which some people learn! Some need more detail, some just need the overview or the picture, and some need a description of the plan, the picture, or the lesson. These will be some of the ways that will be discovered and will be utilized, almost as if it would be too easy for a student to come to the understanding! Yet, it will be.

MUCH OF TODAY'S SOCIETY IS DEPENDENT UPON THE INTERNET FOR COMMUNICATION GLOBALLY. IF THE INTERNET BECOMES UNAVAILABLE, WHAT EFFECT WILL THIS HAVE ON COMMUNICATIONS, SOCIETY, AND ECONOMICS?

Unless there is a total capitulation of electrical power all at once, and if there are not magnetic pulse waves all at once, the communications as you would know them would seem to be intact, or at least they will be recoverable. However, there will be much data lost as there will be magnetic fluctuations. There will not be explosions of magnetic force, but there will be bursts of the same. Energy being released causing electrical surges will also damage certain equipments. For you would find more governmental installations or large corporate installations will be more likely to be affected – complete and utter damage, you see. But there will not be any particular place all at once that would be consumed or would be affected, and therefore, there is the possibility – and we repeat, the possibility – that this will remain somewhat initially, intact in a primitive way.

But there will be difficulties, there will be outages, and there will be damage from natural forces also that will curtail this. But like a cloud in the sky moving at random, as long as it does not touch the ground it can remain, and this body of knowledge has the possibility to remain. This will not be a primitive state, but certainly there will be large difficulties and disruptions. Some centers that are now above the ground will be beneath the sea. Naturally, these will be out of circulation or usage, you see. Everything west of the Rockies will disappear in a very short period of time. All that would be stored in Silicon Valley, or other places where there would be servers and memory banks, they would be affected by this. Certainly it would be a detriment, would it not? But there are some places in the interior and some isolations of this, as there has been preparation for this already. Norway prepares a storehouse of seeds; Washington prepares the Midwest; Russia prepares Siberia; China near Beijing. Different places, different preparations already, you see.

ARE THERE ANY TECHNOLOGIES BEING DEVELOPED AT THIS TIME OR IN THE VERY NEAR FUTURE TO REPLACE THESE DEVICES THAT WILL BE AFFECTED?

Yes. Suffice it to say that the recording of the same will be in stone, or crystalline forces. Amplified from what is now presently being utilized in crystalline influences, but it would be memory put in stone, as you would understand it. There will be the capability to record hologram, or map, or word, without too much difficulty. The recovery of the same will be a little more difficult, but it would be like a hologram almost; it would 'sing' and give answers, you see.

WHAT MEDICAL CHANGES OR MEDICAL DISCOVERIES WILL TAKE PLACE?

There will be the use of what is commonly seen now as lasers and light therapy. They will be provided special qualifications in pulsing and in trimming and using a thin line, like a thread almost in size, and this would be used for cauterization, which is presently done, but it would also be used to act as a scalpel, you see. There will be sounds upon the body that will cause the cells to return to the normal vibrational rate. This resonance between cells will lead to the ability to keep the body youthful and provide much in the way of body-building at the cell level, and it would cause certain influences in the body to be destroyed, or to be negated. This light therapy or use of light and sound will require pathology, but it would be seen as erad-icating a body of disease, and applying surgical procedures upon any body that would be formidable and correct.

There will be, indeed, the adaptation of that which once was. That is to say, more of a combination of treating a sick person holis-tically; spiritually, taking into account their attitude mentally, assess-ing their emotional states (which are both constructive and destructive states), and then the physical condition. Understand that vitamins will be assigned numbers, rather than letters. Understand that vibrational medicine, which is now seen as energy medicine, or tapping medicine, or complementary or therapeutic touch, all will be understood, that there would be the advent of stimulation on cer-tain points on the body, for instance, that would change the construc-tion of the body, speed up the mending of bones, or amplify the filtering and eliminating systems of the body to affect the functions of the glands by different-colored lights and frequency.

As once was in the Temple Beautiful, in what you would call the Atlantean experiences, before the fourth destruction, there was the amplification of the sound of the body, or the frequencies about the body would be enhanced, isolating disease in the body, amplify-ing the genetic code or genetic vibrational rate in the body. This, too, will come about in what would be considered the Renaissance itself. For, even now, there is examination of light therapy to remove disease from sores on the mouth, to lasers being used for operative purposes, to what would be sonic scalpels, shall we say.

Rough-cut gemstones used for surgical purposes, like Flint, or other waferous stones, suit the body much better, and healing is much quicker than a steel, sharp blade, because it is non-intrusive on the body, where the steel is more adverse. Using implements such as natural scalpels, wafers of stone, you see, or crystal, sound and light, medicine, as you know it, will not exist! It will be so different that it would not even be close to what is taking place today! Why poison the body to try to cure it?!

Today's conditions in the body are usually due to illnesses hiding out in the body, corralled or suppressed by medications, as if the medication would be a jailhouse and the disease would be an inmate. Disease does not actually become eradicated or overcome in the body; it is simply subdued until the death of the body, at which time it consumes part of the body until it terminates itself. In the future, this will not be allowed; and, indeed, looking back, this time will be remembered as a time of remorse and shame for those who would be understanding. For those who have ears, let them hear.

But to the question, medicine in the future will not be as you have it now; there will not be tablets or injections of any kind in the body, for this is, in a way, ridiculous, save for, on occasion, when the body needs some assistance in this crude manner. But, in the future, more light therapy, more natural therapies; the use of sound upon the body and light upon the body, as once was, will be returned, you see. The vibratory rate of the body will be assessed and will be amplified, where needed. As you would understand medicine in the future, it would be to understand preventative maintenance of the body, not rescue or rejection of the body. Now, it should be understood that there will be surgeries, indeed. However the accelerated rate of healing will be ten times the present speed, because there will be the use of sound on the body. The lower vibrational rates cause bone to grow; the higher cause tissue to erode or deteriorate. This kind of sound will be used to heal the body, where necessary, to remove tumors, cysts, and all sorts of attachments that the body normally grows, you see.

Medicine will be much different and the healers in the future will be well trained in the priestly qualities, in understanding the soul and the spirit of the human form, and how to amplify it in order to cooperate with it, and give it what it needs, rather than give it what is believed it needs, or attempting to tell the body what to do (which is the current use of drugs, as you know it; albeit necessary at this point in time). In the future, there will be more cooperation with the entirety of the self. See?

WILL HEALERS OF THE FUTURE BE MAINLY TRAINED IN METAPHYSICS?

Today there is currently a dissatisfaction with Allopathic medicine, and, as such, there is already a reaching out to the Oriental medicine. You would find that there is a condition of change in attitude of those who even study medicine itself, for, truly, there are those who have the opinion that if there is such a thing as a disease, then the disease should be able to be handled or eradicated; if it happens for some disease, why not all; after all, disease is a thing; it has a life, and if it is alive then you can kill it and it can be eradicated. The problem is that there is not the will to eradicate disease, nor is there the understanding that disease is not eradicated in a body; it simply hides in different places in the body, waiting to break out of its corral, so to speak.

There are some degrees of difference in which the disease would be destroyed when certain chemicals are touched upon it, as in medicine itself. But here, you would find that disease in the future will be such that sound and light will be used upon disease much more than they are now; and as such, medical understandings will change, as there are those physicians, even now, willing to do anything to provide a healing remedy for their patients! They are willing to do this, because they see no other way to have it take place. Therefore, as you might expect, there will be a greater understanding in the microcosm itself; fractals and the understanding of fractal law will prevail here. But already there is a premise of light therapy, vibrational therapy, and the stimulation of the physical body through the nervous system by therapeutic means first, rather than chemical natures first. This is the proper way to proceed. As there will be a continuation through the millennium itself, you will find that there will be an understanding of life and how it exists in a physical body, and how it can be amplified – which it can be – and how it can be focused or directed. Not by brute force with bandages, scalpels, and medications, but with other means that would appeal to the healing forces within. This cooperative nature will be shared with other groups, people, and individuals, for they seem to be ready for this type of cooperation. See?

WILL THE HEALING ARTS BE USED AS A FORM OF BARTER IN THE FUTURE?

More like a trade-off, one family helping another. The people in these particular fields would need something else. They would not, as they did in the old days, perform surgery "for a chicken." Instead, they would have some services professionally supplied. But they would look to have power or electrical power developed. Therefore, wind, sun, and solar aspects will be some form of bartering where the power will be manipulated from the outside surfaces coming into the middle of the process and then to be delivered to the unit itself. This particular form of use will be considered stable, for now and for later, you see.

CAN YOU GIVE ANY ADVICE TO THOSE WHO WISH TO BECOME HEALERS?

This particular form of healing, we assume you mean the spiritual aspects, in what would be to use the body's chi energy, or the aura fields, the chakra - the spiritual aspects of healing. Then it would be to understand that doubt helps to negate the outcome; to attempt to remove doubt from the mind, to have no expectation (other than complete and utter healing would occur) is something to contemplate or to practice. Try to take the self out of the way, so that there is no reflection of the doubt that is in the mind of self. This will allow the changing, a metamorphosis to take place, so to speak; and, indeed, there would be improvement, as you would call to the healing forces. For the building up of the energies within the self – the electricity within, shall we call it – will be enormous, yet will not have a heat or vibrational effect that crude electricity now has, as you would hang onto it, you see.

WILL THERE BE A GREATER ACCEPTANCE BY THE PUBLIC FOR LAYING ON OF HANDS HEALING, THE CHI ENERGY AND THE ABILITY FOR PEOPLE TO GET INSTANTANEOUS, MIRACULOUS HEALINGS?

It is already taking place. Yes to the question. There will be a continuation of those influences you would understand as therapeutic touch, Reiki, spiritual healing or compassion healing, balance healing. The intention is to change a person's "mode" by changing the energy around them, and this affects the chemical nature quite well. One can continue to use their natural abilities, and it will be more readily accepted as time continues to pass, and as the amplification for the healing occurs, there would be more of those that you would expect to be, as Biblical changes in the healing form. You would also find inventions would be in the world where light and lasers are used to perform healing techniques on a body, you see. Although they will already be here, they will be identified with improving the brain function, the electrical/magnetical impulse, as well as blood flow and other flows of fluid – brain stem fluid within – you see.

IN THE SOCIETY WE LIVE IN, MANY PEOPLE CONSUME DRUGS AND ALCOHOL AS PART OF THEIR REGULAR, SOCIAL ACTIVITIES. WILL SUCH PATTERNS OF BEHAVIOR PERSIST IN THE FUTURE?

Indeed they will; they will not be so severely used, however. Wine and spirits have always been used, and always will be, from ancient times to the present! Understand, what is found in nature has its purpose. The problem with humans, as you know humans, is that they take those things to excess. They have little or no discipline. All things found in nature have a purpose, and, taken reasonably and prudently, they can provide a service that will be helpful to the body. Everything has a constructive purpose. However taken to excess, everything can become destructive, you see. Put limits on desires. Yes, there will be those who misuse these things you would call drugs or stimulants. These are the weaker individuals we speak of.

WHAT WOULD YOU SUGGEST AS AN IDEAL CAREER IN THE NEW AGE?

It all depends whose ideal you wish us to reference, you see. Ideal jobs would be simply ones that would be in food production, water production, and in those that would be in entertainment, as you would call it. Occupations will range from food distribution and water distribution, to education and light manufacturing you see; as seen now, it will be as then, only different, you see.

What sources of power will be used for transportation as well as for powering devices?

There will be the use of those devices that will cause stone to float; there will be also those crafts that will go through the air and the water at the same rate. There will be those devices that will float or will defy gravity, as you understand it; in fact, there will be devices to disrupt gravity and allow the gravitational influences to be controlled – upward to float, downward to be attracted down, side by side to be attracted to either way, you see. There will be the use of those crystalline influences that will generate vibrations that will be used for surgical reasons or healing purposes upon a body, and it will be found that radiation in certain, lesser capacities will be used as a great healing tool, you see. You will find many things that you now understand as poison, or difficulty, or things with prohibited uses, such as Nightshade, will be found to be quite useful to bring relief when given in small amounts in a controlled way, and it will affect a person naturally. These types of understandings will come forth.

But understand the power devices will come from the disruptive influences that will allow metal to float in the air. Navigation will be different upon the planet; it will be done with the same means or mechanism that is used by birds in the air, or fish in the sea, you see. Humans, as you know humans, will be much more resilient, and they will use their inner understanding for direction and for self-healing. The human hand is a wonderful instrument to provide, therapeutically speaking, healing touch, as well as telekinetic changes in a physical body. This will be well known and utilized to speed up or accelerate healing in a physical body; a broken arm will be accelerated to heal in a matter of hours, where it would take weeks before!

PLEASE COMMENT ON HOW PROFESSIONAL COMPETITIVE SPORTS SUCH AS HOCKEY WILL CHANGE IN THE FUTURE.

There will be such sporting events similar to now, but rather than those that would be combative, they will be sporting events that will be cooperative, you see. There will be sporting events, of course, that will be competitive, but the intention will be not at the expense of the other side. You might understand it as the difference between a football game, where there is much in the way of competition (or even warfare) and what would be a party game, in which many people would simply bat or touch a balloon around the room. In the latter, everyone watches the balloon, and as the balloon gets closer, the closest one takes a hand and hits the balloon, and it goes in a different direction. This incorporates enthusiasm in everyone who is in the room; everyone is included, rather than excluded; and everyone gets to enjoy the event. In professional sports now, there are more of the combative aspects that still relate to the primal instincts within humans, as you know humans. And therefore, you will find that somewhere between these two extremes will come a game that will not be contradictive or destructive, or harmful; but, rather, one that will be exciting and will show the use of the body and its coordinated effects, but in a cooperative way.

Specifically, hockey will continue in the future, but it will not be played on ice surfaces; but, rather, it will be played on cement. It will continue to provide entertainment in the same way as today. However, those sports that cause harm, injury, or anger will fade away, but those that provide skill and coordination, individual effort, as well as team cooperation, you see, will prevail.

PART SIX

৵৻৵

The Golden Rule

SOME BELIEVE THAT THERE WILL OCCUR AN ASCENSION OF THE ENTIRE PLANET TO A HIGHER FREQUENCY OR DIMENSION. DO YOU SEE THIS HAPPENING?

There is a belief that there will be the invisible ascension of one hundred and forty-four thousand. Certainly there will be those who will pass from their physical lifetimes during this time, but there will not be a mass rising or, ascension, that some will be taken into the heavens above for a temporal time (or even a permanent time) to higher dimensions. Rather, this confusion would be that the changes in the minds of those one hundred and forty-four thousand would be such that they will alter the probability of the influence from the dimensions above. We do not see, nor do we find the mechanical capability to permit people to flee from this time of testing or teaching. And therefore, we do not see an ascension of a privileged few, out of the several billion people who live upon this planet, that they might escape their destiny! It does not make sense. The very purpose of living in the world at this time is to enjoy these circumstances and these extremes, so that there can be an evolution of the soul to a higher dimension, to a higher consciousness.

To those minds who would expect some sort of physical mutation, we do not see this occurring. To those minds who may expect that there will be an ascension from one vibrational level to another, so that there is a disappearance in the primary or first dimension and the appearance in another dimension, this, too, will not happen. To those who are more of the understanding that there is a change taking place in the consciousness of the peoples upon the planet, then we would address this: for the planet itself will not ascend or descend; the planet has its place in the solar system, and the solar system within the galaxy, and the galaxy within the Universe. The planet itself will, indeed, be adjusting or changing. For there are certain dimensions within dimensions. You might see it as certain areas within a country, and as one travels through the country, and they traverse through these areas, they would have a different sense. The population may speak the same language, but a different dialect. The people in one part or area may do the same thing but in a slightly different way (or a totally different way). There is a flavor, there is a practicality, an understanding, a usage of what is taking place in that area. Therefore, you might say, there is an understanding or a consciousness.

Now, as this planet spins around the sun, and the sun migrates through the Universe as it spins around its own central point, these areas are traversed, and there are certain feelings, vibrations, or levels of consciousness that might be considered. Those who would see this as a change in vibration would be closely aligned to this. For there is a practical formula and certain influences are in certain areas of the Universe, and whatever living being goes through these areas, they are influenced by this flavor, or this understanding, or this practice while in that area or region.

We do not see the planet disappearing, transmuting into vapor, or appearing on the other side of some vibrational wall, or a higher octave, as it might be understood. We do see the peoples upon the planet altering their thinking; those things that are more important to them would be what is more in harmony with the understanding of everything being connected to everything else – or the Law of One. It is the understanding that this time is an ascension to a higher level of consciousness or compassion. For if you take a descending level of consciousness, it is a selfish consciousness in which all aggrandize themselves, pleasure themselves, and seek pleasure at the expense of all others. The reverse is true; it is those who are on a conscious, expanding path that come to the greater understanding. The greater understanding is that all are one. Everything is connected to everything else. It is the spirit of the human, as you would understand it, that causes movement or vibration to take place. The higher the vibration, the more harmonious the person, the substance, the material form can be and therefore closer to the Divine.

However, we do not see this happening as you have given us direction to observe. We do see, however, that it is a consciousness, it is an expansion of truth, enlightenment, and what you would call harmony or a closeness one with the other; a uniting rather than a disbanding of human minds and hearts. To this end, therefore, you may say it is a higher octave, a rising up, an advancement, but it is more to the level of consciousness, to the compassion of the soul, to that part that makes the spirit do good, you see.

We would encourage those who aspire to be good to do the best they can at living their lives in this place, but not to think they can escape the outcome or the circumstances of what is headed this way. Rather, be prepared and embrace the changes that are coming. Do not live in fear or think that there will be some temporary reprieve or rescue. It is a teaching and a testing time. For those who are within the parameter of this opportunity, enjoy it to the fullest. Take advantage of improving the self to the greatest degree. Do not fear the time, nor run away from it, else you will miss a great opportunity!

WOULD IT BE FAIR TO SAY THAT THIS LEVEL OF CONSCIOUSNESS IS WHAT IS
MEANT BY THE SECOND COMING OF JESUS THE CHRIST?

To the higher consciousness or the teachings of the Christ, this would
be in accord with the same; the Second Coming would be, indeed, a
rising up of those minds and those hearts that would believe the
teachings of the Christ, but have the understanding of His mystical
concepts and capabilities, as they might have them themselves. But
here, it is key that the consciousness of the Christ is the compassion
that each would have for the other in an unselfish way; loving un-
conditionally, being humble, and being, indeed, kind and loving to
all things in a practical way. This is in reference to this, the expansion
of this consciousness that would be Christ-like or the Christ consciousness. To those who understand the advancement of expanded
consciousness; those who would have studied in the East would understand the concept in the West. Those who have not may have difficulty in comprehending that the Christ consciousness is that which
is unilateral, available to all, you see!

However, there are some who would think it would only be
allocated to one soul – Amelius, or that one you would call Jesus the
Christ. But, in essence, this is a misnomer. This level of consciousness
is desired to be shared among all who take on the flesh, so they can
advance themselves, and, indeed, come closer to the face of God. In
part, we would agree with the statement, but make room to allow
that it is for any person who would come again, and would demonstrate the same as had been demonstrated before, you see; unconditional love, a human being experiencing the highest experience a
human being can indeed encounter; to be living the life spiritual,

fully realized, and yet still in the flesh, you see.

IS THERE ANYTHING HAPPENING AT THIS TIME IN THE MILKY WAY GALAXY THAT IS DIRECTLY AFFECTING THE PLANET AT THIS TIME?

There is a concentration. There is a coming close to the center of the Milky Way. There are those islands or spaces in the Milky Way that the ancients would see and refer to as the donkey dipping its tail into the pond or the sea. This is the end of what would be the known activities or experiences. The Milky Way might be seen as something of a "recording place." For all time, the Milky Way has been observing. To the question, yes, there is plenty taking place in this huge array that is called the Milky Way. But in fact, it is a conglomerate of huge land, worlds, planets, substances, atmospheres, and life. Yes, there is something happening here, but it is not of any major interest to this place you would call the Earth. It is just one dot in the sky, so to speak. But those souls that enter this place, some have come through this dimension, you know, and some have stayed to learn a little before entering or after entering here. It has an effect, not in the way you would think.

PLEASE COMMENT ON A PHENOMENON WHICH IS REFERRED TO BY DIFFERENT NAMES; IT IS SOMETIMES CALLED THE HARVEST, IT IS SOMETIMES CALLED THE QUICKENING OR THE ASCENSION. IT IS THE IDEA THAT IN THIS APPROXIMATE TIME PERIOD, THERE WILL BE AVAILABLE FOR MANY ENTITIES THE OPPORTUNITY TO RAISE THEIR VIBRATION AND MOVE ON.

As we have already given, this Renaissance period will be, indeed, a combination of those aspects; it is a renovation period and a reconstruction period at the same time, but it is also a time of bringing forth new ideas and concepts. If you look to the Milky Way, you would find it straightening out from its slight leaning off the mark, and what would be the "donkey dipping its tail into the well" (Mayan belief, you see), would indicate a point of awareness. It would be an increase in the understanding. Yea, it will be a desire to understand the truth of the heavens above. As it is seen, the microcosm and the macrocosm are the same; this concept will be seen as the ultimate truth between the two extremes.

However, to the question itself, you will find, indeed, that this is a time in which the old is coming forth or returning; the end of that period of ignorance, an end of that period of contest or conflict, you see. Humans, as you know humans, are increasing their awareness and their search for the spiritual truth in earnest. That which they will perceive first will be the difficulties in their character, their nature; the individuality as well as the national and race minds. For as you would turn on the light at night, you would see the creepy-crawly creatures, the insects on the pathway; things you could not see before. But in time, the path will be cleared and, indeed, the Renaissance, the time of returning to those points, that origin of Love, to be loving and to be compassionate, these are now being reached out for, or touched upon.

To tie these concepts together, understand it as the destruction or tearing down in order to rebuild or build up, but it is the development of the human mind through this Renaissance period, that these extremes – one in the darkness, the other in the light – will occur. It should not be surprising to comprehend this, as it would be the law of nature itself. But humans, as you know humans, do not necessarily follow the laws, as you would expect!

What can we do to elevate our consciousness so that we might as-

CEND THROUGH THIS PROCESS?

It would be to be compassionate one to the other. It would be to understand there are consequences to your actions. It would be to understand that you are not alone in the Universe, as you might think, nor do you have dominance over the planet, as you might think! The planet is an alive, sentient being, you might understand it. It has a different understanding of life, as you would know it, for its term of life is eternal, or at least it seems to be. As you come to the greater understanding that you are insignificant in the grand scheme of things, then you begin to take significant understanding of youself and you learn to love. The best is to be loving and peaceful, to have no enemies, to have no one coveting your property. The best is to be naked in the world with nothing. But humans, as you know humans, tend to need things.

Humans, as you know humans, learn by example. Be the best example you can be, and you will teach just about anyone, whether they have difficulty or not. The key is to continue to make the attempt. As you would find, there would be humans who understand what it is like to be a human, and there are others who think they are humans, but they also believe they will live forever and there will be no termination of their life. Those who are privileged to understand the termination process usually live a full life; those who do not, create mental chains and do not allow themselves to experience the fresh air even one time.

PLEASE DISCUSS THE PHENOMENA OF CROP CIRCLES, AS THEY SEEM TO BE APPEARING MORE FREQUENTLY?

To some degree, there are hoaxes in which there would be willful minds that would make ornate geometric patterns. These should be discounted, for they are not too extensive and there can be found string and boards and other implements that would be used in this.

To those that are, indeed, outside of this, these would be influences from the other dimensions you would call invisible, or that which would be just above or beyond. The intention is like the lines that would be drawn in mountains in the south in the ancient civilizations. They would be markers in time, but also they would be aeronautical influences or waypoints, or what would show direction, you see; especially those that are large and have the tendency to have two or four circles outside of the same. These additional mobile or random moving spheres or shapes tend to coordinate with geographical directions; they can be seen as a bit of a map, you see. However, to those lines that would be used in the past, and those stones in which would be carved figures, these would be also the recording of certain thoughts, certain influences, you see.

Therefore, we would find that there is a degree of extra-terrestrial, as you would call it, marking and giving guidance or direction. Now, these do not give direction like you would understand a road map. They give direction to certain places of energy or ozone radiation, you see. As such, there is a supplemental influence that allows this form of magnetic, anti-magnetic and electrical stimulation to occur, so that there is a defiance of gravity. The fuel for this is somewhat similar to ozone and that is why there is the touching of trees or shrubs, with the ship itself that might come from a different or far-away dimension.

However, to this particular question, you would find that, for the most part, these crop circles tend to be man-made, for hysterical and humorous reasons. For those that have designs that would tend to be complex, and have four additional carriages or appendages, they would tend to be what you are looking for as communication from the higher dimensions or the galaxies beyond.

WHY ARE WE SEEING MORE CROP CIRCLES, AND WHAT DO THEY MEAN?

You would see these as provocative symbols or signs that will lead to a greater understanding that the world itself has within it a certain intelligence. This array would be a communication device, if you will. There is a telepathic communication from other entities or groups in the center or the opposite side of the galaxy (for those that would have understanding or memory).

IS THERE A CORRELATION BETWEEN THE HOPI BELIEF IN THE FIVE AGES OF HUMANKIND, AND THIS TIME PERIOD WE ARE ENTERING?

We assume you are referring to the advancement through the various levels of consciousness that humans go through, and they can be described as the five heavens in the Mormon religion, or the fifteen dimensions in the Hindu, or the several dimensions recounted in *The Torah* or *The Qur'an*, or in other religions, you see. For the Hopi and their five Ages or dimensions, yes, this would be the changes that people go through in their advancement; they either advance or they decline. But as you would move to this, the fifth one, this will be the crowning or the threshold for the human condition, to improve. In other mystery schools, mystery societies, those that hold to the old ways (and there are many!), there is always an advancement, through the four corners, to that of the fifth, which would be the apex, like that of a pyramid.

Humankind surrounds and "walks" through this dimensional change, altering the cloak that blinds it, as it moves forward. But as there is the advancement specifically through these times, as it goes through from the fourth destruction to the fifth new world, this would be in accord with the Hopi prophecy, as well as that of the Mayan and Aztec, the Filipinos, those from Easter Island, Ethiopia, and the central points of the Congo, even to the belief in the religious centers of Russia. These would be in accord with these times, for they tend to converge at this time.

HAS A NEW AGE THAT YOU HAVE CALLED A "NEW RENAISSANCE" ALREADY COMMENCED, OR WILL IT FOLLOW THE EARTH CHANGES?

There are already changes in the planet, as you can see. There are certain groups who are attempting to prepare for such times of difficulty, and there are those who are prepared for times in the next ten years and beyond. There is changing within the attitude, within the thinking, of many in the world, as you know it. You would say that the world is changing, and has changed, and some of the features have been disasters in the banking community, in the financial community in which warfare has taken place. To the electronic fields, there have been great changes. There have been certain discoveries and changes within medical protocol. There is now a change in drinking water that is widespread. You would find that certain applications in regeneration of power through renewable resources are now widespread. Fifty years ago, such things would never be considered. Thirty years ago, they were simply on the drawing board. Ten years ago, they were implemented. Presently, they operate efficiently and without much notice! There are many things common in this day that were, just a scant few years ago, considered ridiculous.

Yes, the world is changing. People have not noticed. But here, the consciousness to clean the planet, to conserve the planet, to reduce pollution; all these ideas are two generations in the making. Yes, the world has changed and the Renaissance has begun and in earnest, within the last year or two or three. For the attitude is now one of cooperation. There is much fear and despair in the world, and out of this will come peace. For it will not be warfare as it has been in the past century or so; instead, it will be out of necessity that countries will cooperate. But what has to change is the way business is done. Greed needs to be suppressed; countries taking care of their own people in an equitable way, then trade with other countries in an equitable way. Good business is simply businessmen keeping their promises, you see. But the world has changed. It is a time of extremes. What happens in one extreme will be countered by equal and opposite extremes. Have you not noticed? This is a time that is deemed chaotic by many. Uncertainty and fear run rampant in some countries even now. Ancient Europe is not stable, in body, mind, or soul.

Out of this chaos will come leaders who may benefit personally, or with their unselfish purpose, and all the people in the world will benefit. This has yet to be experienced, and this will take place as there is uncertainty, and as the face of the planet changes its shape. See? This is not too far down the road. Yes, the world is changing, has changed, and will continue to change in more extreme ways, in shorter periods of time than would be expected. The planet's weather is greatly affected. People in the world are greatly affected by the various sound waves that go through their body, and they know not why. The planet has gotten smaller and smaller; disease is rampant, and can be communicated around the planet within forty-eight hours. Such speed of communications, such speed of disease, such speed of comprehension - all the people in the world making up their mind in one day - can alter or change the direction of the world (and, if you would have a mind to understand, they could even stop the rotation of the planet!).

Yes, the world is changing, but not necessarily is there going to be a line in the sand where the world one day will be one thing and another something totally different. Steps are being taken, leading up to the teetering point, and the axis will shift, you see. This will be the major comprehension of what has been taking place. For there is a certain sense of complacency in the world, even in the face of disaster, repetitive disaster. Very few are stocking up and preparing for the disaster, for they refuse to believe something extreme is going to happen! These are the same people who live under the smoking volcano, and when the volcano blows its top, they are surprised, and they are consumed in the lava flows themselves, you see.

Wisdom takes observation. See this as a time in which the world is changing. Mark down on a piece of paper the steps, and you will see that within the last ten to fifteen years, much has changed. Who would have thought certain things would happen? Who would have thought that the precious metals would be unobtainable for the average person to purchase? Who would have thought that the planet is shaking and quaking like a shivering child at night? Only those who would have ears to hear and eyes to see, and the vision to see the future, you see.

WILL ORGANIZED RELIGIONS HAVE LESS INFLUENCE THAN THEY DO NOW?

There will be a move towards a single religion or single consciousness, and this will have the greater influence upon the planet, for it will be a way of salvation, you see. The organized religions you speak of are waning even now, for they are riddled with hypocrisy, with failure. And, as such, the old religions based on fear are now being scoffed at, you see, and are themselves in fear of their people. To the question, there will be a mentality that will combine politics and religion, as you know it, into one practice. When you have morality, and you have legality, you have peace. Justice must come forth and be applied equitably.

To the question, they will not have much influence, for some will disappear; some that are now seen as powerful will have no influence in the world, for they will be abandoned you see! But for a time, yes to the question; there will be dogma and old ways or customs will be changed, but very slowly, in some quarters, you see. Otherwise, there will be a new religion that will encompass the compassion of the Christ, the wisdom of Moses, the law of Mohammed, and the tolerance of Krishna. See?

WHAT WILL THIS NEW RELIGION BE LIKE?

In the shortest of terms, it would be the practical application of what would be called the Golden Rule. There will be two forces, as always in the world of duality. There will be those who wish to believe that to be one with all things is the proper way, then there is the other faction that will disbelieve this and will attempt to control all things, for their own personal gain. These two factions have been since the beginning of time, and they will continue, for there are those that will take, and those that will give. But in this time, the religion will be more of a practical application, as to morality, as to justice, as to compassion. There will be a lessening of control over people by their status, by their sexuality, by their sexual habits, by their preferences, or by their status in their community, or what they would occupy their day as a vocation. The old markers of status will be removed, and it will be seen, yes, that some are more responsible and have higher positions of authority or responsibility; but that the equality will be seen that they are all souls, each in their own way, living their existence, finding their way in the light. This will be the difference: that they can be high or low on the rung of society's ladder, but that they will be seen as a soul – some more evolved than others – but still, the humility, the similarity, and the spirituality will be identical; some enlightened, some not, but all on the same path towards perfection.

When you have this understanding, then it does not make sense that you should take advantage of one another, or that you should steal from one another, or that you should murder one another. It just does not make sense! This will be part of the new religion, for what is done in the physical world is temporal; any who hoard, any who have property beyond their vision have it only temporarily. Then, it is given back. Those who make use of what they have for the greater good in the time that they have it will be blessed. Those who have just to hoard will be cursed. The question is: will you be willing to cooperate, will you be moral in your business dealings, just in all things, or will you succumb to temptation and engorge yourself on the physical appetites? Limits on desires, will be one of the call words, you see, one of the creeds that will define what will become the one religion. For it will not really be rules and regulations; it will be the understanding of the Laws of Nature and the Laws of God, and there will be no conflict between the two.

WHAT PERCENTAGE OF PEOPLE WILL BE ACTIVELY PARTICIPATING IN THE RELIGION OF THE LAW OF ONE?

About half as you would know it. More practically, a third would be actively engaged.

SHOULD WE EXPECT TO SEE MORE ASCENDED MASTERS AND AVATARS COMING
INTO THE WORLD IN THE NEXT FEW YEARS?

They are already here. But yes, you would find those minds that
would help guide from above, coming still. Yes to the question.

ARE ANY OF THESE BEINGS IN HIGH POLITICAL POSITIONS TODAY?

You might not find them in places of political arenas, but you may
find them in places of economic or places of institution and commerce, you see. But the understanding would be their willingness to
help, the willingness to preach and teach. And, as such, you would
find them more in the area of the practical aspects of the world in
commerce or business or supplying goods, you see. In the political
realms, they would not be highly visible here, nor would they, indeed,
be able to be compassionate. Their passion is to provide, is to give
away those things that are good to all others, you see.

WILL WE SEE MORE ACTIVITY FROM ANGELS, ARCHANGELS, AND OTHER HIGHER
BEINGS DURING THIS TIME?

If you are referring to their presence and being visible, yes to the
question; there will be furthering their activities in the world as they
would be needed, would they not? And there are more who would
pray to them and give them sustenance and substance to come into
the world, as you know it. Yes, you will be perceived of those apparitions and appearances of those who would come into the world carrying weapons, perhaps, for they are best known for some sort of
weaponry, you see. But primarily it would be their intention which
is honest; no deviation. They will be participatory in the lives of in-

dividuals, both famous and not-so-famous; they would be coming into the arms of those who would be neophyte or beginners, you see. Yes, we would find much activity here; they will touch upon the waters, touch upon the Earth, as they have in the past. It is their time to do so, you see.

DURING THIS PRESENT TIME, THERE HAVE BEEN MANY REPORTS AROUND THE WORLD OF MARY THE MADONNA MAKING APPEARANCES TO PEOPLE, WHETHER OR NOT THEY ARE FOLLOWERS OF HER. CAN WE EXPECT TO SEE THIS ACTIVITY INCREASING OVER THE NEXT FEW YEARS?

As it would be seen prior to any difficulty in the world, as you would know it, there is a preparation and a time that offers caution, or calmness, or a coming together to be prepared for certain things. Yes, we would expect that other things could be done in this regard, as you suggest. You would find there is now an urgency taking place; what that would be similar to that which has taken place in Yugoslavia, and that that would now be in Herzegovina and Croatia. There would be further apparitions in Spain, France, and in the bordering states of the Mediterranean itself. There is an urgency, here, to cooperate and to help one another. Peace or karma will be said to the world itself, and there will also be some apparition into that of Rio or the area of Brazil. This will be seen in the sky.

You would find that these phenomena are a direct result of those prayers, for this is a time of woe, and to those of the Catholic countries or minds, this entity administers once again, to those who are of like mind. There will be difficulties and trauma that will cause people to wail and to fall upon their knees, and to pray in earnest. This, of course, will heighten the apparition. But understand the prophecies given in Europe, to the children: the last is about to take place, and this will be most disturbing, as there will be some loss of life in just about every country in which the ocean touches the shores, you see. However, expect this to be a time of opportunity, of uplifting and of enlightenment to those minds who seek to find their way through their religious points of view. Yes, there will be more phenomena, and they will be seen clearly!

WHAT ENTITIES KNOWN AS THE APOSTLES AND THE DISCIPLES ARE REINCARNATED NOW?

As we would examine this, there would be seven, possibly eight at this point. Their function would be to come together from different regions in the world like certain icons, barons, or kings and kingdoms, and there will be an attempt to cause a certain blanket of peace to go across these lands themselves, you see.

WHICH DISCIPLES OR APOSTLES?

Matthew, John, Simon, Stephen, Peter, Thomas, the other Peter, and Ruth.

CAN YOU GIVE US INFORMATION ABOUT THE THIRD INCARNATION OF SUPER AVATAR SATHYA SAI BABA?

It would be scheduled for about six, possibly as late as eight years from this point in time [2011]. He will be known as Purdi Sai. He will wear the turban and sit in a large cavern or room and there will be many cushions. It will be seen as a place of luxury. He will be more materially wealthy, such as Krishna might have been at the time. In his just previous incarnation, the entity was the most powerful of the three. Shirdi Sai Baba came as the teacher, as the wanderer. Sathya Sai came as the teacher, and as a confidant to large industries, politicians, and organizations, but also was one of the people. During his time for preparation to this time, it would be the most powerful of the three, as it was needed.

In the next incarnation, the entity will be more like a counselor, more like the aristocrat, and engaging those intellectual minds who would be putting forth a new consciousness into the world itself; one that would be more to the prosperity of everyone in the world itself, you see, attempting to eradicate poverty. In this next existence, the entity will live a little more luxuriously, you see; have a little more deluxe everything in its life. And, as we have given, he will have a tendency to be surrounded by large groups of people. The comparison will not be the same, for the lifestyle will be different, as the world itself will be different. India will be an oasis that many in the world would wish to incarnate in or wish to live, even if they come from different countries, you see. It will be a beautiful existence.

IS INDIA THE LOCATION WHERE THE REINCARNATION WILL OCCUR?

This will be to about the same place which he has now left, you see. We would find him into Bangalore and Puttaparthi. He may come in from the north, but he will arrive in the old places, you see.

WILL THE VATICAN IN ROME PLAY AS SIGNIFICANT A ROLE AS IT DOES NOW?

The Vatican itself will always be a light; it will be a remembrance of those things and a holy place itself. It may not be as extensive as you would think it would be, for there are many who will turn their backs on their old religions. The religion, as they see it, is based on fear, you see. What we see in the world is there is a tendency that there will be a subtle reference or understanding of these places, but it will be amplified in a different way, you see, without the connotation as is now seen.

WILL THE CATHOLIC CHURCH STILL EXIST IN ITS CURRENT FORM WITH POPES, CARDINALS, AND A HIERARCHY?

This may not last too much longer, for this will not be in the same way, in the same manner. There is a failing in this form of control or organization, for it is based not on the individual, but based more on the observation of the individual from afar.

WILL THE OTHER GREAT RELIGIONS OF THE WORLD, SUCH AS ISLAM, HINDUISM, OR BUDDHISM BE CONTINUING, OR WILL THEY BE CHANGING OR EVEN DIMINISHING IN THE COMING DECADES?

These who follow the Golden Rule will continue to exist. The most compassionate among those, those who practice non-interference or intervention, who tolerate all forms of belief, are the early Krishna or Hindu religion. The world is coming to a similar point, where there can be the incorporation or the understanding of these healing forces or consciousness. This particular consciousness is such as you would call it, the Christ consciousness. It will tolerate and incorporate the truths of the great religions of the world; for all religions know, in part, and all see, in part, you see. But as there would be a time passing, there would be a shedding of those frivolous inconsistencies, and there will not be a need for priests at the front of the hall, but rather, there will be those coworkers who will help those who believe, find a place, you see. And as such, we find this is taking place even now.

WILL TIBET REVERT BACK TO ITS OWN SOVEREIGNTY?

We can see some agreements with both the social leaders and the re-ligious leaders. There will be division between the religion itself, as to the Buddha, and to that of the Dalai Lama, but there will be, in the future, a harmony or a coming together. Therefore, to the ques-tion about sovereignty, after some time (perhaps a generation or ten), there may be the return to this. See?

WHAT CAN BE SAID REGARDING THE RAPID AND RISING GROWTH OF THE PRAC-TICE OF WITCHCRAFT AND PAGAN WORSHIP LATELY?

To some degree, these would be the remnants of the ancient Druid and Atlantean consciousness, you see: the Law of One would be more exact as to this, the consciousness. There was, at that point in time, the Law of One, being those who would follow the compassion, being considerate and compassionate of the feelings and circumstances of others. These would be those who would be considered on the path of Divinity, being self-aware. There were others who were on the path of Belgal, those who would be the followers of the Son of Belgal. These would not be caring of individuals, but would be more for the aggrandizement and position of themselves, to selfish concerns, to the exercising of extreme pleasures for their own sake. This would be at the great subjugation of those Things, that would be laborers; less than human, but in human form.

These would be the remnants of these decisions, these reli-gious points of view that are now becoming prominent in the world, as you would know it. For the great religions of the world have been, indeed, to some degree, adulterated, or, to some degree, they have become stagnant. As such, what is about to take place in this, the Renaissance period, will be improvement on all levels! Look to the economic Renaissance that is taking place. The renovation or destruction that is taking place to the world's great currency will now spill over into the hands of the other currencies; but more exactly, to what would be the gold standard. Look to the conditions in the religious points of view, including the scientific, the arts, and those other influences or levels of society, including justice, and you would find that this is a period, a time in which people are seeking to find the truth.

Hence those of the natural religions or points of view such as the studies of Pan and other forms, from Sufism to that of the Wiccan and otherwise, these would be a return to the simplicity of understanding nature; not attempting to control it! To be in harmony with nature, so that, once again, that pivotal point that is fast approaching may turn the tide, and the world need not fall into a destructive, corrosive and fiery end, or circumstances. Instead, it may be relieved and can avoid these disasters if there is a change of heart, of mind, and of soul. This is why there are such improvements into these religious points of view that seemingly are touching upon the Law of One, or that of the sun-god Ra; the one religion or point of view from ages past, as recounted in the Atlantean experience before the destruction of the world. Those who are learning to control nature, or harness the microscopic, the atomic world, know not what they deal with!

In this sense, there is a resurgence of those who are reaching out and looking for hope, and these, the natural religions, are the memory in the soul mind. It allows them to come to a simpler time, to a time of understanding, a time of being in harmony with nature, and nature in harmony with themselves. If you look, this has been leading up to this point in time for the last few decades you know! However, the resurgence of the understanding is to understand the simplicity of religion, the point of view that would be considered natural, but also to control those intuitive, metaphysical aspects in the development of the telekinetic and clairvoyant points of view, that would be hand therapy, manipulation of matter, and to elicit those minds that are in discarnate form. What other religion welcomes this, you see?

WHAT CAN BE SAID OF THE THEORY THAT THERE IS NO EVIL; IT IS ALL JUST ENERGY?

Let us use the word 'consciousness' and you might perceive the answers a little more clearly, you see. For there is no such thing as evil, as you may understand it as a two-horned being with a tail. Evil is a creation of humankind. When humans prey upon other humans, or when there is no compassion, where there is no love, this absence of love is, indeed, what you would call evil. In the Universe, is the moon evil? It does not have atmosphere; it must be evil! It cannot sustain life in the human form; yet, again, evidence that it is evil. There is, indeed, no evil force or energy in the Universe, for in the beginning there was only the vibration or the word; a thought made vocal, or a frequency; the primary or original frequency, you see. Evil is destructive. Evil is the absence of love. Evil is a destructive force. Now, it can exist simultaneously with the constructive force, and does! But usually it is the will of a person or of a group of people that causes the destructive and inhumane forces to exist. No alternative frequency vibration or substance; just simply humans and their activity towards other humans. Evil is the absence of love.

WHAT ARE SOME IMPORTANT QUALITIES THAT WE NEED FOR THE COMING ERA?

The ability to forgive always. The ability to express compassion to strangers and known individuals alike. The ability to forgive and forget in a Divine way. And the ability to hope and to achieve in a material way. The combination is such: look to the sky for guidance, look to the ground for sustenance, look to the path in front to be hopeful and full of new adventure, and look to the path advanced as to times traveled and lessons learned, or built upon, you see. This will be the practice of those in the world who will bring their talents to be communicative, to be inspirational to others, that they might inspire them to accomplish more than they would on their own. Teaching, of course, would be most important, and those abilities to find water or to be able to live off the land, to some degree, also would be helpful.

FOR THOSE ON THE SPIRITUAL PATH, WILL THERE BE ANY UNIQUE CHALLENGES FOR SPIRITUAL GROWTH DURING THIS TIME?

There will always be new challenges, as there is an advancement of the soul. They have a tendency to be accelerated or sped up during this time, however, and there would be more of an engagement, a vitality as these events are unfolding, or coming closer and closer. Yes, you can expect these times to be more intense. However, the lessons will be the same. The intensity is different, and they may involve larger groups of people at the same time.

HOW IMPORTANT WILL IT BE TO MEDITATE IN THE FUTURE?

As important as it is today, you see. To communicate with the higher selves, to communicate with the dimensions above, and to be able to find within yourself that essence of who and what you are, meditation is, indeed, the key. It is important to come together in large groups, for as minds come together, the meditation is amplified, and the benefit is also multiplied. It is important that more than one mind comes together, you see, for then they comfort one another.

IS IT TRUE THAT WHEN MORE THAN ONE MIND COMES TOGETHER IN MEDITATION, THERE IS A SYNERGISTIC EFFECT, MEANING THAT THE TOTAL IS GREATER THAN THE SUM OF ITS INDIVIDUAL PARTS?

We would agree with this, yes.

CAN YOU OFFER A SUGGESTION TO HAVE MORE VIVID AND CLEAR DREAMS AND RECEIVE INFORMATION ON EARTH CHANGES?

The first is to select a point of interest, then to read or look to available media, or a book, or engage in interest in a general direction. This will focus the mind in that area concerned. Then, as there is the entering into sleep, the body should be rested, not tensed, nor should it have stresses from the day left in it. As the body enters sleep, then utter what is desired for the dream:

> Please advise me on Earth changes and let me see
> those things that are going to take place, and let these
> visions or sightings be vivid, and let me remember
> or understand them as they occur. Amen.

Such a prayer, or one similar to the same, can be uttered as you go to sleep. Then, as there would be an examination of it - the event you are seeking- the recording of the same would be helpful. Primarily to be calm during sleep, to be focused at night to your point of interest, then to recall the same; even in the middle of the night, wake up and record it or note it, you see. Going over the recorded notes you made, over and over again, perhaps an in-depth description of what was given in a dream could be said or stated.

You may take other things that would be helpful to induce sleep: a warm glass of milk, some warm honey, herbs that would cause the self to be drowsy, like Slippery Elm tea, you see. Anything that coats the stomach allows the dreams to be either more vivid and enriched with information, or the dreams might be more like the nightmare: running through the dream, when undigested cheese might be in the stomach, you see. Take care what you eat prior to sleep, for it does influence the mind, and, therefore, the dream states. But focus the mind, pray for the area of concern, and then record the same.

YOU HAVE MADE MANY REFERENCES TO THE RELIGION OF ATLANTIS KNOWN AS THE LAW OF ONE. IN THIS DAWNING OF THE NEW EARTH, WHAT WILL BE THE ROLE OF THE LAW OF ONE?

There is the attitude or the attempts of those to reunite or invigorate, or (you might say) resurrect what would be the Law of One. The Law of One is an attitude, or an understanding for those beings who are compassionate; those beings who understand that as they are united with everything, that everything is conjoined, that everything has an attachment one to the other. Then they can understand that the Law of One is a law of compassion and consequence.

Those who are compassionate are finding their way and re-membering their experiences with that that you would call the Divine or that that you might call the Law of One being God Almighty. And the attachments, the associations, the experience of getting closer and remembering from whence they came, those souls, those minds, those hearts would be attempting to come closer and closer to touching the face of God Almighty. Therefore, it is the Law of One that is the understanding of remembrance, so to speak, that all are, indeed, attached or united, and they are attempting to come closer and closer to that that you would call God Almighty.

The Law of One is the understanding that there is one God and that all are one in the eyes of God. Understand there is a thread that flows through all things; an energy or force that causes the smallest particles you could see, perceive, or understand to move. This ambient, coherent force is what you would appeal to as God itself, at its most fragile or suggestive level. This thread reaches out through every heart and mind on the planet, as you know it, in all its varied ways, shapes, and forms, and it reaches out through all living things (including the planet itself), and from there to the solar system, the galaxy, and the Universe beyond! Thoughts are motivating, thoughts are real, and they are the influence of these smaller particles, these small essences of things. What is seen within them, this force, is God itself (if you would understand it from a certain perspective). The microcosm and the macrocosm are the same; take steps down and steps up, and at each step you would find similarity. Some would call this fractal understanding, but is better understood as, "As above, so below."

The Law of One is an association; it is an understanding, it is an attitude, but it is more to understand that there is a law, a certainty, that all are appended, united, attached, interacted with, or otherwise one; one, with each other! And what one does to another, this is affected to all, including that one who instigates the cause or the consequence, you see. The Law of One is a law of perfection. The Law of One is that that all will seek unto the Divine understanding of themselves, and to the Divinity or the invisible forces you might call "from above;" as they harmonize, and become associated with you, so there can be the greatest human experience of all: to be the Divinely awakened, fully realized while in the flesh. See?

IN THE FUTURE, WILL THERE BE AN OPPOSITION TO THE LAW OF ONE?

The answer is affirmative; as there is now, as there always has been. If you would take the human race, you would see that there are two opposing forces; this is, after all, the world of duality. You would have those who would be in accord, those who would be compassionate, those who would have the same feelings for everyone as they would for themselves. Those who would be in opposition to this are those who wish all things for themselves at the expense of others. There is no compassion, nor is there caring. You might say there is a disconnection between those who would be selfish, and seek their own aggrandizement at the expense of others. For instance, in the Atlantean times, they often had those Things, or beasts of burden, you might associate them with, and they were slaves, and their life was one of drudgery. The Things worked specifically at certain functions so there could be the comfort and the pleasure of the Sons of Belgal. Their selfish aggrandizement was based on the suppression of those Things or those souls that were encapsulated in these bodies that would be like beasts of burden, you see.

In this regard, you would see in the future, as in the present, there are two opposing forces, Light and Dark you might say. But if you would look at the human race, there are those who are giving, and those who are taking; those who share and are content in their cooperation with each other, their caring for one another, and those who are not - those who only wish to consume for their own personal pleasures, all that they can, even at the expense of the comfort, safety, and welfare of those who would be lesser beings. It is like a race of masters, supported by a race of slaves, you see, to give you some idea.

There will always be opposition, but as the pendulum swings from one extreme to the other, the opposition in this time (the Sons of Belgal) will be subdued. There will not be the warfare and the selfish consumption as there has been, but rather, there will be an orderly process, shall we say, that the consequences of things will be observed and expected, so that deliberate decisions and deliberate actions will unfold and there will be certain outcomes or responses, that are predictable, you see. And these consequences will be favorable to most.

As the pendulum swings to this extreme, expect there to be a closeness, but it takes a willingness of all who are upon the planet *now* to choose which side they would be on: selfish or unselfish.

THE EDGAR CAYCE MATERIAL REFERENCES A GROUP OF ENTITIES AS THE SONS OF "BELIAL." IS THIS THE SAME GROUP AS THE SONS OF BELGAL?

As of the same. B-E-L-G-A-L. The original spelling would be three lines, a circle, and a spike off the circle. The Sons of the Law of One were represented by a sunburst, just so you have both spellings. Three horizontal lines under the sunburst and a serpent underneath the three lines. The sunburst would be spiky or radiating arms out, as in what would be seen in the sunburst of Ra-Ta, or what you might see in the Mayan or Aztec realms. A sunburst represents the rays of sun; "Sons" of the Law of One, radiating out through and to all things. In Egypt, you would see the sun with lines radiating out from it in the hieroglyphs or in the carvings or reliefs, especially associated with Ramses and Nefertiti. This is again a similarity to the Sons of the Law of One; the rays radiating out to and through everyone, and everything, you see. You would also see winged images in later Egyptian activity, symbolizing protection surrounded and given out to all. But the feathers would look like the rays of heaven, especially when you see these on totems; the bird being on the top, with the wings or arms outstretched.

This is the sign of protection and unity, the sun radiating out to all things, to and through everything. You would see that the sun itself does provide life to everything, and so does the spiritual life, giving life to everything. Everything in the world requires the sun, or the vibration of light; even though at the deepest levels of the ocean it might seem nonexistent, there is light. The vibration or frequencies cause the cells to activate and the nervous system to vacillate or function. It causes movement. If you take a bell or a tuning fork, and you strike it and hold it close to the human body, the body can feel and will soon resonate at the same frequency as the bell; it shifts or alters (though not permanently, of course). If you take a Buddhist singing bowl and strike it in such a way, it, too, vibrates, and the frequencies can go through and to a body. Striking a drum, or using an instrument, or a human voice even, the body can feel the frequency going through it. This frequency instills life in all things. And if you can do this with many things, and you realize that light is the finest vibration of all, then you can come to the greater understanding that the cells themselves are stimulated by light or vibration, and they are alive! Therefore, all are connected through this sound, or vibration, or movement of frequency through them, you see?

YOU MENTIONED THE IMAGE OF THE SUN USED IN THE NAME 'SONS OF THE LAW OF ONE.' DID THEY SEE THEMSELVES AS 'SONS' OR AS 'SUNS'?

Let us give it to you in such a way that it combines the two. "Sons" refer to genealogy, but also it can mean that are all one, united, related, as all sons are related (although men and women were equal at that time). They are related to the sun itself, the giver of all things, that Universal, single thing; the Word, or Light, or Soul, you might call it, or the sun itself. But understand they are connected through life that emanates from light or vibration, and in this way, the sons are like cousins, brothers; they are, in a genealogical way, members of the human race, members who have, like a fraternity, come together.

Your clarification is such that we refer not to those who are related in a way that they are descendents of the sun god, but rather that they are descendents of those who have chosen the singleness, the Law of One, that all are one, and the Law is Light! See? The sun is the giver of light, and therefore is mid-way in the heavens between those who are on the Earth and those beings who are in the heavens above. But it is light, and therefore represents the heavens above.

COULD YOU PLEASE ELABORATE ON THE SONS OF BELGAL?

In the time of Atlantis, the Sons of Belgal were those minds who were filled with self-aggrandizement, those minds who lived in the world at the subjugation of others, including those beings you would call the Things or the slaves; those that would be less than human, you see. Those who enjoyed their opulence, their decadence, their prestige, their personal wealth, these would be the Sons of Belgal, for they had in their own mind the activities or the purpose to hoard or to gain for themselves. They attempted to use and be using. These would be the minds who would not care or have callous thoughts towards other beings. Those who have great power and personal prestige, and who show some form of compassion towards those who are suffering are the opposite. This is the difference! One group in the world, as you know the world, was fearful, and they preyed upon one another. One group was not fearful, but compassionate, and they assisted one another. This assistance would be what you would re-member in the "Good Book" as the Golden Rule or "do unto others as you would have them do unto you," with respect, you see.

This is the difference between these two groups of people; one existing for their own existence at the cost of everything or every-one else, and the other who would give away most things and would impoverish themselves, yet were still caring of those who would be left behind. See?

This is a time of new beginning. This is a time of change, and as a time of change there is the opportunity to make great advance-ments or to make great mistakes. No need to be impatient, but, in-deed, there should be the expediting of those things that would be considered knowledgeable. Preparation for families for such times will be to become self-sufficient, and indeed there will be pride in the hearts and minds of those who take onto themselves this attempt to alter their habits, their thinking, and their purpose. To those greedy souls that have come into the world and have remained here for the last five thousand years, now there will be a time for them to be collected, encapsulated, and held away from the human race, as you know it.

BY WHAT PROCESS WOULD THESE SELFISH SOULS BE ENCAPSULATED AND PRE-VENTED FROM INCARNATING?

We doubt very much that there would be a comprehension of the process in this, the finite mind. Understand it as simply a barrier or prevention that they would not be allowed to enter into this, the time of peace; for here, it will be a time of regeneration, as has been predicted from Krishna, to what would be other ancient understandings – Moses, for instance, and that of the Essene, and to those of the Native cultures, here, that have seen a time of great calmness or peace. For at this point in time it would be advantageous to reincarnate, for many souls to make advancements. There will not be even competitive sports; there will not be allowed any competitive combat or victory and defeat, so to speak.

The process is simply that there would be a barrier, and they will not be permitted, you see. For understand, thy God is a loving and just God; there are no injustices in the world, as you know it. There is a time and a place for all things. This, the Thousand Years of Peace is about to take root at that point in time.

IT IS SAID THAT THE GREAT PYRAMID IN EGYPT USED TO BE COVERED WITH SHINING STONE THAT COULD BE SEEN LIKE A BEACON IN THE DESERT FROM MILES AWAY, AND IT HAD A STRANGE LANGUAGE ON IT. WHAT WAS THE LANGUAGE AND WHAT DID IT SAY?

These would be symbols of the one God. Often there has been said there are many paths up the mountain, but only one peak. This is a crude interpretation of some of these things. This would be a golden capstone you speak of; it would be what would be representative of the association with the spiritual aspects from which humans have evolved, you see. Prior to the entering into the flesh, there was somewhat of a migration of those minds that would be caught up in the material, but prior to that point they could come and go in the material aspects. Hermes built the tri-vehicles, or the pyramid. Prior to that, the consciousness would be expanded and understood, but when there was the construction of the same, the language would be Atlantean, similar to that which is seen in the Pyrenees now, spoken almost in the same fashion. The combination was both of the Egyptian and the Atlantean, you see, more to the sect from Poseida; for here, these would be the intellectuals, or those of the priesthood, you see. They were the same carvings that were on the Temple Beautiful. The use of the terrible crystals would have the same markings as here: the capstone on the pyramid, you see. When the limestone and the gold would be together, this was a shining tribute to the Divine, to remind each and every soul from whence they came, that they are whole and part of the Divine themselves.

Unfortunately, changes occurred, but the consciousness and the understanding did not. The storm is over, the sun comes out, the Age changed. It did not extinguish the truth, nor should it; just the records were lost. This is why the temple itself was decimated and the limestone was taken and used by those who were ignorant of the same, for their dwellings, their hovels, their places, you see. Unfortunate! But it was the time; to dismantle those things from antiquity was to erase them from the consciousness. But even doing so, it has not erased the remembrances of these times. See?

DOUGLAS JAMES COTTRELL TALKS ABOUT THIS RELIGION OF THE LAW OF ONE AND HOW PEOPLE SHOULD LIVE THEIR LIVES. HOW WILL HE AND HIS ORGANIZATION PROMOTE OR MAKE THAT INFORMATION KNOWN?

The mortar, the boards, the bricks, the metal, they will make none of this; it will be the people who inhabit these material surroundings. Make no mistake, it is the people who communicate through Divine inspiration, and through what would be the dedication of their inspiration gained from the Divine that will accomplish this. When will this be done? It is being done now. There are many that will come together for a purpose that would be common; that purpose would be for mutual protection, safety, well-being and love. We do not speak of carnal love, for this is unimportant. We speak of love that is unconditional; that which is Divine love, you see, that lasts for Eternity, and is, indeed, the light for each soul to find its way back into the fold from which it has wandered, you see.

The time is at hand; the light that exists in this temple will shine out like a beacon on the beach and it will be far-reaching. But it begins with a few people deciding to get along with each other, and to figure out ways and means to do so, so conflicts are resolved earnestly, emotions are not erratic or extreme (save for love), and there is mutual respect and accord for each other. When one is hurting, then others may come to aid. This type of well-being is, indeed, the compassion of the Christ; this is, indeed, the Law of Ra-Ta; this is, indeed, a return to the ancient, single religion of mutual respect, partnership, fairness, acceptance and tolerance. Some might not believe the same, but they certainly will have within themselves the same values, you see. For instance, does it matter that one has a favorite color that is blue, and another that is green? Nay! But there are people who will argue the point: one is better than the other. Not so in harmony, where both can agree that it is a *preference*; the preference is equally important one to the other. But there should not be conflict, combat, or even conversation that would debate this. Each has his or her own preference. Then, mutual respect allows another to do whatever it is they do, for it is their business, and the other should not comment, judge, critique, or criticize; not one word!

This is the truth of the Law of One, for those who can do this, stay and maintain it for one whole day, they will be on the right track. But it will take two or three or four generations of such practice to make it into the society as we have commented and you have directed us to, you see. However, it is the way. To love one another is to tolerate one another. It is to respect each other like you would respect yourself. See?

WHAT DO YOU MEAN BY THE "TEACHINGS OF RA-TA"?

Ra-Ta was the sun-God in the ancient Atlantean and Egyptian religions in the times of antiquity. Ra would be that one who would be the leader, the prophet. Look to the Temple Beautiful and the Temple Sacrifice in Atlantis. Look to the ancient temples when the Nile flowed east and west, rather than north and south. It was at those times that the Law of One was the law that would be practiced, you see; when there were lighter-than-air ships in use; when there would be gravity and anti-gravity forces that would move objects. There were luminous walls that would be lighted without light, as you would know it. These would be the ancient times before the previous destruction. Ra-Ta would be considered the priest exiled from the Atlantean land Poseida or that of the island Atla, and made his way to Egypt, you see. He stayed in exile until there was a recall, you see. This would be ten thousand five hundred years prior to the entering in of Jesus the Nazarene, you see. Who was Ra-Ta? The worship of the sun, Ra, you see.

WHAT EVIDENCE OR PROOF DO PEOPLE NEED TO BELIEVE THE LAW?

Where there is evidence for a certain belief, or a certain practice bears benefit, then you have proven the law! Impatience is a problem with humans, as you may know. Teaching patience helps save the soul. It curtails errors or actions that might be violent, or destructive, or disruptive. Evidence of understanding certain concepts helps keep the peace within the mind and heart of an individual. Proving that there is assistance from above, in the various forms helps all to believe that what they are believing is not simply words from those who would be in authority; but, rather, it is the truth, and this, indeed, is what all are looking for. If they can bear something, and they know it is the truth, they will endeavor to bear it to the end, for they *know* it is the truth.

All the world is a temporal place. This is understood, but, in fact, it is not readily believed. The practice of the Law of Love or the Law of One will help all to come to the greater understanding that they are connected with each other and all things, and, by having respect for all things, they will treat all things as if they themselves were being treated, or hoped to be treated. This is the Law of One: to find their way back to perfect harmony with God Almighty; to be in harmony with all things in a loving and practical way; to be at peace with all things, to be at peace with the self. Then they can live their life in such a way that it would be productive. Greed, lust, vanity, sloth; all will fade. But while there might be times of justifiable anger, there will be no times of slander or violence.

The group will come to the understanding of how to be in Love with themselves, with God above, and all things. The Law of One is to be in harmony with all things. The Law of One is to understand the kinship of those who are in kinship with each other, for their own gain as well as for the gains of others, while other aspects of gain for the self would be in opposition to the Law of One. There are those who would, indeed, gain for their selfish interest, their own aggrandizement. They would believe they are right, and because of this, they would cause strife in the world and enslave nations. If there can be a return to the old ways, that each and every one is the same, then you would have evidence that there should be a reason to do this. For humans, as you know humans, only learn by example, and when they see, feel, touch, hear and understand, then they can believe. Because they have evidence!

Show them the truth and give evidence of the truths, then they will come, as they have been before; an enlightened race of people willing to cooperate with one another, that they will, indeed, deem in themselves that the success of another is their own success, and they will not be jealous or envious of the same.

SPECIFICALLY, WHAT EVIDENCE OF THE TRUTH CAN WE PROVIDE?

That they can get along; that they accept each other for what they are; that the differences between the group are obvious, but there is a single intention, and that intention is love; to be loving, to receive love. That the fulfillment of each other is encouraged, so that if one moves forward in some area, there is not jealousy, there is a move forward. They do not take advantage, for there is no greed, but they are willing to help one another for the simple virtue of being able to help! And then the whole group succeeds, you see.

However, at this point in time, it is how to get along with each other. As the different patterns of people (there are one hundred and forty-four) would be classified and understood, then individuals are able to see their strengths and weaknesses; they would not blame one another for their weaknesses, but would look within and try to train or strengthen themselves and overcome their own weaknesses, while at the same time offering their strengths to the betterment of themselves – yes – but also to others, or to the world. In such a way, you have cooperation.

As in the old days, the enlightened society understood the

laws of nature, and they utilized the same. Fusion is a law of nature, and it can produce unlimited sources of power or energy, cheaply, so that none would be enslaved by one holding the authority or the item and everyone else paying for its service. Such sources of energy can be given freely, that all would benefit, and not only a few! This is a hard lesson to see; that giving away something for the benefit of all produces benefit for the inventor or the individual. But all things being equal and in harmony, there is more gain this way than there is monetarily – which, again, is temporal and must be left behind.

Learning how to cooperate with one another, taking the various differences and utilizing the strengths while overcoming the weaknesses in the group is the place to start. This will help each and everyone take the steps to understand their soul and to come in contact with those invisible things, and to realize the spiritual aspects of themselves. For this will be the demonstration of the group: that they have some authority to benefit a body physically, mentally, emotionally, and spiritually; that they can change the environment of those who are in difficulty; whether it is loneliness, or finances, or some other aspect, the environment can be altered or changed. But most importantly, it will encourage individuals who take the steps, to show them the steps, to allow them to take the steps, and this light will be the way that attracts many!

The purpose, of course is to change the lives of each and everyone who comes into the group, who is initiated into the group, and at various levels of initiation they are given more authority or understanding - but they will have proven their proficiency in the former degree. This way, there is time that each can improve. There will be certain guidelines or examinations that one has come to a certain elevation or proficiency in their understanding. Truth is what each is seeking! To be happy and feel loved inside will motivate them and will be their desire. All desires are good, but putting limits on desires is to be in harmony with the Law of One. Remember: the Law of One recognizes that you are, in part, a piece of the whole; therein when you see another, do you recognize yourself to the betterment or to the opposition of this?

Establishing such regulations and observations, one will see that the compassion develops within the members of the group and they will be able to prove their proficiency in this. By certain tests, or actions, or activities, or attitude, they will prove themselves. Those in authority will watch over the proficiency, and as they see certain improvements, then the individual may move up to the next step, or the next degree. However, this would be established by those who have the capability to do so.

What is important, at this point, is simply coming together. This group is attempting to incorporate the Law of Attraction and Manifestation. The critical mass being formed, all things on the periphery will be attracted to the center like a magnet, like gravity itself. The problem will be in satisfying each and every individual, and therefore it may be necessary to make inquiry as to what the individuals are expecting before they enter into the organization or group; and as they amalgamate, as they wish to graduate, there will be other observations and examinations, and a declaration of that which they wish to accomplish. It should be considered a patient progress towards enlightenment; that the difficulty will be that many will be in a hurry, you see, and the group will have to compensate for the different belief factors – attempting to amalgamate them into a new language or terms that would be general, not specific to any other term - details that would be worked out by those who have skills to do the same. The intention is to make the individual more than he or she is, to bring peace in his or her life, thathe or she might

---

enjoy all aspects of God: health, wealth, and peace of mind. "Cast your nets wide, that you will catch but a few!"

Build upon what already has been established. Being the charity of giving love and healing, establish a healing community in this location. Then reach out to any and all, hither and yon, you see.

Can you offer a prayer or a mantra that we could say to change the destiny of the world for the better, which may even lessen the effect of the Earth changes that have been predicted?

The prayer would encompass gratitude for your life, a request for repentance, and a request for forgiveness. The prayer can be carried out in such a way that it can be repeated, and then there can be a simple adaptation of changing the ways of any who would wish to.

God Almighty, I ask for the intervention of the Divine forces above. I ask because I am grateful for my life. I ask because I am aware that I am part of this Universal world, solar system, and dimension. I ask for forgiveness for myself, and for the actions of those who have made transgressions against this planet and/or the peoples upon the same. I ask that the Divine intervene with love, compassion, and forgiveness, so that there can be a softening of the hearts of those who are upon the planet, seeking darkness, destruction and death, that they might be held up in their pursuits, that they might be changed from this direction, that they might relent and then repent, and then seek to do good in places, and with people, and with the tools at hand; to bring construction, and love, and building, and harmony, and peace into the

*world again. I ask for this place to be, once again, what it
was in the beginning: a peaceful place, a loving place, a
place that accepts all, no matter their limit, no matter
their intention. They are accepted into the light and the
warmth of love; Divine love, unconditional love. I appeal
to that that is 'That That It Is.' This is my prayer.
Let us all become the prayer and live our words! Amen.*

This should cover just about any particular nation, people,
religion, or belief, in their own way and through their own customs,
to comprehend that you are appealing to the Great Beyond for intervention in what might be a cosmic plan already in place. But by appealing, you are altering the formula. As the formula is altered, so
will the outcome of those events be altered; events that are testing
or teaching the people upon the planet to be more Divine and compassionate, and to have a singleness; that singleness to be a godliness, that godliness to be humanity, to be humane to each other. See?

Start with your ten closest friends and offer this prayer as a
gift; or, start with three people you know who will repeat the prayer.
Understand it is not volume, but quality. Prayers said without sincerity are wasted words. Prayers said with sincerity are heavily
weighted. In addition to giving cards or notes to people, you may
also use the Internet and let it be like a wide net being cast; throw it
broadly without expectation, but do give some explanation as to why
it might be considered, and that you would ask for some participa-
tion. But when you have the world in harmony with a single thought,
the world shifts or changes, like turning the steering wheel on a car,
or the rudder of a ship; it does so abruptly.

Start with a few friends or associates, and have them, likewise, use the power of three or the power of ten. But ask them for

sincerity, and ask them to pray all at the same time. Start slow, and then allow it to accumulate so that when it is recognized at the higher levels, there will be no condemnation of it, nor rejecting it out of hand. There will, however, be an acceptance of it, you see.

WHAT CAN WE DO TO HELP DURING THIS TIME?

There is currently great difficulty in the Canary Islands. There will be flooding in the Mediterranean. There will be changes in the temperature of the planet as landmasses will start to appear. The oceans will rise, and old shorelines will become sea-beds. Let this be part of the message. Let this be part of the evidence that this Law of One can be in harmony with understanding the future occurrences; the prophecies of the future will validate the group's intentions, as would be the miracles in changes of matter, or bone and muscle, you see. To be in harmony is to, indeed, understand the physical world, and that the mind can alter the world; and it is, at this point in time, that the urgency is given, that humankind is spiraling down a path of great destruction.

There is still time, if people change their ways, their attitude, their thinking, then there can be salvation and the world need not experience total destruction, that there can be a reprieve. Seek the Hopi Indian prophecies and other Native American prophecies. Look to Easter Island as tombstones or a testament to the landmass that once was in a westerly direction. Look to those influences in Egypt, and the Pyrenees, and Arizona, and you will find evidence of the civilizations that hold remnants of the Atlantean; and as such, the culture, the benefit of the Atlantean races are now emerging, as many come into the world who lost their lives then. They are now attempting to find their lives and to continue on bringing this new/old understanding forward.

Your mission would be: attempt to alter the course that human nature is on, from one of great destruction, to a reprieve. And although there will be a shift in the face of the Earth, this reprieve will save many, and the loss of life need not be so great, and the effects of these destructive and changing forces need not be so extensive. This would sound like a noble cause or something to accomplish, to alter the course of humans from its present spiral downward to a possible movement to a more productive harmony and achievement with the Divine! For the Divine is in the invisible. The Divine beings can only observe, unless they are asked; can only participate, when they are prayed to. They are willing, if those who are in the flesh are willing.

This would take some effort; more exactly, it will take some example. Many can be saved here. The world can be altered, and the planet can be put back to rest, for the human mind - and the combination of all those minds in the world at this time - are directing the course of the planet's actions and activities.

It might seem like a great effort, but the Law of One begins when a few people come together; when they are of the same accord, the same intention. When they are participating for the benefit of the group and each other in the group, and they care about one another, their demonstration of caring can be considered their initiation. Those who come for their own selfish means are of the temporary mind and are failing. Unless they can be altered or assisted, then they will need to be rejected. Learning how to accept and reject would be the first step. However, accepting those who would be of similar mind, similar accord, is not a matter of simply accepting those who are popular or easy to get along with, but there is something inside of each that would be recognized, no matter what their personality. Establish how to recognize this. Then, watch how they change, how they become acclimated to the group's understanding, and how they have a desire beyond their own to be part of the group and to make the group prosper. Then see if they are consistent in their attitude, or their intentions. These three steps will allow selection to be made of those who would be worthy, those who would be desiring to be part of this group. These who would be in harmony with each other would be in harmony with the one.

All things come to one thing, and that one thing is love. Those who share the same definition, the same understanding, are, indeed, part of the one! All others who take this and use it for their own selfish purposes, whatever that might be are not quite in harmony; they may actually be in opposition. Learning how to deal with this would be just as important as how to select from the many who would come. They will show their true nature in time. Be not in a rush to admit or reject anyone. Time will prove their intention. Judge by their actions, not necessarily by their words, for they may be mixed up in their vocabulary, but their heart might be pure, as to the intention to be part of the one.

Take the steps. Time is passing by. Messages of hope, messages of light need to be outgoing. Hold regular meetings at least once a week to discuss self-development, or to define the Law of One. It is just as important that it is defined by the minds in the group as it is to simply make a proclamation of the same, for the eternal and ancient truths will bubble up, you see. The first objective is to attract those who wish to avert the prophecy of the Hopi Indian (that the world is spiraling into oblivion) and that, perhaps, this next disaster of the world can be softened or averted. This would be a good place to start.

As we would look through the minds that will be gathered

here, we would find that there is a degree of sensitivity, that all are becoming aware. Feel the planet, feel the hostility under the ground, feel the hopelessness of those minds and those hearts who are in jeopardy. Feel their plight, and you will have some understanding of how the angels above weep for those who will be no more! Humankind can come together as the same kind, if they view themselves in kind. Regrettably, they might not, in certain areas or regions. But understand the sensitivity of the planet, and the sensitivity of those souls who have inhabited the flesh upon the planet, and you will have a greater understanding of who and what you are, and your affinity with nature; that is to say, affinity with the world as it is. Realize the times that are taking place are special times, indeed!

In what would be seen would be the changes you are expecting; however, the improvement to your *soul* would be what you are not expecting. But understand that the world moves slowly, and the soul is inspired (or takes on and is invigorated) by these challenges and influences that come into the world! In order to improve your soul, it is not to regret, or to express sorrow, or to become angry or even murderous; but rather, to simply control yourself. For any who are on the spiritual path know how to control themselves so that they are not provoked into getting off the path through violence, murder, or any form of aggrandizement, you see, one to the other.

Look to the core of the world itself and you would find that this particular core reaches down from the top through to the bottom; it cools in the bottom and it boils in the top. Attempting to mix what is given would be helpful. But as we see it, the world is continuing to alter its direction; there are changes taking place in the crust *even now*: the collapsing of chambers, where there has been the removal of oil and gas, and you would find that the world itself is replenishing rather than destroying itself, as you would know it. To those who have ears, let them hear; to those who wish to make something more of the world, do not be afraid! Live life to the fullest, and there will come a degree of salvation, you see.

You will attempt to understand the microcosm and how it relates to the macrocosm, you see. There is a thread that runs through all things, that point of consciousness that can influence the smallest particles that can be perceived, as well as the largest particles that surround you in daily life. When you have control over this, then you can control much; but, more exactly, you can control yourself.

Keep your integrity. Come together in a group, so there can be the attraction of other minds so there can be an explanation of these things that would be pertinent. Being prepared, and talking about being prepared, and coaching and advising others on how to be prepared, while in harmony with all things, is difficult indeed! Keep the integrity of the group together, heart-to-heart, mind-to-mind, and this group will multiply, and your message will be amplified, and the fun will continue. When you have light-hearted, light minds, usually you have success.

DO YOU HAVE ANY ADDITIONAL INFORMATION OR A FINAL COMMENT THAT WOULD BE HELPFUL AT THIS POINT IN TIME?

Understand we have listened to your instruction in the beginning [to gear answers to the average person, for the purpose of education and enlightenment] and we have attempted to give what would be meaningful to a certain mindset, understanding, or level, without causing minds to engage in this topic in a fearful way. Indeed, there will be those changes in the world, as you would call it; there will be the Earth changes. This is not the first time this has been discussed, nor given, nor attempted to be found out by certain individuals who may already be associated. The purpose of this is to understand that the world is going to go through some difficulties; there is no misunderstanding here. For those who have ears, let them hear; for those who have eyes, let them see. For those who are blind, for those who do not care, it is unfortunate that they will suffer the most.

As you would draw near to the greater understanding, let there be the preparation for times in which people do not or cannot come together and comprehend the actions and the responsibilities for their actions, that they are affecting the world itself. For the Earth has ears! It has an attitude. It has opinions. Try not to think of it as just a rock, but think of it as part of yourself. Psychometry is an example of how thought can permeate matter itself. When you go into a church, you can feel the awe in the building, for you would hear the prayers of all those who have gone before. Thoughts are real things. They reside within real places. As you begin to come closer and closer to yourself, you come to understand that everything is one. There is a thread that connects all things, allowing each to go through their steps or to take into themselves their destiny. This requires the wisdom of the soul. For sometimes people put themselves through situations when they are in jeopardy, even to the point of losing the life, yet, there they are.

As such, learn to love and to be loving. It is a time in which you can fall in love, be in love, and sustain love. This particular point is now. There is no turning back from this point. Coming together, assisting one another, and having a tribal or unity mentality will save many. The generosity of those countries which have plenty to offer to those countries that are having difficulty will be seen as the New World Order. For what will come of this is a new form of business, a new form of trade; and as we have given, trade will be east and west, crossing the countries that would lie north of Italy (Spain itself), and there the trade will take place to the West still, as it would be maintained.

What is being taught here? What is the lesson? *How to get along with everyone.* How to be fair and just. How to love one another, as you would love yourself, your family and your country.

Indeed, you will be able to see the pattern, as you would see the pathways across the Northern hemisphere. You will see in South America disturbances on both coasts. Lemuria will try to rise again, lying in a westerly direction from Peru. The planet will wobble. It will flip, or it would go in a lazy figure-eight configuration. This has yet to be determined, but once the waters start to slosh in their basins, they will progress, and the sloshing will increase so that the eastern seaboard of the Americas will be flooded many times. And each time, the oceans will move back and forth, and Africa will seem to shrink in size, maintaining its same shape, but because the water will rise around the outside of the continent, it will shrink. Many times you will see this sloshing of water back and forth.

Many times you will see the world change, but understand: pray for the planet, pray for the people upon the planet, and pray for the self that you can meet these things that will be deemed chaotic by many, but by doing so, you will meet your purpose. When there are those Earth changes in the world, as you know it, indeed, very quickly, the world will alter or change itself. The crust will break up in some places, mountain ranges will be flattened, and flat-lands will be made into mountain ranges. If you take a pie, and push the crust of the pie together, it causes ridges to be formed, but if you pull the crust apart, it causes the ridges to go flat. If you push it back together again, one part of the rift will slide under the other part. These are the changes that will take place in the world rather quickly.

This is why there will be the changes in those who are about the planet. Some countries will simply start all over again, for they will be reduced to their beginning levels. Those that change in the twinkle of an eye will be inspired, shall we say, through this energy that comes into the world. For radiation can come from space, as it has recently from the sunspot activity or plasma, and it has changed many on the planet. For some, physical loss of their life has occurred. Others have been transmuted to a higher level of consciousness and awareness, and this is seen by their emotional expressions being enhanced. To those who go through this time and remain in control of themselves, they will change themselves vastly. There will be a physical, metaphysical, and spiritual awakening or change within them. For, as it has been said, they will be "woken up," and they will perceive the light. In this way, they will have a different understanding. It will not be dynamic. It will be subtle. But as they are awake they realize, almost as if by memory, who and what they were, who and what they are today, and what is needed. They will understand their connection with the Universe, the universal mind, and other minds that they wish to choose to be associated with, you see.

No one can say this or that must be done, for each possesses his or her own free will or free choice. There will not be a twin planet, but there will be a different planet. This planet will change its face quite drastically. Those who maintain some consciousness will, themselves, be maintained. Humans, as you know humans, are about to go through a change that brings out their spiritual nature; awakens them, you see. And for some, this means they will continue assisting and helping in bringing in the New Age, the New Millennium, the New Law of One. As it was before, it will reinvent itself again. And there will be many who will understand. They can hear a rock speak, they can understand and hear the thoughts of another's mind, and many will come to learn from this.

This is a time in which the world is about to go through gyrations, and go through that which it has never seen in recent history. There are many who will be shocked, caught off guard, and many who will panic and scream, and think the sky is falling. There are many who profess great fundamental faith, but, in essence, they blame difficulties in the world on some dark figure. They do not take responsibilities for themselves, nor do they understand that God, which is a loving and just God, can allow things of change to happen. But if they look around in their own lives, they would see that when someone goes into a household, and wishes to renovate the house, one tears down the walls, expands the rooms, perhaps, and does things that seem to be destructive to anyone who would look upon this from their perspective and see only the big steel bin on the front lawn, walls and ceilings torn down, and garbage thrown away. But the building materials that were once taken into the house, and applied with great pride to make it a beautiful place, are thrown away to make room for new materials. Although it looks like destruction, the old is being discarded because it is a renovation; out with the old, to make room for the new. The same is taking place in the world.

Never lose sight that what is taking place in the world at this point in time, by thy God, (which is a Great Architect in the Universe) is, indeed, a renovation. This is not an end time; it is a renewing time. It is taking out the old, the unfashionable, or that which once served the household well, but now is a deterrent and deteriorates the household itself. When those aspects are discarded – the old wood, walls, floors, and ceilings – it makes from for that which is new and beautiful. This is why there are difficulties in the world, as you know it.

CHAPTER SEVEN

᪥

The Law of One

WOULD YOU PLEASE EXPLAIN THE LAW OF ONE IN GREATER DETAIL?

It is as it is stated; it is that all are One. Not possibly, not circumstantially, not in part, not by privilege or bias, design, by might or force. But it is in the understanding in the minds of humans (as you know humans) the finite mind can comprehend it as an association. It might be considered integrity that all humans are One; they are all brothers and sisters. In the physical world, they may have come from different backgrounds, but they are all human. They are not part human and human. They are all human. Therefore, they are all One.

The opposite to the Law of One is the Law of Singularity, where each soul isolates itself in a physical body, and each physical body isolates itself from all other physical bodies, and the process continues to be one leading to darkness, loneliness and death. The temporal body does experience death. The temporal body is taken on by the soul individually, and it is given up individually. To understand the rules in the physical world is not the same as to understand the rules in the spiritual realms.

But to the finite mind, to understand all are One is to associate that there is a consciousness, there is a divinity, there is a soul mind within each and every body that is eternal (it is indestructible), that has commenced in its existence since the Beginning and will continue its existence until the End. Each mind is of the same; on the soul level, all are equal, all are One. They came from the same Source and they return to the same. If you look at it in the analogy of water (the essence of life), then you will begin to understand that water in a mass can be an ocean, but you can take from the ocean a single drop. That drop is an individual when it is outside of the ocean. When it is immersed back into the ocean, it is no longer a drop. It is an entire ocean. A simple, single association (or amalgamation) if you look at it that way. The drop has become the ocean.

The willingness to separate can be that of the finite mind, and that is to the Law of being singular or isolated. You might call it "selfish." The willingness to return back into the ocean is the Law of One. It is a consciousness, it is an understanding that you know you are part of the whole. There is no doubt. There is no intellectual query, debate, or wonder. When the drop decides to return to the ocean, it knows what it is doing; it desires to return to the whole again, and it takes the action to do so. In this action, it ceases to exist as a drop, and instead of no existence, it becomes a greater existence. It becomes an ocean! Substitute the word "consciousness" and you have an understanding that the finite mind can comprehend, in this metaphor.

The Law of One is simply that that is a Universal understanding that all minds are connected; all souls are One. They have simply decided to separate, to experience (in their own way) free will and free choice. And as they continue to do so, what is it that they continue to do? To separate further and further from the Christos, or the centre of consciousness, and they stream out across the Universes, through all the dimensions, and they get lost. Temptation, aggrandizement, the lust for their individual satisfaction, it blinds them and they lose their way. To understand the Law of One is to find their way back, to amalgamate, to return to a critical mass as they once were. To become enlightened, yes. To become cooperative and to surrender their individuality, this is the process that leads them to understand the Law of One. Those who are willing to do this are unselfish; they are full of compassion. They are unified and they cooperate with each other, do they not? They coexist in the same great consciousness. Those who do not are the Sons of Belgal (Belize, you might call it). These are the ones who separate and continue to separate, thinking that their existence is, indeed, the greater existence, because they are, in their own minds, aware of themselves. Like a seed (or a drop), they are aware of their individuality. They refrain from joining the greater consciousness and the reason they refrain from doing so (no matter what the excuse might be) is that they are reluctant to give up their individuality. They know not the beauty of joining the whole. A drop becomes an ocean. Think of the vastness of this! The seed must die, that the plant might grow and become more.

To understand the Law of One is to understand that the self can become more (can become all) in its understanding and its experience; that along the way, there must be the willingness to accept each other, to learn to get along, and to behave in currents of love. Those who refrain, or do not, are against the Law of One. They are for their own singularity, aggrandizement, and they are trapped in the material worlds, you see.

Again, the Law of One is a consciousness to understand that all are One. They are One mind, they are One soul, and that those who attempt to amalgamate are in harmony with the Law of One; not that they must surrender who and what they are, but that this consciousness is added to the whole, and by doing so, they become greater in their own consciousness.

The Law of One, therefore, is an association with all other minds who are of the same mind, and that mind is love. Love in all its various forms can be understood and can be practiced as compassion, cooperation, gratitude; it can be practiced in many ways. They are all constructive, they are all beneficial to each other and to the Universe itself. In short, they are all in harmony (willfully in harmony, you see).

In that that might be considered the Law of One, it is that all are of the same mind, the same consciousness, the same heart, the same belief, and they practice their existence in the same way. They intrude not on each other, but they welcome each other. Like many drops in the ocean, they have a common ancestor, a common future, a common existence in the present moment. Somehow, they know they are individual drops, but somehow they are the entire ocean, united. There are many variations, but there is only one consciousness. The Law of One is a willingness to embrace that consciousness, to be loving under all circumstances, to be willing to learn to love even those who are difficult to love; for, you see, it is easy to learn to love those that are easy to love, but learning to love those that would commit even the most heinous crimes, this is, indeed, learning how to love. The Law of One is love.

WOULD IT BE FAIR TO SAY THAT THE LAW OF ONE IS THE LAW OF NATURE, AND THEREFORE INVARIABLE AND IMMUTABLE?

It would be. Yes.

WHERE DID THE LAW OF ONE COME FROM?

The same place that gravity originated, magnetism started, and motion and vibration commenced. It began in the Word. In the Beginning, there was only the Word, or the vibration, and out of this vibration came all other vibrations. The Law of One was, in essence, One. It only became the Law of One when the essence of One was divided, when those in the Christos decided to leave. Once they were aware of their own free will and free choice, they created the Law of One; they left it behind. Then, they attempt to find or return to it, you see.

WAS EARLY MANKIND STILL AWARE OF THE LAW OF ONE, OR WERE THEY BECOMING SO ENGRAINED IN PHYSICAL MATTER AND MATERIAL THINGS THAT THEY WERE BEGINNING TO FORGET?

They were aware of the common ancestry, the common communication between minds (for it was not of the spoken word, you see), they were able to move in and out of the forms rather easily. It was not until sometime much later when they were trapped or engrained in the physical form that they could not, at will, jump out of the form. At that point in time, it became extremely difficult for them to migrate from one to another, to another; and, as such, they resided within the form until physical death took place.

AT TIMES SUCH AS ATLANTIS, WAS THERE A BOOK ON THE LAW OF ONE, OR WAS THIS INTERNALLY KNOWN?

There is always scribes, always words; for unless something is marked down, it cannot constantly be referred to. In this time, there would be certain pillars, obelisks, that would be carved or marked with certain symbols; existed then, exist now, and will exist in the future, for humans (as you know humans) have to write something down. See?

WOULD YOU BE ABLE TO SPEAK OF THESE CERTAIN RULES OR TENETS OF THE LAW OF ONE?

They are evident, even now. They are: to be in harmony with all things. They are: to be respectful and courteous to all others. They Are: to be of service, is to be in harmony with creation. To help and to be of service is, indeed, to be creative. Do not adulterate the mind with worry or fear. Let the heart be pure and innocent. Do not fabricate stories or make judgments about anyone, unless you have personal knowledge of what is taking place, or what has taken place. Understand that mistakes take place, and when these mistakes lead to regret, then the person has learned from the lesson and there is no need for punishment. Understand that the Divine carries out its own form of punishment and reward. It is always better to help, than to hinder. There is always a positive solution for any difficulty that may befall the self.

This should suffice for the time being.

COULD YOU GIVE US SOME WORDS ON HOW THE LAW OF ONE RELATES TO OTHER SPIRITUAL LAWS, SUCH AS THE LAW OF KARMA, THE LAW OF GRACE, OR THE LAW OF ATTRACTION AND MANIFESTATION?

To the question itself, you are asking how all laws relate, one to the other. It is obvious, is it not? These are certain practices that open the spirit, open the eyes of the soul to that that lies beyond. Think of it as a human looking down at their feet, or a human looking up into the sky. There is a huge difference, but they are still doing the same thing (they are looking). Depends on what they are looking for or expecting; depends on what their attitude is, and how they apply these laws of nature, or creation. For one can positively create, or one can negatively create; depends on their attitude (or even their preference).

The Law of One is to understand that there is no escaping each other. Each soul is bound together. Whether they accept it or not (whether they know it or not), does not really matter. The fact is that there is a connection between each soul. Those laws you recounted, as to the Laws of Gratitude, as to the Laws of being Humble, as to the Laws of Mindfulness (as in that of using the mind to gain), understand that it is God that gives the gain. The human does the work and prepares itself, but the gain is always from God.

COULD YOU GIVE US AN ANALOGY OR A METAPHOR TO DESCRIBE HOW MINDS AND SOULS ARE LINKED TO ONE ANOTHER?

First, there is no real location in the physical body where the mind might exist, is there? No one can say where thoughts come from, nor where they go! Nor can they say where a chain or line of thoughts have been linked together, where they have come from, and where they go. There is this question of knowledge, of wisdom, in that that would be considered the invisible. Yet, you believe it, for you experience it. To measure the soul, to understand that the minds are linked together, is to look for evidence that this occurs, that there is communication between the various minds or individuals; there can be a consciousness that is expressed singularly and collectively. In order to measure this, you would need different instruments than what you would currently have to measure length, mass, weight, temperature (if you will).

In order to comprehend this is to understand that the meta-

physical or spiritual experiences can demonstrate a connection between the two; but here, telepathy or clairsentience (or even clairvoyance, or other of the mystical skills), they demonstrate this
communication, this access to information.

But simply, humans (as you know humans) need each others'
company! When they are alone, isolated, it tends to affect their balance or their sanity. They cannot help talking about one another, either critically or enthusiastically. They need physical touch, they need
affection. This might be seen as to the exchange between individuals;
the demonstration that the minds are all linked together is to understand that there is a pool in which all souls came from, and they will
return back to that pool again. Call it a "pool of light," if you will.

To measure this is simply to explore the Akashic Records,
where all knowledge is stored, and then to see the access that each
and every entity has to this storehouse of knowledge, and how they
can understand or know things about one another. For all of the life
is written and recorded: every whit, every word, every note, every
experience, you see. Like a spider's web, all minds are linked, like a
strand on the web. What happens to one part of the web happens to
all; if you pull one strand and release it, the whole web vibrate. This
can be seen in human nature. As one nation is provoked, the whole
world react. Now that there is the confirmation of the Internet, the
re- action is instantaneous; the same (if you will) predicted as it was
in the past, but the acceleration is now evident that the effects occur
much faster.

All minds are One, for it is the basis of human nature to care
for each other, to require physical touch from each other, and to con-
verse or communicate with each other, all on the physical level. But
in that that is on the spiritual level is that they can share dreams,
they can see the future that is yet to be, they can speak or communi-

cate one mind to the other (and usually is truthful, expressed without circumstance, without deception).

WHAT DOES IT MEAN TO BE IN HARMONY?

It means without friction; it means cooperation, courtesy, respect. It means there is no individual differences, no matter what. To be in harmony is to be cooperative. To be in harmony is to understand, as an individual soul, you have your own existence, you have your own progression, you have your own destiny. But you choose to walk with others in the same way. For instance, to be in harmony is a long column of people, various shapes, various sizes, various ability, and they are all walking along the same road; some a little faster, some a little slower. But as they walk along the road, they do not bump into each other, they do not push or shove. Some do not lag behind and others do not run ahead. Like a wave, like a ribbon, like a stream, they merge together and they walk along the road, each sharing the road, each feeling the experience in their own way, and yet, they are a ribbon of people, moving along the road all going in the same direction; no one feeling more superior or inferior to either others or themselves.

To be in harmony, therefore, is to simply be at peace and moving in a similar direction as all other souls would be moving; towards that as the Christos, returning home from whence they came, to being in love with love, you see. There is no sadness, no darkness, no despair. There might be challenges and excitement and uncertainty, but it is the willingness to move on, to experience that that is yet to be. To be in harmony is, therefore, more than a consciousness. It is, in essence, the experience of the experience, accepting all and accepting the self. To be in harmony is to be united, like the drop in the ocean. That "glue" that holds it together (the integrity, one drop to the other) is Harmony. See?

WHAT IS THE DIFFERENCE BETWEEN SELF REALIZATION AND FULL REALIZATION?

To be self-realized is to understand the capability of the self, a certain consciousness. To be fully-realized is to be aware of the association outside of the self, or the Universal Consciousness, and to know the difference. One operates within the sphere of knowledge (as of the self); the other operates as to the Universal consciousness, and the self realizes it as a cooperative nature, not a selfish one, or a preferred one. Simply that it is One.

WHAT DOES THE PHRASE "HUMANS AS YOU KNOW HUMANS" MEAN?

Is it not clear? Humans, as you observe them, have a certain expectation, or they are certainly predictable. To understand a human from a human perspective is to understand people, as you know people. However, to evaluate or to understand the entirety of the human is to take upon that of the consciousness of the soul, and to see it as similar. In seeing it similar to the self, there can be a comparison. On the spiritual level, there is no comparison; there is an observation. The value, the association, the acceptance of humans, from a human perspective is far greater than that that is accepted on a spiritual level. For in the finite world, there are occurrences, preferences, desires. To the spiritual level (or realm) there is none of that. There is simply an awareness one to the other, and the acceptance one to the other. See?

DOES THE CONNECTION ONLY EXIST BETWEEN SOULS, OR ARE WE CONNECTED

The connection is to all things in nature. For humans (as you know humans) have been given dominance over the world itself; this is why a mind can influence animals, or plants, or even insects. A powerful mind can bend the spoon, calm the wind, raise the temperature, divert a storm, start a growing season, amplify the radiance of the sun, improve (or not) those things that are outside of the physical self, or that are found in nature (as you know it). A weaker mind can be suggested or told what to do by a stronger mind; a stronger mind has the responsibility, knowing not to interfere in the weaker mind.

WHAT IS THE PURPOSE OF PHYSICAL LIFE?

In that that can be easily understood, it would be to understand that life itself (in the physical sense) is but a breath in the life of the soul. You would find humans (as you know humans) have, to some extent, misunderstood. They carry about their life as if they would live forever, and they would be immortal. Yet, each, in its own way, is living a terminal life. It will end.

In that of the period of the physical birth to the period of the physical death, this time allotted to each and every entity is that time that is allotted for the perfection of the self; to engage in what would be considered circumstances or experience to overcome the weaknesses, the inadequacies (yea, the difficulties) in self, in order that there might be that of the "true self" manifested. Some would call this the Christ consciousness. Some would call this the perfection of the soul. But it would be, indeed, a cleansing process, and whether this time (as to the life, in the physical sense) is a day, a month, a year, a century, it is, in all probability, the exact amount of time needed for the soul to continue to perfect that cleansing process in order that it might return from whence it came (as to the Godhead itself).

For, you see, each soul makes the sojourn through the world of materiality in order that it might overcome the temptations, might overcome the lust, and the tendencies for extremes; yea, overcome the selfishness for itself; and that the Original Sin (the sin of separation) ultimately is overcome. Then the soul, with its full cloak of understanding, with its sword of truth, and its shield of faith can enter back in to what would be Heaven, the Father, the Godhead and, as such, they would be perfect.

HOW MIGHT THIS PURPOSE OF LIFE BE ACCOMPLISHED BY INDIVIDUALS?

It will be accomplished, although it might take some a turn or two at the problem (yea, in others, many turns at the same problem). It must be overcome. For as one would build their house of blocks, each block must be laid firmly and squarely, builded upon one another. There cannot be in any difficulty, in any adversity, that that you would know as crookedness (as shortness, as you would call it) here, stumbling blocks. You will find that as each meets each, they would, in their own sense, attune themselves to overcome the inadequacies seen in themselves. They would then find that their purpose could be considered complete if they would willingly accept adversity and willingly understand that problems are but the stepping stones to success.

WHY IS THE PURPOSE OF LIFE TO RETURN TO THE GODHEAD?

This is in overcoming the Original Sin, the sin of separation. For, you see, each soul longs for that, as to its completion. You would not find any who does not feel a little alone, a little unassured. You would not find any who is not looking for that completion, that ultimate capacity; and, as such, that harmony and that peace in the mind (as well as that peace in the heart). And only when there is peace in the mind, and peace in the heart can one truly find its way back from whence it came, to that that is the giver of all peace, the giver of all life. And, as this is done, the trip is complete. It is not a matter of if, or should, or must. It is a matter that, sooner or later, each soul feels the need to return to the Godhead itself, and, indeed, seeks it out.

DO INDIVIDUALS HAVE THEIR OWN SPECIFIC PURPOSES OF LIFE, OTHER THAN ATTAINING THE GODHEAD?

You are speaking of the different pathways towards the Godhead itself, and in this vein, this is correct. You will find that they have several ways up the mountain, but there is only one peak. It does not matter which trail a soul follows, as long as they attempt to ascend towards that that is the end result (the peak of perfection, the highest point, that that can be seen as true completion). Yes, to the question. You will find, here, that there are many things that each soul in each sojourn must overcome in order to make the self whole, as they would be willing to do this, as it would be their free will and choice. For no Man can say this or that must be done. But in examining the pathways of each entity, it is that they attempt to aspire to that point that would lead them into that that is beyond. As such, yes, there are many pathways.

DO OUR CLOSE ATTACHMENTS TO OTHER INDIVIDUALS SUCH AS A CAREER OR MARRIAGE INDICATE A JOINT PURPOSE OF LIFE?

You would find that those groupings (families) would offer, here, the better (or greatest) opportunity to apply the God principles in everyday life. You will find that this is affirmative; that, here, others are attracted towards the self. For, you see, the weaknesses in self will be the strengths in another. Whether it is a marriage, a partnership, an association, that that is seen as to a grouping or any alignment of one or more entities will be a balancing of these strengths and weaknesses. Now, in certain undertakings, there will be a degree of common evolvement, here. This would be an overcoming or achieving the purposes that are similar in the lives of each of these entities who have gathered.

As such, in a family situation, you will find it is the offering, here, of the greater ability. For, you see, the ideal would be to overcome the strengths and weaknesses of self to create a balance or more perfect state. And this can be done by the mirror or reflection of that that is seen in the other (as to the family member, you see). And usually families are not very diplomatic, one with the other. They tend to be blunt, and to the point, and, as such, this would offer that pinnacle of truth that is necessary for the evaluation. There would not be much colour, but there would be direct communication, here.

As such, yes to the question, here. Associations or groupings are usu- ally found with common purposes (as to souls in a family, in a partnership, in a company, in a corporation); we go as far as saying that even in the living areas individuals have gathered, here, to share in what would be a commonhood of experience. For instance, neighbours in a house. The houses on a certain block will have a certain similarity. The city will have a certain consciousness or similarity. The province will have the same. The nation will have the same. The race will have the same. As such, it is not by chance that one enters a race, enters a nation or country, and chooses a province, and a city, and chooses a house on a certain block, and chooses a certain family. Indeed, it is not by chance. Indeed, it is by all conditions fitting into that that is necessary for the individual to overcome that that it is attempting to overcome.

PLEASE DESCRIBE THE PROCESS BY WHICH SOULS FIRST TOOK ON PHYSICAL FLESH ON EARTH?

Then you would need to go several millions of years before this point. When those souls came through the dimensions from Banar and others, and hovered around the planet, they saw unto themselves those forms, although they were crude in nature, and they took upon themselves, using their powerful minds and their ability to create, to make accessible those forms that they later inhabited. See? Here, they cleared up the animal part to make it more accessible for their entering in, or to possess the form itself, and the soul would be conscious within the form, able to experience all of the emotions, all of the physical satisfactions, you see. In this process of defining a form, it would be the creative forces they had within; for here, in this pristine state, they were closer to the Godhead and had creative/co-creative ability (shall we call it) to change matter by their thoughts, by their interventions, or direct interference, see, in which they provided what they needed in order to experience physical matter. They did inhabit trees, and stones, and other objects in this dimension, but it was the humanoid beings to which they found the greatest satisfaction and they could experience the emotions and the appetites in the physical form. It was not quite suitable; it was crude, and there were animalistic set-backs. And, indeed, by entering into physical matter, there was more than they intended; it changed their basic understanding.

Therefore, to the question, the souls had the ability to select a vehicle in a humanoid form or way. They improved the vehicle, the humanoid-looking form; they inhabited the same by taking possession of it, by incorporating their consciousness within the same (a sort of co-existence, you see). However, the body would wear out, and they would have to recycle. The problem being that, in time, the human appetites, temptations, and the extremes to which they experienced physical life adulterated themselves, and they be- come less conscious. They lost their way. They became engrained in matter, until the present day. See?

DID THIS OCCUR ALL OVER THE PLANET OR IN ONE PARTICULAR AREA?

There was the original five races that would come into the world, and they were distributed amongst the five races, you see. Therefore, yes, this would be at the similar time all over the world, but in different forces or factions, you see. Therein, the influences would be the same. From the Heavens above, they entered into the world. They gained dominance over the world, and became entrapped by the pleasures or temptations of the world.

YOU REFERRED TO SOMETHING KNOWN AS "BANAR." WHAT IS THIS?

It is of the dimensions above, you see.

SO IT IS ANOTHER DIMENSION, A SPIRITUAL DIMENSION?

As of a place, yes.

WHY DID SOULS ENTER THE PHYSICAL DIMENSION?

In the beginning, there were a group of souls that decided they would leave the Christos [for] new experiences, individual control, individual understanding gripped them, and they departed, and they filtered out into the Universe, into the dimensions and into the worlds below. They were co-creating wherever they went, but they desired this existence, in different, temporal forms, and sooner or later they became adulterated and lost their memory from whence they came. However, inside there is still a tendency that says, "We have to go here! There is something we must do! Who is this..? What is that...?" And ultimately, they face all those questions, all those fears, all those individual experiences, and when they have done this enough times, then they begin to ask, "There must be a better way..?" And they move on through the other dimensions; not like children, but like who they think they are.

DID THIS ACTION TAKE PLACE IN THE BEGINNING, AT THE POINT OF CREATION?

It happened in the moment that they were given free will and free choice; they became self-aware and, at that moment, they left. This is recounted in *the Bible* as Adam and Eve became aware of their innocence; they covered themselves up and then they proceeded to leave Eden. See?

WHAT IS THE CHRISTOS?

It is pure love, unconditional love. It is the nourishment of all souls. It is the originating point. It is the end point. It is the Alpha and the Omega. It is that that it is. See?

WOULD IT BE FAIR TO SAY THAT THIS IS THE CREATOR?

The Creator, or Creation, or the Universal Mind, or the Universal Consciousness; as of the same. Affirmative.

WHAT PERCENTAGE OF SOULS HAVE NEVER LEFT THE CHRISTOS?

Why bother with this sort of question? This is immaterial, for the finite mind cannot comprehend the same.

WHAT DO THE FIGURES IN THE ADAM AND EVE STORY REPRESENT?

Adam represents the first soul that would enter into this dimension (as you would know it), Amelius/Adam, the same (Jesus the Christ); the first soul that entered into this dimension. Eve represents that of the fracture that occurred within that, as to the consciousness of the world itself. This is not a woman (or "woe-man"), it is that that causes the downfall. This would be as to that that would be the fruit of the Tree of Knowledge of Good and Evil, that, here, there became a separation from that that would be the Heavens above, and humans (as you know humans) became aware of their duality. Prior to that point, there was no duality. There was only love, and in the dimensions of love, there is no other emotion; for emotions (as you would understand emotions) are of this dimension in which you would understand the world or the planet that is lived upon as being part, as being only possessive of all the other emotions. As one transcends or leaves behind the world (as you know it), there is an ascension back to that that is pure and unconditional love. Again, all other emotions are of the lower realm. In the Beginning, there was only love. In the End, there will be only love.

The fruit of the Tree of Knowledge of Good and Evil is the duality, the comprehension that there is a duality in the first place.

This is that that would cause the downfall. The Tree of Life is that that is eternal. It is that from which the sustenance of the soul continues. It is that that you would understand as being awake in the spiritual Heavens or dimension above, hence the term "Gods like us" are used in the texts [e.g. Genesis 3:22]. It means for those who are fully awake, self-realized, fully-realized (Avatar beings, you see), those that have wakened up to who they are, as they were in the Beginning, you see.

The Serpent represents that as to temptation. It represents that as to the downfall of Mankind. It represents, in body itself, that that would be the carnal aspects of humans (as you know humans). It represents the descending from that of unconditional love into that that would be love that is tainted, adulterated, or altered, so that it fits in with the material world and the love of things versus that as to the immaterial or eternal aspects of things, where there is no materiality, that brings pleasure as does that in the world, you see. For here, in the eternal, there is only that that is: bliss, you see.

The downfall, the Serpent, represents temptation, and the delivery of the same. It also represents those minds that are of the lower realms that are encouraging the downfall or the descension of other souls from the higher realms of bliss and unconditional love to that of the lower realms (which is to the carnal, to the materialistic, to the finite, you see). This inflames the ego. This engulfs the soul itself, and is that that embellishes the perfection.

It is the element which humans (as you know humans) must overcome. The delivery of the fruit of the Tree of Knowledge of Good and Evil to that that would be Eve, which represents that that would be part of Man in the material realm, and that that is tempting to Man (as to Mankind or Humankind) in the world, as you know it. It steals the enlightenment, mask the truth, and blinds the light from which every soul may see by.

We are giving this in such a way as you have instructed; there is more that could be given.

IS IT FAIR TO SAY THAT SOME SOULS ARE STILL MOVING AWAY FROM THE GOD-HEAD, OR ARE ALL SOULS MOVING BACK TOWARDS IT?

They are in between. Some are expanding and returning. Some are descend- ing to the finite realms, and others are ascending to the in-finite. If you wish direction, some are moving down, and some are moving up. They are in a constant sea or pool of flux; best to see this as a pond, and in the pond there are lights. They look like firefly lights (for those who understand the insects that are illuminated), and they are in constant movement, turmoil, mixing and waving, bobbing back and forth. They are still in the pool of water. Occasion-ally, one or two will jump out. They will land on the shore and be-come aware of who and what they are.

Does this make sense, into understanding the direction of a soul? It is in flux in this world, in this dimension. It is encapsulated. It is in flux, and, on occasion, it becomes aware of where it is, and then it jumps out of this chaotic, constant, moving or revolving, you see.

IS IT POSSIBLE TO APPROXIMATE HOW MANY SOULS ARE IN EXISTENCE?

As many stars as there is in the sky, times one thousand.

WOULD YOU AGREE THAT THERE IS A DUALITY IN HUMANS, OF WANTING TO BELONG TO THE WHOLE, BUT BEING AFRAID OF LOSING INDIVIDUALITY AND INDEPENDENCE?

Indeed, we would agree, for it is the basis of human evolution. All their existence (as individual souls) is to continue in the continuum as separate, while at the same time they are attempting to amalgamate, unite and become One; the Law of One. Yet, they resist, yet they desire. Any emotion other than love is but temporal in this dimension. The only emotion that continues on beyond the earthly planes is love; all others are shed and left behind. As they understand this, then they would understand that love is the way in the spiritual existence or dimensions above. To be loving is to be advancing!

However, to the question: those that attempt to remain, individually, individuals are doomed to repeat on the wheel of reincarnation. They are doomed to swarm in the pool of consciousness until they realize that they are in the pool! And then they might step outside of the pool and take their place along the shore. Then they would begin to advance their consciousness.

Yes, we would agree to this analogy.

DOES AN INDIVIDUAL MAKE A CONSCIOUS CHOICE OR SUBCONSCIOUS ONE?

It is a waking up; it is becoming aware of yourself. When you become aware, you become realized, and then you become self-realized, and (in time) you become fully realized. Then there is no indecision. You willingly see the greater consciousness and you embrace it. It is a waking-up process. It is a matter of touching upon love and being in love with love to such a point that there is no indifference, there is no question. The self willingly adapts and becomes the whole again. For realize the drops emerged from the ocean in the first place, that they might experience their existence as individuals. The returning from whence they came is a reversal of that that is already taking place. There should not be any fear, or any fretting of loss; there needs simply to be the awakening, like Buddha and others. They became awake. They became aware of who they are. They became aware that they are the ocean. Then, there is no uncertainty, procrastination, or vacillation. There is a huge desire to become the ocean again.

Is it fair to say that prior to such an awakening taking place, that humans would typically feel isolated, alone and disconnected from one another as opposed to feeling that they are part of the whole?

As of the same. Affirmative. For how can one be part of the whole, if they still are thinking as individuals? See? You cannot think yourself becoming the whole; you must accept it and become the whole. Therefore, it is no thought process. It is a transmutation, you might say. Like one piece of cloud joining another piece of cloud, seamless, the two fragments have become One. You cannot distinguish between one part and the other, for they are all the same, just bigger. And the essence, therefore (the willingness to become part of the whole) is, indeed, the purpose for which all the previous existences have been lived, to come to that return point. When you have gone in all the directions, have lived all the lives, have experienced all the life lessons, the only lesson left is to reunite from whence you came! Willingly, you see, for no one can be forced or coerced in this.

Do our thoughts and our minds create this veil of separation?

To the understanding, to a certain degree; yes we would agree, the understanding that thoughts and minds can be separate; they can perceive of themselves as being separate; they see themselves as being separate from all others, and therefore their view is limited in that they become isolated like a capsule, separate and distinct. If this is the meaning of the question, yes to the question.

HOW DO WE BALANCE CREATING PEACE AND CLEARING THE MIND VERSUS THINKING THAT IT IS A NATURAL PROCESS?

How you think is a natural process. What you refer to as the thinking in which humans (as you know humans) attach emotions onto their thoughts, to be in the stillness of the mind, in this form of thinking, is indeed, the highest form of thinking that can take place. However, humans tend to attach emotion, or their own bias, or their own understanding on something. They have to! They do it all the time. It is difficult not to have an opinion or to place a judgment. If we were to say to someone, "atomic energy," there would be half the people that think it is good, the other half think it is bad, and yet, most of them have no idea what atomic energy is! They have never seen it, touched it, experienced it, or have any close association with it.

To have this consciousness, to have this understanding, one has to observe from the outside, and to be the subject on the inside. A sort of observing-the-self, observing-the-self, you see.

IF THE NOTION OF SELF BEING SEPARATE IS AN ILLUSION, WHERE DOES THIS IDEA COME FROM?

The idea of self being separate is something of an assessment of the self; it is a values system, one in which people look within, in an introverted way, or they look without, in an extroverted way. It starts with the beginning. The soul takes onto the flesh, and all things in life are selfish, are they not? You have to breathe and eat, you have to accept and reject, and, indeed, only the self feels whatever is around it or near it! This would be engrained in the personality of the self in what would be the expectations of life, for only one soul takes on one body. It has a single purpose. There might be exceptions to this, but to give it in such a way, that once a soul, migrating through the ethers, comes to a body that is suitable, it does take it on, and sets aside other purposes, you see.

Can the awakening experience be compared to the Kundalini awakening experience?

To be aware is to be aware. To be self-realized as to what the self truly is, and, at the same time, to be fully-realized so that there is no question; there just is. The Kundalini experience is something that helps a physical body get in contact with the higher realms, by exerting, here, certain frequency (shall we call it) that allows the human body to blossom into the spiritual body which it possessed, you see. The Kundalini is the chemical, reproductive cells in the body that move through the body and trigger secretions in the glands itself, which cause certain alignment and, therefore, a certain vibration that is very pleasing to the physical body (erotic, or even sensual). This transfer or transmute itself into that of the force that awakens the glands in the brain (the pituitary and pineal) which are like doorways or windows to that that would be the dimensions beyond this earthly one, you see.

Knowing that, it cannot be compared to a sensation. It is as to the spiritual association at the highest level and what you speak of is that that is the association of the energy at the lowest level. See?

Is awakening a gradual or a sudden experience?

You may be totally cognizant that you are One with all things in an instant. This is true. However, the process usually takes a little longer than a spontaneous recognition (although this can happen, and has, to many). Often it is a profound experience that is not easily dismissed as a figment of imagination or some other result of some other cause.

To the question itself, it usually takes earnest effort to be awakened in a controlled fashion, and it is advisable to go slow, otherwise there would be mental abrasions, you see. And, as such, developing and utilizing this dominant energy within the self does take some effort, but it can happen spontaneously (and has).

WHO WERE THE SONS OF GOD AND THE DAUGHTERS OF MEN MENTIONED IN THE BIBLE?

It would be considered, here, those who would be the pure souls. For understand when there was the breaking away (that would be as "the Good Book" would account it as the war between the Satan, Beelzebub, and that of God) did not mean that there were two characters, here, fighting it out in Heaven. It means simply there was a separation of thought; those that would enter for selfish means and those that would enter for unselfish means. As those who broke away from – call it – that of the grand formulation known as God, they would, here, become the Daughters. Those who would enter (for they did break away also) to retrieve would be called the Sons of God. The difference being that those who would be as to the feminine aspects entered here into the flesh; and here, for lustful tendencies, lost their right as to their knowledge of whence they came (their direction, so to speak).

The others returned and attempted to allow the others to return to whence they came. It would be known as way-showers. However, those who entered the Earth to be the teachers (the guideposts), these, too, became tempted by the flesh, and soon lost their consciousness (although it was not done complete). As such, there remains within the heart of all Men that that is to the Sons and Daughters of God and of Men: that of the separation to- wards the lustful or selfish tendencies and towards that of the unselfish tendencies (or spiritual tendencies) and this war is maintained within each and every mind. Ultimately the way-showers will return, and they that would be the original separators from God will return also, for they will have the trail clearly marked, the path clearly shown, the stars will guide their way.

THERE HAS BEEN REFERENCE TO THE SEVEN BLESSINGS. WOULD YOU TELL US WHAT THEY ARE?

There is only one blessing. All others are derivatives, or fractions of the same. The one blessing is to have the love of God, and that love is to be loving to God in the first place. If you understand this, then you will understand that coincidence, chance, gain is always a result of that that has been given first. If you want rewards to come to you, then you must do something first, then you will reap the reward (not the other way around).

IN THE GOLDEN AGE OF GREECE, THE PHRASE "KNOW THYSELF" WAS INSCRIBED ON THE TEMPLE OF ATHENA. WHAT WORDS OF ADVICE WOULD YOU GIVE PEOPLE WHO ARE TRYING TO KNOW THEMSELVES AND FIND OUT WHO AND WHAT THEY ARE?

In a word, it would be: patience. To know thyself is very difficult. It is a simple statement, but the consequences are enormous. To be on a self-discovery is to begin to look at yourself from several different octaves. To know yourself is a willful practice of looking within. It is a higher level of consciousness to begin to express the notion that you are, indeed, a vast uncertainty, unknown, or an entity more than just your physical body.

To know yourself is to look within, to put yourself in a closet know- ing you have two others there: one, your best friend, and the other, your worst enemy. When you look upon the self in an objective way, then it is a higher level of consciousness, for you begin to assess who and what you are. You begin to discover that you are more than what you thought you were! You begin to discover the Higher Self, that part of the self that is above the animal consciousness, that reaches up to the Divine or Spiritual Consciousness; that you are distinct and separate.

To know yourself is to know that you are, indeed, an entity unto the self – yes – but you are much more than that; that you are linked with other individuals, other minds, other souls, and it takes a long time to come to know who and what you are. But at the end of the journey, you will be knowledgeable of the self, yes; knowledgeable of the personality or the Ego; that part that you might relate to the small "I Am." But then you will begin to branch out and to comprehend the other aspects, the higher "I Am," that part of the self that is related to the understanding of the High Self or Soul Mind.

Therein, you begin to understand the Universe or the Macrocosm, in comparison with the Microcosm, and you will begin to see that they are exactly the same (only on the other edge of the scale, you see)! Patience is required, for as you take this meaningful step inward, it is like walking into the library; at first you are awed by all the books. This would be the awakening or the awareness that you are more than a single book. As you progress through the library, and you read all the books, you gain great knowledge. In time, you will see those books in the back, that are the more treasured knowledge. See? Therein you will find out who and what you are, linked in all time with the past, to the present, and from the present to that that would be the flexible future.

To know thyself, then, requires patience. It requires a long time of self-investigation, and when you know yourself, you will know your strength and your weaknesses; you will know that you are frail on some occasion, but that you are strong on others. You will come to know that you will live forever; that there is that spark of genius within, that that is of God and from God itself (the soul, you see). And through this, you will see that all are connected, all are One, and that, indeed, you need not fear death; you need not fear life! You need to express it to enjoy it fully. If you can do this, then you will know yourself as a human being who has discovered the Divine within and has allowed that spiritual essence to blossom forward, so that you do not rely upon anyone else; you are not co-dependent, you are independent and yet you are part of the same, part of the whole.

To know yourself is to know God, for there is part of the self that is of God and from God, and in the likeness of God. You come to understand, in a personal way, in a close way, creation, and in this attempt to understand creation, you begin to see the different aspects, facets, octaves of the self, and you begin to like yourself, then to love yourself, then to be grateful for your life. It takes a lifetime to know yourself; do not judge yourself until the last day, of the last hour, of the last minute, of the last breath. Then, you might, with some authority, judge yourself. But up until that moment, judge not. Learn by your mistakes, for they are stepping stones to knowledge, to success, to wisdom. Attempt to avoid temptation and others who would present temptation to you. Better to make your own mistakes than the mistakes that someone else will provoke you to get.

The Law of One is a single understanding, yet it is an understanding of the Universe. To "Know Thyself" is a single understanding, yet it take a lifetime to do so, with any manner of authority or consistency. Be patient!

WHAT OTHER PLANES OR DIMENSIONS ARE AVAILABLE FOR OUR LEARNING?

You would find that each entity has the ability to engage in what would be introspection, reflection, investigation, counselling, invention and other dimensions in which there would be other individuals concerned with this particular vein, or, here, field of endeavour. You would find these dimensions or planes would, here, be established upon those that would be of the ability of the mind to grasp the same (as to philosophy, theology, and what might be considered the physics or, here, the scientific). You will find that these levels pertain to individuals who have, in their own right, earned the right to that level or plane and they are willing to help any who would approach them. This is usually done through that of the sleep states. For instance, when one has a problem, they enter the sleep state and "sleep on it" (so to speak). During this period, they travel to this dimension or that dimension, or to this group or that group who are familiar with this problem. And then, if they are willing and accepting, they are given an answer or a solution, to their particular problem. They return back to themselves and then simply carry out their direction, in the physical sense, in their life. See?

As one would aspire, one then becomes the way-shower, or, here, a helper, a teacher; and, as it is better to give than receive, you would find that there are many who are in the body of Mankind who are attempting to help those on the lower levels attain the higher levels. For as the body become healed, then it become better, and it is to the welfare of all who are in the body (no isolation, you see).

Therefore, these other levels or planes can be achieved through states of sleep, through states of meditation, through states of introspection. These planes await any and all. They can be seen as "the great hall of knowledge" with many rooms. For has it not been said, "In my Father's house, there are many mansions"? This refers to the many levels of thought, or consciousness, or awareness (as you may call it).

THERE IS AN IDEA THAT WE SHOULD BE FEARFUL OF THE WRATH OF GOD. DOES GOD HAVE WRATH?

That would infer that thy God is an angry God, is a jealous God, is a re- vengeful God, and is a God that does not comprehend all things, and has not prepared the lessons properly, and that the self has some instruction, some rules, or obligation to the rules. In fact, the wrath of God (to understand it as such) is that thy God is not offended by those who are attempting to develop or advance, and they make mistakes. Thy God is not offended in the human sense at all! If anything, God would be disappointed, if it had human response. For humans, hearing the words of God through the Apostles, or the Disciples, or the Prophets, would know for certain that what is being said would be something that should be followed, and yet, throughout history, they do not.

God is little more wrath, than God would be human. Wrath is a human concept. God is a loving and benevolent God, a God that loves each so much that He has allowed them to do that that they would wish or want to do. They have the gift of free will and free choice. In its wisdom, God has ordained that that which is given forth by a soul should be experienced from the opposite side (or, perhaps, sides). This allows for one to comprehend the full nature of a certain thing, so that the self can perpetuate itself and move on through these difficult experiences, or lessons, so that they can be, indeed, aware of what is acceptable and what is not. By this we mean, God is not full of wrath. God is not impatient, like some parent might be.

God is like electricity: everywhere, and in every mind, and in every body. God loves each and every soul; the privilege of going out into the worlds and the Heavens above, to completely experience all things in the material realms, for the single purpose that when the soul returns, God itself will expand and become more profitable, wiser, more content.

Anyone that teaches God and speaks for God and is assured of what is in the mind of God is a fool, is a deceiver, and is an unbeliever. Thy God is a loving and just God. Each moves forward on its own responsibility. Each receives back what it has given forth previously, not the other way around! See?

WHY DO SO MANY RELIGIONS TEACH THAT GOD IS VENGEFUL?

What is the purpose of religion? If you understand the purpose, then you would understand the words. Who can speak for God? Not a religion, but only the Prophet. Prophets never talk of God in such a way. Prophets always speak of God in the essence of incomplete understanding, for thy God is a loving being. God is love, Love is God. There is no room for such assumptions, or such propagation of that that might not be quite accurate.

COULD YOU COMMENT ON THE IDEA OF BEING A "GOD-FEARING PERSON,"
AND PERHAPS SHED SOME LIGHT ON HOW WE SHOULD FEEL INSTEAD TOWARDS
GOD?

Change the word [fearing] to "respectful." Change the word to be: each should be loving of thy God with every cell of thy body. To be grateful is to be God-like. To be loving is to be God-like, to be filled with love; pure love, unconditional love. This is to be closer to God than any other way. Therefore, any emotion that does not express unconditional love (or love in some form) is by virtue of understanding that thy God is a loving and just God.

When you speak of emotions, you speak of the physical world. There are no such emotions in the spiritual dimensions or realms above; there is only love. Can someone be loving and angry at the same time? Can someone love and hate at the same time? Can someone love and be judging or prejudiced at the same time? Can someone think two thoughts at the same time? No.

What you look for in God is love. God cannot be adulterated, although God is the Creator of all things, and everything you see in the material world has been created for a purpose, and that purpose is to awaken the slumbering soul within each and every body, so that it might cause the spirit to rise up and to assist itself to move closer to those things that are righteous, those things that the entity (or the self) might know as being close to what God would have us do. If this is the case, then prosperity will continue. If it is not, then nothing will continue. Humans (as you know humans) always have a choice.

WHAT IS SIN?

Sin is that that is simply met as being off the mark. You would find that King David was God's most favourite prophet. Why? Simply because he committed every sin...once. He learned by the sins. He found the way back on the mark, and, as such, struck the target true and straight.

Sin is simply being off the mark. It is not that there will be an outrageous God who will persecute and punish any for, here, falling into that of sin. But there is a benevolent Father, a greater consciousness that gently has that of the alignment take place.

Sin is that of an entity who is out of tune with itself, who is off its mark, who is going in any direction but the right one.

HOW DO WE LEARN TO BE ON THE MARK?

This would be done by contemplation, by introspection, by meditation. When one bangs their head on the wall long enough, they soon find out that there is an easier way, and it is simply to stop banging their head on the wall. As this would be done, as there would be that of attempting to put the self in the position of another (as there would be the attempt to "do unto the other as you would have them do unto the self") and to live by this, not that the self would become a doormat, or not that self would become a tyrant, then you would have self attempting to be on the mark.

Be not afraid to make mistake, for mistake is but the opportunity to perfection. Those who are afraid to make mistakes are afraid to learn. Learn from the experience and, as such, in this understanding you will know sin and what is not sin.

HUMANS SEEM ALMOST PREDISPOSED TOWARDS NEGATIVITY. WE WILL MORE EASILY REMEMBER NEGATIVE EXPERIENCES BEFORE POSITIVE ONES; WE USUALLY SEE NEGATIVE ASPECTS IN OTHER PEOPLE BEFORE SEEING THE POSITIVE. CAN

YOU COMMENT ON WHY WE ARE SO FIXATED ON NEGATIVITY AND, IF POSSIBLE, HOW THIS COULD BE OVERCOME?

Usually it is a matter that humans (as you know humans) feel they are not receiving something they ought to receive. It is their spiritual poverty that they are showing. They do not understand that the Universe fulfils each wish, each desire. It is to understand that their own mind is as powerful on occasion as that of the forces that are bringing the solution to their health problem, financial problem, or some other suffering. But it is easier to suffer by remembering the pain, by looking towards that that would be harmful and distressful.

Humans are of the finite mind, and the finite mind looks always for the problem. The infinite mind looks over all of the finite situations, attempts to direct itself to the best one. As it finds the best one, and in its wisdom continues this understanding, then they grow closer and closer to the God- head itself. Remember: it takes patience, tolerance, love and forgiveness (which are all due to the self), in order to ascend to that level of consciousness in which the self is fully awake. Humans (as you know humans) are reluctant to do so.

COULD YOU PLEASE EXPLAIN WHY HUMANS TEND TO DISSUADE OTHERS FROM BEING SUCCESSFUL, FROM TAKING RISKS, OR DOING NEW THINGS?

This is not the case. There are many humans who encourage others, who advise them freely, and who advance them, and give of their own time and resources. When you make such statements, you should not say it is as if it would be blanketing everyone. While there might be an attitude in some degree that is shared with this, these pains, these feelings that "misery likes company" and, therefore, those that are in pain like to cause pain, it give them some justification, or some excuse for their circumstance. But it is not true that all are this way. There are many, in their own way, who encourage, who sustain themselves through the success of others.

To this end, however, in understanding those that are in the pond, they are milling around, thinking they are inadequate in some way. They are not appreciative or grateful of what they have. You may see them with hands full of ice cream and chocolate bars, and yet they want more. The reason these souls are in pain is that they are usually not in harmony. Greed is an example of this. They may have much, but they want more. They want to be supreme, or the most powerful. Their Ego is inflamed. They aspire to do great things, and be recognized by all as the most important. Their Ego is inflamed and their head has grown. Is this the way to enlightenment in the infinite? Nay it is not. They do these things because they are full of those things that they think they ought to be. Although they may have done much good in the past (and they will in the future), by holding such attitudes, or thoughts, they can, in their own way, delay their progress.

Impatience, vanity, self-aggrandizement, self-importance, these are all the weaknesses in the character. And they are, at this point in time, demonstrating their weakness. In time, they will grow into that that would be a wise and humble Man. They would not allow themselves to tarry on the weaknesses of their soul or character. They will be filled with compassion.

HOW MIGHT THE TRUE MEANING OF BROTHERLY LOVE BE UNDERSTOOD IN THIS DIMENSION?

It would be to understand that in all humanity, in every human that you see or meet, that you are a part of this. Understand the human race as a body. Understand the self as a cell in that body, and then you would understand that as there is a difficulty on the cell (as to any body), there is a difficulty in the entire body.

Brotherly love is that of the continuity between cells. Love is that of the thread that holds Mankind together. For, you see, although there are different cells in the body, and there be different members in the body, each member can hurt equally. And, as such, if one member hurt, then the entire body hurt. For no member is an island unto itself, no Man is an island unto itself.

As such, in understanding brotherly love, know the wisdom in the statement that ye should do that unto others that ye would wish them to do unto the self. For you see, striking the blow against the brother is, indeed, striking a blow against the self. For humanity (or Mankind) must cleanse the body, must, in its entirety be perfect in order that the race, in order that the consciousness of the race-mind and that of the races can become One. Only through this, understanding that brotherly love is, in actuality, love manifested towards the self, but directed at others can one truly understand the meaning of love. For, you see, would you cut off your arm to, here, spite your nose? No. Then why cut off another to spite yourself?

If it would be clearly understood, what is given out is directly re- turned and applied toward the self, if this would be understood, if it would be recognized and believed, then you would find that the world would be a much better place. It is not that each should fear that they should hold back, else they suffer, but that they should have respect, that they should have understanding that no matter what condition the other human being may be in, if he be the most vile and debased creature, still within that flesh and blood lies that that is of God and from God. It is of the soul. And this is that spark of humanity that has the ability to return love. For, you see, God loves all.

Does not the sun shine on the good and bad alike? Is there not love of any mother for her son or daughter, no matter what crime they may have committed? And this is how love should be seen; accepting the individual with its weaknesses, but attempting to recognize that spark, that genius that is within each and every entity, but knowing it is, likewise, toward the self, part of the self. For as each human is a cell in a living body, know that the body is of God and it is Divine.

HOW MIGHT AN INDIVIDUAL BEST UNDERSTAND THE EMOTION OF LOVE?

It is easily seen. Love is that of understanding the needs of self and having those needs given to self, understanding that the needs are the same in each and everyone else. Love is pure. Love is of God. To understand love is to understand God. Know that in the Law that if you love all others, then you love God. God is love. Love is God.

For each to truly understand this, they must engage in different circumstances and experiences in order to overcome those of the animalistic emotions: those that would tend to put self above another, those that would attempt to separate self from another. When any can understand the needs of another, then they have a good foothold on understanding love. To understand love truly is to forgive seven times seventy. To understand love is to make concessions for the weak, but to stand up to the strong when they are in the wrong. To understand love is to be compassionate and forgiving to- ward the self (indeed, as much as you would give to any other). This is all accomplished through experience, through what some may deem the 'curse' or the 'problem,' when in actuality it is the blessing for self to overcome self.

To understand love is not hard; to be loving is.

DO YOU HAVE ANY ADDITIONAL INFORMATION ON THIS TOPIC THAT WOULD BE HELPFUL AT THIS TIME?

The Law of One is such that everyone realizes they are One. Who would harm their own flesh? Who would cause pain to themselves? Who would steal from themselves, or take something away from themselves? Who would be that that would be so foolish that they would destroy themselves? Those who are not of the Law of One, this might be their path. For those that are, indeed, moving forward in the Law of One, they understand that to do some good for others, to help or assist, to be of service to others, to help another one up the ladder, one step at a time, to allow others to go to the head of the line first if/when they are in need, to be generous, to be loving, to be helpful; this is the exact steps one must take to benefit themselves.

Who would say to the fireplace, "Give us heat, and then we will give you wood?" The misguided and foolish would, of course. Those that are full of greed, and self-envy, narcissism; misguided, finite minds, these might. But if they say, "I have the fireplace, now I will put the wood in the same. I will prepare the fireplace. I will take the initiative and ignite the contents, and I will be patient until the wood burns, so that there will be heat. I will do all the preparation. I will work, and then I will share the heat that comes from the benefit of the fire burning, which I have had the presence of mind to engage, to build, to provide, and then to share." This is the essence of wisdom, of compassion, of love, of understanding that an individual's actions can benefit many, beyond that that he or she would even expect to benefit (and, usually, without expectation, the benefit is given or shared).

To those who are impoverished spiritually, and they weep and cry, "Why is there no heat in the fireplace," and they have not lifted one finger of their own to do something about it, then pity them indeed, for they have cast themselves out. Yea, to those who would, with their own will, benefit all others unselfishly, continuously, and without merit for their own safety or resources (those that do such sacrificing, or here, work, even under adversarial situations, for the benefit of others), these are the ones that are welcomed into the warmth of thy God Almighty's bosom, who are nurtured by unconditional love or bliss. For they have seen the light; they have seen eternity, they have walked on the path of God Almighty, and they are rewarded, as such. Yea, it does not matter who did what, who said what, it only matters that one survives, and they survive well. See?

For further guidance, it would simply be: to be understanding of the self, to be patient with the self, and as this could be done (as this would be done) then you would find in that of the years that would pass, as one would grow into the understanding (as to the wisdom), then you would find that the greater perfection could take place. For there is a season, and there is a time in that season for all things.

Understand that the life is but a breath in the life of the soul, and that the soul lives for eternity. And if you are of the soul, and you live for eternity, what is the rush?

CONCLUSION

❧❧

by Douglas James Cottrell, Ph.D.

Can you perceive the future?

If you are like most people, you will answer, "no." Many believe that the future cannot be seen, because it has not yet occurred. But let me ask you this: have you ever had a dream about an event that came true? Have you ever had a *feeling* that something was going to happen, and it did? Did you ever "just know" that something was going to happen, and then it did? If you answered yes to any of these questions, then your answer should be that you can, in fact, perceive the future; either through precognition, premonition, clairvoyance or clairsentience.

It is logical that if the future was not foreseeable, *no one* would be able to see it, and future predictions would be mere guessing games. However, many people – from the Maya and the Hopi, to the prophets of the *Old Testament*, to Nostradamus, Edgar Cayce, Ross Peterson, and Paul Solomon (or myself) – have seen the future exactly as it has unfolded (sometimes decades or even centuries in advance of the event). Many credible people have reported to me their feelings, visions and dreams about a future event that, in time, came to pass.

There is plenty of evidence to suggest that credible information has been gained about the future before it happened. Many people, just like you, have reported to me information about future events which is in line with the ones described in this book. Some have had dreams in which they saw cruise ships swept miles inland by tidal waves. Some have seen land rising out of the sea, forming landbridges and new islands. Others have reported seeing volcanoes and fire devastating the countryside (one person describing it as a wall of fire). Many have had dreams warning of tough times ahead, and some have even been warned about what to stock up on now.

Numerous people in different places and at different times have made predictions similar to the ones made in this book regarding future events which have yet to happen. If you look at the appendices in this book you will find a listing of some of their works, including those who have created so-called "future Earth maps." There are similarities among the predictions, with enough difference to suggest that people are not being inspired by one another but are actually independently seeing similar information.

My motto is: "faith is built upon belief, and belief is built upon evidence." If many people in different places and at different times are being given the same information, then it must be evidence of truth. By any measure of logic, if something can be done once, it can be done again.

Do you believe in prophecy? Some believe that these predicted Earth changes may not happen in our own lifetimes. This is a fair statement. However, evidence is suggesting that changes have already begun. Some have noted that supervolcanoes like the Yellowstone and Long Valley calderas in the U.S.A., Laguna del Maule in Chile, Santorini in Greece and Campi Flegrei in Italy are showing signs of activity. Earthquake experts have noticed increased seismic activity all over the world. Weather patterns are changing, with some areas reporting the coldest temperatures on record, and others reporting the warmest. NASA notes that the global temperature has increased "1.4 degrees Fahrenheit since 1880." On NASA's Global

Climate Change website (climate.nasa.gov) they remark:

> *The oceans have absorbed much of this increased heat, with the top 700 meters (about 2,300 feet) of ocean showing warming of 0.302 degrees Fahrenheit since 1969. The Greenland and Antarctic ice sheets have decreased in mass. Greenland lost 150 to 250 cubic kilometers (36 to 60 cubic miles) of ice per year between 2002 and 2006, while Antarctica lost about 152 cubic kilometers (36 cubic miles) of ice between 2002 and 2005. The global sea level has risen about 17 centimeters (6.7 inches) in the last century.*

Recently (January 2015) an article was published with the headline, "Earth has Shifted: Inuit Elders Issue Warning to NASA and the World." In that article, Inuit elders attribute the recent extremes in weather to a shift, tilt or "wobble" of the Earth to the north. This echoes a remark made to me over a year ago by a friend in Norway that their stars had "shifted south."

If you need evidence that times are changing, you need only look around you.

The question becomes: "what can I do when a prophecy of the future is given to me?" I believe that information that is given in a prophecy (or a clairvoyant viewing of the future) is something we may change; otherwise such information would not be given, and there would be no such forewarning or opportunity to amend the outcome. Therefore, we should heed the warnings and be prepared.

If we look at these monumental changes that are coming, at first view it seems like it is impossible that we could lessen the impact or change the outcome. But we forget about our Divine spiritual side, or the soul within. You have a direct connection to all that surrounds you: your physical environment, as well as your spiritual one. You are connected with the living planet itself, and every other living being upon it.

That said, then our collective consciousness or mind-set determines what is going to happen to us in the future. The future is dependent upon decisions and (more importantly) actions that we make *today*.

We live in a world of duality. We have before us, always, the choice to do good or to do "not so good." We do a dance between the extremes of light and dark, positive and negative; the two pillars, the yin and yang. Sometimes we help another, in which case we are an angel. Sometimes we hurt another, in which case we are a demon. Most times we are somewhere in between, attempting to find our way, and to find balance.

The proper way is to act with compassion and respect, and not to allow the temptations of the physical, material world to distract us into selfishness and self-aggrandizement. By living – *living* – the Golden Rule of doing unto others as we would have done unto ourselves, we live a life of service, on the spiritual path. It is a choice. It starts with each one of us.

As humans we might not know what is going to happen (and we might not need to know). God Almighty has several solutions or destinations, but we possess free will and free choice. The exercising of these spiritual gifts determines the outcome. I believe that a spiritual journey usually starts with some event in life that causes a person to look for help in the heavenly dimensions or the Great Beyond, or when they call on God Almighty for help. Our spiritual connection to the Divine is our guiding light. Solutions to all our problems can be communicated to us through our connection to the collective consciousness for direction and guidance in the present moment.

Can the destiny of the planet be changed? Yes!

If the Earth is proceeding along a certain course or path, that course will lead to a particular outcome. If we are all collectively moving in one direction and one of us takes an action to divert us off that path by a slight variance, we are no longer moving in the same direction to the same end. If *just one* of us decides to change for the better – *just a little bit* – then we change the entire planet's destiny; for all that is needed to change from the original direction is a course change of just one degree! As one person makes a choice to change his or her path, so changes the collective consciousness!

It is rather amazing when you think that each of us has such power to change the entire course or destiny of our planet for the cause of good. But it begins now, in the present moment.

You can change the world! You have powerful spiritual abilities or gifts – whether you believe it or not (or know it or not). Start changing the course of the Earth by changing the way you do things each day. Be kinder and more compassionate, and you will change the world greatly. You should also set an example for others to follow and that would be a blessing for them. Remember if fifty-one per cent of the population had the same beneficial intention, there would be an instant transformation for the better.

I believe together we can surmount this time of uncertainty by simply applying compassion to one other, one person at a time. Put yourself in the other person's place before you decide what you're going to do. Your actions always have consequences. Considering what the consequences will be in the future will help you make good decisions in the present moment.

I had a dream of spiritual centers springing up all over the world, united in a singleness of purpose. I sincerely hope to see that vision become a reality in my lifetime.

The best advice I can offer you is: understand you have direct communication with God Almighty through your dreams, visions, meditations, and all the other intuitive/spiritual gifts or abilities you possess. I encourage you to develop your spiritual abilities. Record your dreams daily for guidance from above. Many people are being forewarned of oncoming Earth changes through interpreting their dreams. This will be your best source for guidance and solutions to problems or to make decisions.

You should not be afraid of what is going to happen. It is a Divine plan unfolding as it should. You should be prepared for times when there may be shortages of food, water and other staples that you might need. The time to act is now; not next year or hereafter. Be practical in your pursuits and follow your inner guidance.

The Oracle once said: I give you prophecy because the Divine has given it to me to do so. I cannot discern which processes to give, whether they comfort you or alarm you. It is not my place, for I am only the messenger of the Divine. The Divine gives me these prophecies so that we might have eyes to see, and ears to hear, and know that we can avoid suffering.

I believe that by changing our habits and how we treat each other (and this planet), we might be able to soften what is going to happen. God Almighty is a loving and just God and wishes none to suffer, save those who choose to do so. If you heed the words of the prophecy and become prepared, you may prosper and survive. If the prophecy is fulfilled, you will be comforted and safe, as you will be prepared. If, however, the prophecy does not come to pass and the predicted crisis and calamity is averted, then what have you lost in being prepared?

Nothing.

Each of us has a soul that has chosen to enter into this world at this time. Yes, it is an extreme time. It appears to be a chaotic time. There is much sorrow in the world, and negativity is widespread. But it is our karma to be in the world right now, to face these challenges head-on, and to test our ability to be compassionate, even in the face of adversity.

Over the years, I have come to understand that the Cosmos provides ways and means for everyone to find their inner way. There is always hope. The only requirement is that you are willing to surrender yourself to the Divine and trust God Almighty will wake you from your slumber.

Continue to be of service to others. You have an opportunity right now to grow spiritually like never before. We are on the verge of a new Earth!

May you enjoy all aspects of God Almighty: Health Wealth and Peace of Mind.

May peace and love be with you always.

Douglas

THE
APPENDICES

APPENDIX I

⫷⫸

The Hallower: Updates 2013-2014

The following are excerpts from a series of Quantum Meditation readings by Douglas James Cottrell given between 2013 and 204. Some cover upcoming Earth changes, while others focus on economic projections and potential for military conflict.

FROM A QUANTUM MEDITATION SESSION
NOVEMBER 28, 2013 (JL QUESTIONING)

IT WOULD APPEAR THE UNITED STATES STOCK MARKET IS ON THE VERGE OF COLLAPSE. PLEASE ADVISE.

We can see the market going up a little further, to about the sixteen thousand, seven hundred point. Then we would find somewhat of the barometer reaching a peak.

DO YOU SEE IT FALLING AS LOW AS NINE THOUSAND?

We are consulting with other minds that are observing or have interest in this market, as to this, as to the exchange itself... we are watching it.... We have the number nine thosand, four hundred and ninety-one, as to a bottoming point.

IS THIS ALMOST A STRAIGHT DROP THAT YOU ARE OBSERVING (A WEEK)?

Not quite that quickly, but steps, or stages downward, here: down to eleven, down to twelve, down further, bouncing around. Almost straight down, but, here, with steps; almost corrective influences or possibilities than any sort of rally would be met with severe pressure. Not straight down, but zigzag steps down, you see.

WILL THIS TAKE PLACE IN LESS THAN A THIRTY-DAY PERIOD?

It would be a little longer. We would see this as a possibility into the new year itself. However, there will be some concern on Christmas, as to the day, the holiday, then there will be some lingering and some vacillation about the first week. If it would be weak, and very weak in the first week of January, then you can see this expressing in a downward movement the value of the marketplace. Yes, to the question, in as much as it might be, to the next thirty- plus days, you see. Into the month of January would be the turn-around point. Either there will some intervention by those financial institutions - the Fed bank or so - or there will not. This is uncertain at about the day sixth or twelfth, of January.

ARE YOU SPEAKING ABOUT CHRISTMAS, 2013?

We are expressing to the month itself, you see. It could extend past this point, as we have given. There is still some upward movement. We are looking at these times in this month, the month of January.

Look toward the Christmas, and if there is a crisis, then you will know it is this Christmas, or it is next. But here, look to the key, for the Christmas crisis, something will happen during the holiday.

Then there will be some vacillation or some intervention by the Federal bank, or there will be some withdrawal. It will start in Europe, as there will be some crisis in Spain. Then you will have the pieces together and the timing will be correct.

I WAS THINKING THIS WOULD HAPPEN IN APRIL, MAY, OR JUNE OF 2014.

Look to those steps, as we have given. The timing is not off; we are looking at events. There will be an isolation policy from the Chinese that will be in the news. This would the forerunner of a flight to take money out of the country. We have individuals here, attempting to ignite or to cause an explosion in this point, or in this time in the marketplace itself. You are perceiving this, as we see it.

FROM A QUANTUM MEDITATION SESSION
NOVEMBER 29, 2013 (JL QUESTIONING)

PLEASE ELABORATE ON THE PREDICTION YOU MADE RECENTLY REGARDING THE CRISIS AROUND CHRISTMAS?

This will come from China, as there will be somewhat of an aggression towards the West. The West will be unsure as to how to react. This will be the tipping point, and the gloves will be off, you might say. As we have given before – as has been given by others – when there is that of the Chinese moving westward with force, then it would be as to the beginning of conflict. This is in part what we are referring to, but this will have an affect against the Americans, and there will be some confusion in the White House.

IS THIS MOVE RELATED TO THE RECENT DESIGNATION WHERE CHINESE AIR-

SPACE WAS DECLARED OVER ISLANDS THAT ARE CLAIMED BY JAPAN?

As of the same. There is an advancing military influence or strengthening that is taking place. There is a separation or a removal of dependency from the American currency, and has been taking place, for some months now. To the question, this is affirmative.

DOES THIS AGGRESSION INVOLVE THE SHOOTING DOWN OF AMERICAN MILITARY PLANES?

We do not have a specific incident on that particular point in time, but as we extend forward, we can find some challenges to the airspace being met by the West, and there will be fly-bys or near misses, or, here, missiles fired. Affirmative.

THE UNITED STATES' RESPONSE HAS BEEN TO SEND SUPPOSEDLY UNARMED STRATEGIC BOMBERS OVER THAT SPACE, ON SUPPOSED ROUTINE TRAINING MISSIONS. COULD YOU ELABORATE A LITTLE BIT MORE ON THAT?

Your elaborations are correct. We have several planes in the air when there would be missiles fired and we would find this as challenges to other influences that relate to resources, monies, and industrial imbalances.

This move by the Chinese is firm. This is not done theoretically looking for hypothetical gains. This is an act to expand its territorial borders, and it will continue in other directions. For, here the world seems to be at it knees, economically. There is, indeed, weakness in the military, in the Americans. There is limited funds. The Chinese are basing their calculated movements on poor economic ability to support the military (and other factors, of course). However, they have no intention of retracting this space and they will view it as an invasion and, indeed, this will cause confusion, for, here, this show of force by the West is weak. It is like going to the enemies who have shields and throwing stones, hoping they would retreat.

This is a concerted effort calculated, and it will be a demonstration of that that will continue into the years ahead; as we have given, as the Chinese move westward, they move to gather resources, territory, property to regain their own empire as it once was, you see. They wish to be, again, and they will be, for they are fast becoming, if not already, the leader in the world economically, and as they continue to expand their population, they will continue to reach out in all directions. Russia will be next. Then it will be more towards that as to the Philippines, and to the Koreas, and even to the borders of India. For they already have merged the old clans in the north; Nepal and those other areas, you see. This will continue, calculated, methodically, they are attempting to regain their old borders, that would include as much of the Pacific Rim as possible.

To the question, however, yes, this is not shadow boxing. This is concerted efforts, and the Americans are worried of what we have just given; they, too, expect to happen. The Japanese are weak with their domestic problems. They are decimated with their atomic fiasco, and they are in no way capable of defending themselves militarily. The hatred between the Chinese and the Japanese is eternal.

To the question, yes, there is no training mission here. It is taking up positions. But, again, the weak side is the West. We see missiles in the air. We see several planes at the same time. This could be the timing, if not on the day, it will soon take place.

WOULD WE EXPECT THE USE OF CONVENTIONAL ARMS OR NUCLEAR WEAPONS IN THIS OFFENSIVE?

Simply missiles, in the conventional sense, although they will be powerful. We do not see explosions, or dirty bombs, or the use of force to the extreme measure; more conventional, if you can call it that. Direction.

WILL ANY OF THESE MISSILES LAND ON THE UNITED STATES?

Not at this time.

This will be a defence of their area. They are attempting to put a curtain up around the border, airspace, waterways, and, of course, landmasses. Wherever they can expand, wherever they can incorporate a little more land, this is their mission: to expand their borders. They have already captured resources in far-away places, and they will continue to own hard resources throughout several nations. It is a matter of time. Those weaker Oriental races will be incorporated, willingly, we might add, to the protection of the Chinese. But the influence will be economic, the might will be the dollar (more exactly, the currency, gold itself) and, ultimately, no one will really beat them back, or fend them off. They will be able to do whatever they wish, but they will not be militarily aggressive, violently, but they will defend their territory; for they know they can, and so does everyone else. Shows of force, training maneuvers are like warning shots, meant to frighten off weaker adversary, but if they do not frighten, then the warning shot is a waste. How can one beat shields with stones, you see?

WILL THE UNITED STATES PRESIDENT GIVE IN TO THIS THREAT?

He is attempting to accommodate too many people. Indeed, the entity is at- tempting to have all sides and interest groups come to a common point of view. To this end, we do not find the President able or willing to use military forces, beyond that that would appear to be resisting or a show of force. The advice he is receiving from different military people is conflicting. His decisive intentions, therefore, will be to threaten, but no real intention to go to war. How can one throw stones at shields and expect to frighten them away. As such, the entity will not take the next step and be the aggressor. But there are hawks in the military that would like to do this, but they are handicapped with financial restrictions and shortages.

To the question, however, the President himself will continue to vacillate, for he has no clear plan and he tends to listen to those who would be hawkish. But again, threats with the Chinese are like words falling on walls. To the question, we do not see a military aggression, or the heart to do so, in the mind of the President at this point in time; just too many people attempting to advise or direct, and there is no clear outcome or purpose. For the Chinese are, indeed, becoming the banker to the West, and there is something ironic in this, you see. One cannot attack the banker's house, and expect the banker to be kind. However, this is a different point.

As we perceive it, there will be confusion in the White House.

IS THERE AN IMMEDIATE NEED FOR MILITARY BUILDUP IN THE UNITED STATES?

It does not appear that the Chinese will be aggressive in order to provoke military conflict. They are methodical. It is like a robot taking steps: they are well calculated, and when they take the step, they do not retreat. We do not find, here, military confrontation in a frivolous manner. We find the West attempting to determine what is going to happen. There might be some show of force, as there has been with Korea, but the Chinese are deaf. They are unresponsive to threats.

To the Americans, there will be some intention to build up, on the west coast, services, ships, and long-range bombers. These will be stationed on some of the islands in the middle of the Pacific as well, but these will all be shows of force. There is a readiness, but we do not find the Chinese interested in military expansion or conflict to America, or Canada, or Mexico. There is no need, see? They will simply stand pat on their own property, and if the Americans want to come to them at their own expense, then they will be welcomed, and there would be a shield, or there would be a repulsion, but there will be no retreat, and the Americans would fail in any attempt to do so, or any other nation for that matter. The logistics are against them.

But you will see a buildup, here, of at least ships and personnel who would be on the ships. They will be used for different rescue reasons, for there will be need to do so to some of the islands, due to weather problems, you see (but this will not be considered at this point in time). Humans, as you know humans, usually do the right thing but for the wrong reasons. Italy itself will soon suffer a folding of the land, and fissures will appear in the middle plain of the same, and this will distract everyone.

However, to your question, yes, expect ships and personnel buildup, but there will be no need to defend the coast against the Chinese threat, for it will not really be a threat to the coast at all.

WILL THERE BE A COMPUTER-BASED HACKING ATTACK AGAINST THE WEST?

It is already taking place, as you have pointed out, and will continue to do so. Whether there will be a major shutdown, this is not certain, but certainly there is constant warfare taking place in cyberspace. Yes to the question, even now.

It would appear so. There will be other conditions of disparaging news coming from Japan and from Italy.

When Iran and Iraq are one heart (and it seems like they are getting close) we see a certain suspicious peace maintaining until a certain time. Hostilities are increasing, hot-blooded minds and hearts. One moment.

It appear to be that there will be the use, or at least the attempt to use, small atomic devices – suitcase bombs, as you would know them – and this will act as a trigger point for the Israeli to come into the land of the Arab. We have not clear advancement or invasion, but there is a building up, even now, of forces and they are seemingly at high alert.

As you have asked the question, will there be the invasion of Israel into Iran, we have here, threatening movements, and as we continue the possibility increase that the Israeli will turn into the beast itself, and that of the Iranian will be frightened. We have this en masse, land, air.

Yes to the question, but we are not certain as to the time; some trepidation here, some intervention, but ultimately there seems to be an all-out movement from Israel into Iran. Like a beast, it will go through the whole country. There will be no limitation of simple border transgressions. This will be throughout the whole country.

This is a little further down the road, at this point. Look for more disruptions in Turkey first. There might even be the mushroom cloud in Turkey, then there will be no restrictions for the Israeli to move, towards their old nemesis, you see. For here, the Iranians will get the blame for this explosion in Turkey.

QUANTUM MEDITATION SESSION
DECEMBER 10, 2013 (RA QUESTIONING)

IN THE NEWS, KOREA HAS JUST INDICATED THAT THEY ARE CREATING A NO-FLY ZONE OR PROTECTED ZONE OF AIRSPACE, SIMILAR TO WHAT CHINA HAS RECENTLY ANNOUNCED IN THE SOUTH CHINA SEA. IS THIS EVENT IN KEEPING WITH THE OVERALL PATTERN THAT YOU FORESAW IN THE CHINA PREDICTION?

In recent times, we have indicated difficulties between that of the Japanese and the Chinese, and the Americans who would seem to be taunting or push- ing their authority over certain areas or islands that would be between China and Japan in the pacific, you see. We are not specifically referring to the Korean question, but, as such, this would be part of the overall intention to confound and confuse the Americans, as we have given in the previous communication. As you would see, that of the Koreans are attempting, with some degree of gleeful expectation, that the Americans are being isolated, embarrassed, and that their alleged tyranny in the world is now coming to a close (or at least it is being challenged).

To the Chinese, there is some disdain that the Koreans are attempting to walk down the middle of a rather delicate and explosive situation or circumstance between that as to the sides being taken; China on one side, looking to have its territory repatriated and the rich resources that would nearby lie off these islands, and that of the Japanese who, having at the end of the war, maintained their cultural and historical ownership (if we can call it that) to this territory or region. Also, that they do not want a staging place or military presence near to their homeland than was possible.

As such, the Koreans are like the erratic cousins attempting to taunt the Americans, without regard to the Japanese and Chinese questions for territorial rights and privileges, and that even that of the military might of the Chinese is scheduled to make a presence – not an invasion, but a presence – in the general area, bringing back, again, fears from the Japanese that they will have a friendly enemy on their doorstep, and that there will be the loss of resources that would lie beneath the water itself.

Therefore, to the question, in some degree this would have been our examination to the Chinese, American and Japanese question taking place in the Pacific, in that vicinity of the world. To what is taking place in Korea now is little more than a sideshow or irritation and distraction by the Koreans towards the Americans. The Chinese disapprove of this, but they are not willing to have the Koreans do too much more, or to remain in their share of taunting of their share of embarrassing the Americans, you see.

You will find this will spread a little further westward towards that of the Arabic nations, and (as we have given before) Iran and Iraq will be like one heart, two sides beating one to the other. This, too, will be an attempt to embarrass, confound, confuse and complicate the American's question: a sort of diversification, causing a splitting up of forces, assets, and resources. It is not wise to fight a campaign on more than one front, and this will look to be as if the attempt will be to do this the same: to, here, to hold up the Americans, to split their attention, and their resources (also here, to some degree, to deflect some attention to what is taking place in Japan).

As we examine different aspects here, there would be great resistance in the South, for that of the North to rule. We would not see this taking place in the immediate future, if this is the question. We do not see reconciliation or an attempt to do so from any military or economic point of strength, but rather when there would be some natural disasters in which the land will be washed over by large tidal waves. Then you would find there would be more of a willingness to coexist, and there might not be considered north and south, but more like east and west; the west being a little further advanced or capable than the east, you see. For the east will tend to have great destructive areas or regions along the same, you see.

IN THE FIRST READING ABOUT THE CHINESE [NOVEMBER 28, 2013] YOU DE-SCRIBED THE PREDICTION AS A "CHRISTMAS PREDICTION" THAT WOULD HAP-PEN EITHER THIS CHRISTMAS (MEANING 2013) OR NEXT CHRISTMAS (2014). DO YOU HAVE AN UPDATE AS TO WHEN THE ACTION FROM CHINA IS MORE LIKELY TO TAKE PLACE?

As we have seen in this particular area (or what would be the timing of the same), the focus of certain events would be closer at hand, and there will be a squeezing in time of the planet itself. This would be taking place in the earlier part, or the next few weeks. Concerning the Mass of Christ, there will be some indications and some possible retraction of statements. As we see, there might be some pressures made, or some deals made, in which there would be to the financial benefit of the Chinese, temporarily, negotiations allowing a retraction or a cessation of hostilities. There is the possibility of destructive forces at the same time that may cause complications to any attempt to reconcile or to stand down from any physical force or difficulty. If this occurs, then there will be sore points, or there will be difficulties that would last until the next year, in which more of the forcefulness will come forward as economic pressures will continue to build throughout this year, and that of the Chinese will continue to prosper, and do quite well, from all various sources. See?

IS IT MORE LIKELY THERE WILL BE A DEAL OR A NEGOTIATION TO QUIET THINGS DOWN, OR IS IT MORE LIKELY THAT THERE WILL BE AN ESCALATION?

It seems there will be an increase in escalation. This would be the higher probability.

IN THE YEAR OR TWO AHEAD, DO YOU SEE PROBLEMS FOR THE CHINESE ECONOMY, OR ARE THEY GOING TO CONTINUE AS THEY HAVE BEEN, WITH A STRONG RATE OF GROWTH?

There will be no stopping the economic might of the Chinese. They will continue to manufacture and continue to flood the world with manufactured items. As most of the Oriental organizations or companies have kept their workforce in a certain line or a certain passage, the Chinese itself will continue as the Americans did in the Industrial years, facing the same problems of corruption, of accelerated expansion, of consumerism, to a country that came from an agricultural base. The same will take place here in the Chinese. There will be other nations that will join with them, attempting to keep their currently strong, and to keep their economy moving or busy.

To the question, therefore then, although there might seemingly be some difficulties in which there is abuse to the economic environment, we do not see the country's machinery stopping, but rather the nation will continue to get larger and broader in its influ-ence across the world (if this is the question). Do not expect the Chi-nese to wither on the vine. Rather, that they will expand their presence, and their nationalism, their philosophy, and their way of doing things, as they already are.

HOW YOU SEE JAPAN EVOLVING OR DEVELOPING IN THE NEXT COUPLE OF YEARS WITH ALL THE PROBLEMS THEY HAVE TO DEAL WITH?

As long as they attempt to remain isolated, they will continue to maintain some balance or some possibility of maintaining their exis-tence. Overcoming what has already been suffered – and seems to be continued, here, with large holes in the eastern side, northeasterly directions, here – and those other circumstances that are weakened, here, by those who have little in the way of protection or dress, they will be exposed to more and more – the fisheries, the people along the coast, to those who make a living from the sea – they will con-tinue to be in difficulty and they will disappear. To the continuation or strengthening of the nation of Japan, the sword is stuck in the soil, and as long as this is so, there is the possibility of recovery. The re-covery seems to take place in a rugged way, and from rugged indi-viduals, as you know them.

As we continue to observe what is going to take place, we can find that there would be some associations with the Russians that will come to their aid, to some degree. This would be a long-standing relationship, but there does seem to be some positive benefits coming from the Russians, and the Russians seem to have some technology or capability to stop the poisoning of the water, and of the land, and of the reactor itself. What can be expected, here, is that the Japanese, if they remain isolated and aloof, there will be more difficulties. If they are more open, there will be changes to the way things are done or thought.

YOU USED THE EXPRESSION, "THE SWORD STUCK IN THE SOIL." DOES THIS MEAN, AS LONG AS THERE IS NO WAR?

It is an ancient promise. It is that the Japanese have survived atomic explosions in the past. They have the experience to overcome great disasters and they believe the divine wind has not left them. They are defiant people and they are self-reliant. In this case, they may need outside support from the Americans and the Russians; one time, long-ago sworn enemies now coming forth at the rescue of each.

THERE HAVE BEEN STORIES IN THE PRESS SAYING THAT PRESIDENT OBAMA HAS BEEN RECENTLY PURGING THE MILITARY OF SENIOR PEOPLE AND FORCING THEM INTO RETIREMENT. CAN YOU OFFER ANY ADDITIONAL INFORMATION ON THIS?

There would be some change in venues and there is an attempt to have more loyal to his way of administrating the company, the country, or the organization, or the minds of those who would be the countrymen, you see. If the question is: is there some attrition taking place with old mind and old hearts, the answer is affirmative. However, the timetable is off, and the new folks are having difficulty ascending. As they come into the room or the place, the look is for their loyalty, their contribution, and their ability to think independently. Therefore, to the question: we would find the Americans have brought in new people into old circumstances, and this will be seen as breaking of the old circumstances. Unfortunate!

CAN YOU FORESEE ANY RESISTANCE (MAYBE EVEN UPRISING OR REVOLT) TO THE CURRENT U.S. ADMINISTRATION?

You can expect the same, yes. There are those who would be resentful that they are being ignored, and that there are those who would feel that the administration should be more forthright and more forceful and not so round-about in their sojourns or plight. As we would see, there is a turnabout coming. There is mishap after mishap after mishap. Largely people are taking offence to what is being given, here, on several levels. But as you have directed us towards those of the military or the security forces, should there be further purging of the same, as you are indicating, then there would be some resistance and even retaliation to this, you see.

To the question, however: you can expect some changes to take place without too much difficulties. But if they persist, then that of the Hallower will come; the Hallower who resides himself at the extremes of the planet, you see; the extremes of the country.

PLEASE CLARIFY THE TERM. IS IT "HALLOWER" THAT YOU USED?

As of the same.

WHAT DOES THAT MEAN?

It means the Hallower; an entity.

IS THIS A HUMAN ENTITY?

Appears to be in the world. Yes.

Is this human living in the U.S. currently?

To the area you have directed us to, yes.

How will these events affect gold in the year 2014?

It will be a very strong market. There will be a "golden fist," shall we call it, rather than an iron fist mentality. There will be a holding on to the metals and this will spill over into other areas of resources and real property. As there will be a further movement towards that of jewels – semi-precious and precious stones – the metals that are precious will also become much more precious. What is going to happen is that the market itself will tighten up, and there will be a delivery that will be noted. This will be a delivery of metals to people that might not otherwise expect the same, but also to peoples who would hoard the same and have some considerable wealth; again, a sign of the times: hoarding, protecting, isolating (and this is the opposite thing to do, you see).

It is being said that one of the major difficulties in the current gold market is the imbalance between the paper market and the actual metal market. Will this imbalance be coming to an end in 2014 or will it continue?

More than likely, there will be a movement towards real property, real assets, or real wealth. Therefore, we do not find that there would be a lessening of the requirements of having wealth that is truly wealth; real property, you see, tangible assets. This will continue, as we see it. Those who have focus, they may indicate themselves some way with a tattoo, or some badge, or some recognition, as to their having real assets. Therefore the need to do this would be such that it would differentiate between those that have, and those that have not.

A CALLER ON DOUGLAS'S RADIO SHOW RECOUNTED A DREAM IN WHICH SHE SAW A NEWSPAPER WITH THE HEADLINE "THE PETRODOLLAR IS NO MORE." WHEN WILL THE DEMISE OF THE PETRODOLLAR TAKE PLACE?

You might say, to a great degree, this is taking place, even now. Envision it as arm wrestling taking place between two entities: one trying to pull the opponent's arm into their court. Back and forth they go. This is taking place now, as we see it, and has been, for some time, a struggle. The inflationary influences are great. The economies appear to be moving ahead with good productive aspects, but the factories are somewhat empty. There are small towns that are drying up, and people are becoming a little extreme. As such, you can find, here, that within that of one or two or three years, changes to the petrodollar (as to the control or the demand for its use, as you would call it) would take place. This will dry up rather quickly, as there will be a move away from oil and into metal, and the gold standard would have to be reset. When this occurs, the petrodollar will be no more, you see.

WHEN WOULD THERE BE A PUBLIC ANNOUNCEMENT THAT THE PETRO-DOLLAR IS NO MORE?

There will never be such an announcement. There will be continued erosion here with the Arabic countries, the Mediterranean countries, the Asian countries, all capitulating and leading into the Chinese banking systems in which they will need to have on hand real metal, or gold in their country's banks in order to maintain association with the Chinese, you see.

Do you have any final comment on this topic?

Expect those things at Christmas to be tidings of joy, but also there will be, on the watchful eye of those who do not sleep, there will be observations from on high of certain activities in the Earth that will necessitate the armed forces to be participatory soon. As this would be done, then you would find the place. It will suffer and it will be quiet. There will be political movements, and there will be an attempt to remove certain leaders from their perspective perches, so to speak. The world is now becoming impatient with leadership, and, unfortunately, "might makes right." Expect more of this to take place in the next year or two, especially with the American peoples themselves, you see. Further away people do not seem to count, or have any heart for violence. As we would look forward, we would find, in certain areas of the world, it will be lit up and it will be light and fanciful. In other areas, it would be a starvation, and the world will be without. See?

This is a time to be prepared, but not afraid; to be practical, not to isolate; to enjoy the life fully, for this is a time of great renovation. But, like all renovations, that that is yet to be, after the tearing down, will be worth the journey. The world will not be the same as now, for the face will be different. But the peoples upon the same will have the seeds to produce a thousand years of peace. Those that you know, and those that you counsel will be among them. Patience! But live your life daily fully, you see; not in fear, but in expectation of that that is yet to be. The Hallower is coming. See?

Be an example. Some will listen and some will not. Remember Noah and the Ark. Those who listened, came inside, and those that did not, found their destiny elsewhere. Have an Ark in the heart and in the mind. Be giving, but prudently. Be an example of how all should be, and many will come, many will follow. Many will find their way. But it is a time of extremes. As dark as it might get, it will be brilliant. Light will always be light; always resilient, always evident, and always present. See?

QUANTUM MEDITATION SESSION
FEBRUARY 2014 (JR QUESTIONING)

WHO OR WHAT IS THE HALLOWER?

It is the entity that is coming that will announce to the world that that would be changes in the world. A prophet of old, a prophet of new. It is a consciousness and it is a person. You have been associated with the person before and many are coming together now, almost as if there has been prearrangement made (which there has been). Look to this voice crying in the wilderness (so to speak), uniting the different groups, uniting the singleness of purpose. The survival of the world will be benefitted by this voice. For now, that is all that can be given.

QUANTUM MEDITATION SESSION
APRIL 8, 2014 (RD QUESTIONING)

SPECIFICALLY WITH REGARDS TO THE COMING EARTH CHANGES, I NOTE IN THE NEWS ABOUT TWO OR THREE DAYS AGO THERE WAS AN EIGHT-POINT-FOUR RICHTER SCALE EARTHQUAKE IN CHILE, AND THIS IS THE TIP OF THE SAN ANDREAS FAULT. IS THIS QUAKE AN EARLY INDICATOR OF THE COMING EARTH CHANGES?

As of the same. It would be that, as to the western coast of North and South America, everything west of the Rockies will disappear; some slowly, some quickly. But as you would see a crack along the sidewalk, you do not take the crowbar and start in the middle to separate the two sides. You start at one end and then pry, and this allows the fissure to expand from the weakest point through the thickest point. And you would find this is happening at different points in and along the San Andreas area or that that would be the entire Rocky Mountain range (more to the Americas in the North than the South, but of the same).

Understand that of the continents that resided that would be in the Pacific, lying in a westerly direction from Peru, these are submerged and, here, the weak point is the edge, the hanging on (so to speak) of these continents you would call them. Some would call them plates, tectonic or otherwise.

As such, yes, this would be an indicator of that that is and will be along the western coast, more activity, until such a point that many levers will be at work in many places. And the mountains themselves are, indeed, fault lines where the pressure has been builded up and pushed up the mountains to the heights that they are. As the continents, which are now pushing against the mainland, begin to ease themselves and slip out to sea (so to speak), then, of course, they separate along the fault line and the mountains will collapse, to give an idea.

As such, to understand this particular point, yes, it would be a severe and continuous prying of the plates. Even now we can perceive that there are radiating energies building up and you can expect more activity, more quaking and shaking in this area, in the not-too-distant future, you see. But what happens in one area of the planet, look to the opposite area in the planet and, therefore, you will see that, from this area in the southeast, look to the northwest for reciprocal – call it – quaking or influence. Look to the Pacific Rim itself and you will find that the increase of activity is quite noticeable. Once this was a large landmass that lie in an easterly direction from Hawaii and that that would be the land of Mu and Og and Oz were above the surface. They have now fallen or sunken but they will be repatriated, to some degree. The islands that are in the Hawaii area, are, in fact, the tops of those large mountains that would lie on the great plain in the Land of Lemuria. It will rise a bit. There will be shifting and you will see landmasses here occurring, especially off the eastern areas of Argentina in the south.

The world is wobbling and in its wobble those landmasses that are submerged will bubble up, so to speak, where they once have seen the light of day, and those that are now above the surface will find themselves slipping underneath the surface, especially in low-lying coastal areas. As the oceans raise their level, as the seas rise, the coastal plains will be submerged, and the weight of the water upon those plains will cause fractures and submergence of large tracks of land. Simple, logical and inevitable. But, here, to this area you have directed our attention, we see there is still a pulsing taking place and there can be considered more activity coming here soon.

QUANTUM MEDITATION SESSION
JUNE 21 2014 (JR QUESTIONING)

WHAT SIGNS SHOULD BE EXPECT AS A PRECURSOR OF AN AMERICAN CURRENCY CRASH AND WHAT YEAR CAN WE EXPECT THIS WOULD TAKE PLACE?

The devaluation of the American dollar is already taking place. As to a crash or that that would be an upheaval, you would look towards that of '16 before you would find severe devaluation of the money itself. When you would find that, as to gold itself, rising above that of fourteen hundred in U.S. dollars, be prepared for the value to increase to eighteen hundred. And then within that of a degree of the petro-dollar crisis, which is what you are referring to, you will find that that of the American currency will no longer be used for foreign oil. Instead, there will be syndicates (as there are already starting) with countries which are importing and purchasing the Middle East black gold in gold bullion. This will keep everyone honest and will further separate and remove the strength of the U.S. dollar from the world markets. This would take place within the next two – let us say – twenty-four months, but is already beginning to escalate for to take place.

Look towards the metals themselves, especially gold moving beyond the eighteen hundred dollar mark. And then you would see that this would be a very difficult time and that of the currency itself will be devalued in the world marketplace.

Look also, again, to Europe when you would find conditions of some – let us say – confrontations with the euro, between that of the Greek and the German, that you would find, here, again, some meddling taking place that will affect the price of gold. You will see some disruptions in Spain and France as well. But as this would be a combination of signs, you can expect the American dollar to weaken over the next twelve to twenty-four months and then within that timeframe of 2016, be prepared for upheavals. There may be an assassination that would speed up the process. This is yet to be determined. But as you would see the conflict between the Chinese and the rest of the world, you will see unions between the Chinese, the Middle East, and even Russia (although it would be somewhat of an uneasy alliance). This, too, would be a signal or a sign of economic upheaval in the West.

There will be further abuses of human rights and some confrontations in the south-west of the country. This, too, will be another sign, although it is a marker that is weak that there would be difficulties in the currency. You would find inflation will continue, although it seems to be subdued, or that of the reporting markers have been adulterated; they are not accurate. But you will see higher expenses in oil prices, grocery prices, and taxes. More and more, there will be fines levied for even the most minute infraction of the law. This would be another sign, although, again, weaker. This is already starting and it will continue to be more severe. Look towards that of the American being alienated by the dollar itself to be traded for the oil or petrol products in the world. This would be already occurring, but it would become more severe. Trade east and west between Europe will begin to amplify through Spain itself. This would be good for the West, and it would be a compensating marker or perhaps a rescue. For when there are shortages of gold, and they cannot be delivered, from the West to their European owners, which seems already to be taking place, if it is not complied or if there is further delay, then you would find that the Swiss and the French retaliating and alienating themselves from the West. This, too, will be a marker.

These would be the signs, as you have requested to show that there would be difficulties, assuming you are referring to the currency crisis in North America itself.

WHAT SIGNS SHOULD WE EXPECT AS A PRECURSOR OF THE U.S. STOCK MARKET CRASH, AND WHAT YEAR WOULD WE EXPECT THAT TO HAPPEN?

We would find the ceiling has been reached and that there would be a continuation of lateral or sideways movements. There could be the assassination that would signal this. There could be that as to conflicts militarily, although this would be, throughout the world, somewhat minor. However there is a stretch to the financial wealth or maintenance of the federal government. Look to reports when there cannot be bills paid, especially to the military, as there have been. Look towards that as to reports of counterfeiting being rampant or being repeated in the news.

But, here, when you see the Russian and the Chinese shaking hands, then it would be somewhat as to a closed deal that there would be economic difficulty and that of the stock market will have difficulty in its breath and in its support. Look to those who would be major investors shorting the market. There will not be confrontation or lawsuits, but there will be concern about short selling or "puts." This will be in the news as well. And when there is an extraordinary amount of "puts" (as to put options) or short selling, around the upper sixteen to seventeen hundred figure, then you would see this condition developing, as to the rapid and sudden collapse in some sectors of the market, which will pull down others.

As there have been some direct attempts to hurt America financially, this will not be an outside source, but would be more from an internal panic as there would be a flight to gold. Look at the gold going up, and then you would see the markets as historically has been arranged, that they would be poised for downward collapse. Now the first step would be severe, but there would be a false confidence and there would be a calmness or reports that this bear move is over. Do not believe it. It is but a platform, like walking on the gallows; the trap door would soon open. Look to this within a matter of months, not years.

How low do you see the stock market going, if that happens?

You would see this as to a third drop, the possibility being excessive, spiking downward and upward. It will recover, but not so sharply. Look to the electronic movements, which the markets now seem to be into high speed trading taking place. This will move the market sharply lower with big plunges. As to a time frame? As to a duration of this being bottom? Look to the metals resting between eighteen and twenty-four hundred. When it becomes over two thousand, then the market will have some difficulty in ascending. But the market moves will be rather severe, up and down. We could see this at the eight thousand mark, you see, or lower. The moves are drastic.

WHAT SPECIFIC THINGS SHOULD WE DO FOR FINANCIAL STABILITY IN THE NEXT FEW MONTHS?

Individually, attempt to pay down or get out of debt. Debt, credit card debt, is a great demon. Own your own place. Have with you some portable valuable property like silver coins or gold coins. Silver is about to move upward rather quickly. Silver, called "the poor man's gold," will actually be the trading metal where gold coins or bullion will be the investment or reserve.

Look to the countries in the world that are hoarding the same now – the Chinese, the Indian, the Russian, the Norwegian (although in a smaller way) – and to those countries that would be in South Africa, and also into Australia. The mine shares are poised to ascend with the bullion. Although it will be somewhat of a lopsided gain, they will be affected not so severely.

But, as such, invest in gold companies that have gold in the ground (whether they are producing or not, remains to be seen) especially those that have interests in Africa. Then own the silver coins or the gold coins or bullion, if you would wish. Do not own certificates. Unless you have the metal in your hand, delivery of the metal might be difficult or even impossible. Hold the metal. We are not referring to jewelry (although it would be considered of some value). Stones that are precious or semi-precious stones can also be gathered and kept. If you would, for the future, hoard that as to seeds, seeds themselves will be quite valuable. And any fresh water supplies that you might have on your property should be capped or maintained or be made available for fresh water in its own right will become ultimately valuable.

But as you have directed us within the next few months, be prudent. Look to those things that will accelerate in their value, especially that that would be property outside of large communities or centers. Have four to five acres of land available for the family to sustain itself ultimately. But, again, we have looked beyond the time frame you have given. In the short time, do not panic. Pay down debt so that you are no longer controlled by those who own your debt, if at all possible. Own your own property. Have within yourself gold or silver coins in a safe place. And keep quiet about your wealth, for otherwise there may be the intruders, you see.

Form bands or alliances with others who have skills that can be combined. People you are in accord with. Opportunities to invest in gold companies, buying shares is acceptable but, again, do not leave the shares with the broker. Covet them. Keep them in your own personal possession, else they will be used as collateral to be traded against yourself by the very brokers who own or have them in their hand. This would be a rule of thumb for the next three months or extending beyond. Maintaining the posture for the next six to twelve months will prove to be more substantial. But certain short selling in the market should be seen not as panic time, but it should be seen as a buying time for companies that are solid and have gold in the ground, whether they are major or minor companies. They should have some basis in Australia or in that of the African continent itself. There is some silver benefits in South America. These companies as well.

Any food company would do well as an eye for an investor but we caution to know the difference between speculation and investment. Speculation means you may take all of your money and lose it. Therefore, speculate with little bits, as if you would be gambling. Investment means that you would have a controlled, and positive return, or that there would be not too much uncertainty in those things you invest in. For the time frame of three months, These would be safe, these would be consistent, and although a little patience may be required for further gain, the first and foremost gain you can make is to have no debt. For this is like handcuffs; physically and spiritually. See? For those that have ears, let them hear.

SHOULD WE KEEP MONEY IN LARGE U.S. BANK ACCOUNTS?

We do not see the collapse of the banks. We do not see run on the banks en masse; but, here, it would not hurt to spread the money around. The Canadian banks are one of the safest banks in the world. The Norwegian economy or banks are also safe. Otherwise, those banks that are dabbling in a variety of other interests, stock market holdings, insurance holdings, as well as banking interests, if they are gambling, and they are diversified, they may not be sturdy or strong. However, as the Good Book would say, do not put all your eggs in one basket. If you are holding onto your money, then put it in more than one location. Have easy access to it. Almost within a day's notice you can withdraw or hold your money. This would be prudent, and it would be easy to do.

Pension plans that can be converted and can be based on precious metals or real property, these would tend to fare better than
those that would be upon monetary vehicles which may be subju-
gated to governmental regulation. However, to the question, if the
cash is to be held, hold it in different banks; not necessarily one
major bank, but two or three or more. Or look to move it out of the
country, if it is possible, you see. The Canadians, especially the bank
of [Nova] Scotia, and even that of the Toronto Dominion bank (or
T.D. bank), seem to be solid, and have preparations already in the
North American continent, with their own banking outlets, including
Mexico. As long as there is control of your assets, you can have them
in your hand very quickly, then it should be safe.

**WITH REGARD TO EARTH CHANGES, WHAT CAN WE EXPECT TO HAPPEN WITH
SOLAR FLARES AND ASTEROIDS?**

You will continue to see sunspot activity, and the appearance of more;
this would be into the August [2014] month. The activity for solar
flares are increasing, even now. You would find radiation to the Earth
itself and the effects to the magnetic shield is occurring even now.
However, expect that, as to be more prominent, as to sunspot activity
that will line up in a bottom-to-top or south-to-north line, as they
have previously been from a west-to-east or horizontal line. Now it
will be the reverse. The activity in the sun is rather severe, for that
of the polarization has [changed] and is continuing to change; south
to north, north to south. As this continues, you can expect more flares
and more observation of the plasma striking the Earth itself.

There will be further and greater occurrences of aurora bo-
realis sightings, you see. This magnetic field or influence will be felt,
and people will be irritated and more vertigo or dizzy sensations will

be the result. This is taking place now and will continue for the next several months. Then there will be some relief of the same. But expect the sun itself to be volatile and to be bubbling like the soup in a cauldron. The surface temperature is increasing, due to this polar fluctuation or swapping. This will continue as it has already started, for the next two years.

The time frame is now. The sunspot activity will continue for the next seven months, but it will be a curious alignment of sunspots in a vertical plane (you might say) from an observation point upon the planet. Liken that that has been in a horizontal plane within the last two years. However, fluctuation of heat from the sun and radiation outburst or plasma explosions, these will be frequent and will last through the summer into August and even September and October. The planet itself will feel the heat and you will see the oceans marked as one degree warmer from that that is being radiated upon the Earth, rather than that that would be the volcanic temperature heating up the ocean from within. Signs of this will be outages of satellites, naturally. Major newscast satellites and military satellites will be the most susceptible for they will be in the range of this constant blast of energy forces from the sun; these eruptions, you see. They will be quite enormous, and will be reported as the same; more so than has ever been seen before, you see.

PLEASE COMMENT ON A PREDICTION MADE IN A HYPNOSIS SESSION THAT A CA-TASTROPHE WILL BE COMING TO NEW YORK CITY IN 2016.

We assume that the information is more to the possibility of inundation of water and flooding in the New York City area in the year 2016. This is highly probable and this may extend a little further into '18, but, as we see it, you will find the marker here will be in the Canary Islands. The volcanic activity that is taking place here now, and that of the island-forming that is taking place along the western coast of Portugal, as well as that that would be in the mouth of the Mediterranean Sea, and you could expect that there will be tsunami that will come from the east. When there is certain activity that would be to the Canary Islands, or the region in the western area of the coasts of Europe. You will see also activity in the British Isles that would indicate some shaking and quaking or that of an earthquake activity that would run from the African west coast to that of the British Isles and even further north to the Scandinavian country. This will shake the entire western coastline.

Then you can expect that, as to inundations as to the water coming closer or flooding along that of the Manhattan, Long Point, to the Carolinas even. The entire eastern seaboard will be affected by this. Already there will be indications of some earthquake activity that will traverse from that of the Carolinas and even a little further south, through the Appalachians, higher to that of Montreal itself (or more to that of the Mont-Saint-Hilaire region in the south shore).

Yes, this will be taking place. Indeed, this will be from '14 to '16, as to the hypnosis information you are referring to, and there will be a continuation through that of '16 to '18 in which there will be further inundations of water. But look towards that of the west, towards that of volcanic ash in the atmosphere. This would be an indication of great woe in that of the eastern regions of the country as well. For this will play havoc with transportation and agricultural concerns, you see. This would be somewhat as to the screaming and urgency heard in this hypnotic trance; it would be referred to this volcanic activity unseen and unsuspected coming from the west. We do not have the session completely; we have it through the records of your own mind.

WHAT ROLE WILL THE HALLOWER PLAY WHEN THESE EARTH CHANGING EVENTS START TO UNFOLD?

Just prior to the same, there will be continued reliability on the information given, as it will be given in increments. And for those that have ears to hear, and those that are in accord, they will form an alliance. This alliance will propagate the information; sort of a telepathic, telegraphic, instant communication (if you will) and those that would be in alliance with the same will be somewhat protected by this source, which is an ancient source, and has been an oracle, and has been a protector of years gone by; actually more than eons, you see. And, as such, this will be the reliability that will be counted upon. This will have reports on political, geographical, scientific, and spiritual influences that those who are in accord can be informed, protected, and, as such, can prosper during these rough times. Remember this is a time of awakening. Those that are choosing to do so cannot be harmed, for they will know when and where and what to do. But they will have an alliance. The White Brotherhood would be that of overseeing this influence, and the influence will be shared, provided there is continuation in the human form. As this would be demonstrated, then there will be others who will find positions or will be in accord, and they, too, will add to the record of what is going to happen so that there will be preparation; then there will be survival; then there will be rebuilding; then there will be enlightenment; and then there will be kindness and compassion shared with those who have not listened or to those that have picked up the gun and the club and have isolated themselves with fear.

HOW WILL THE HALLOWER MANIFEST TO HUMANITY?

First, through the reliability of the information given. Then through the hearts and minds of those that are called to serve or to be in accord. Then as there is a continuation of this, a loyalty, a compassion, then there will be seen great miracles and these will be the signs that there has been from the divine a consent or some authority. Then, and only then, would there be recognition that this one is the precursor, the announcer, of those things yet to come, and to that one that will come ultimately to be a light unto the world.

ARE YOU TALKING ABOUT THE SECOND COMING OF JESUS CHRIST?

We are talking about that one that will come, that will be a light unto the world. Look for a strong man in Europe to help with the financial, economic balances. Look to that, as to a world consciousness, in which all the continents will come together in a like-minded, compassionate way.

WHAT PROBLEM, IF ANY, IS H.A.A.R.P. [HIGH FREQUENCY ACTIVE AURORAL RESEARCH PROGRAM] CAUSING?

Understand the world has vibrational rates and if you would follow in that of the understanding of Tesla and De La Warr (and even Velikovsky), you would find that the world itself is entering into a sensitivity of vibration. You would find that these influences you have referred to are affecting the minds of people – the sensitivity – and their sensitivity is either causing them suffering or pain, in which they are then putting forward more violent, self-destructive tendencies, or they are rising above this and their compassion, their spirituality (if you would call it that) allows them to have great recourse to change even the weather (never mind the hearts and minds of others). They have the ability, coming together, to change the vibrational rate of the planet.

For as you would understand the planet as a living mechanism, then you would understand that this vibrational effect can be influenced and the planet itself can be calmed. For it is growing angry, it is full of resentment, with all the hatred and anger and destruction that is now coming forward. This is affecting the planet itself, for every inanimate object has a consciousness. This you have referred to, the vibrational effect of HAARP, is seemingly affecting that of the cycles, even unto the cycles of insects, animals, as well as weather patterns, and to the vibration affecting the plates or the crust of the Earth itself; it is loosening the same, you see.

AFTER 2016, WILL NEW YORK CITY CONTINUE TO EXIST?

It will continue, but, indeed, it will be somewhat inundated with waters – all of the east coast will be – but there will be a move inward and (let us say) a fluctuation of peoples towards the western and northwestern areas. You can expect that as to the White House to be inundated with water. It will be vacated, there will be flooding of the sewers, and the building will be turned back to the populace that you would call "street people." This is yet to be. But this will occur as the destruction or as there has been tsunami or tidal wave affecting even unto the White House itself. But it will survive. It just will not be the capital.

WILL THE VOLCANIC ACTIVITIES IN ICELAND BE AN INDICATION OF ITS IMPENDING DESTRUCTION?

As of the same. This will be one of the places of volcanic ash spewing into the atmosphere. Already there are scientific meetings concerned about these high-level volcanic ash accumulations, which are affecting sun penetration upon the planet, and, therefore, growing seasons. Yes to the question, there will be rapid and sudden expulsion of volcanic activity here as there will be ultimately in the lower realms, into that of Italy itself. Look to the same. You will see the world itself will be more dynamic, in that what happens in one side of the planet, within forty-five days or less, there will be a reciprocal affect on the equal and opposite side of the planet. The planet is not round, as you would know it. It is more like a cinder shape and it is tumbling and the tumbling will continue and these activities will affect this cinder and it will change its shape.

There will be much more land above the sea (or the surface of the same) than there is now below the same. This will cause flooding as more mass will come above. The water will be dispersed over fertile lands or coastal plains that are quite low. Africa and the plain around the same will be completely flooded. Iceland and the British Isles will shrink and may even have great concerns about their own survival. The Scandinavian lands will split in half. The north shore of Europe itself or Russia will disappear; rather severe flooding inland. And, as we have given, already there is flooding in Ireland, Spain and other places. This is happening immediately.

But, to the question, Iceland will be a very difficult and more volcanic-active place than it ever has been before. This is already speeding up in the cycle, you see. Again, look to Vesuvius and Etna, and you will find a greater timing, as to a countdown that the world is about to shift. The wobbling on the axis is already taking place, to some forty degrees. The magnetic north pole is moving towards the Bering Strait at about forty kilometers per year, showing definite tilting and effect of the magnetic poles, which will be followed by the geographical poles, you see. This is when you can see these outbursts in Wyoming, Iceland, Montreal, Spain and Italy, and Argentina, Chile and Peru. This will be the outcome. The Earth will shake and quake and the face of the Earth will change that it will not be recognizable from its current appearance. Expect more and larger landmasses to appear in the great oceans, you see.

FOR THOSE OF US LIVING IN NEW YORK CITY, WHERE WILL BE SAFE FOR US TO LIVE AND PURCHASE PROPERTY?

Anywhere beyond two hundred miles from the coast would be considered safe; lesser than that would be at a higher altitude. Remember even into the organization to which you are a member, Virginia Beach will survive. Although the buildings might topple, the landmass along the eastern seaboard will not change too much. But expect the islands surrounded here or river flowing, these low-lying areas within fifty miles of the coast – especially if they are lower or not very much above sea level – they will disappear. Here, to those that would be willing, within fifty miles at a higher altitude of about two hundred yards or meters and above. They would be somewhat safe. Although there might be inundation of rain and storm and long periods of wet activity, and some volcanic ash influence, they will survive. But in that that is more to the inland of two hundred miles, there will be no difficulty whatsoever. But in the reality, we doubt very much those that would be in New York or Manhattan or the surrounding burroughs will migrate en masse, until the very last minute.

Therefore, for those who have ears, let them pick places that are higher up. Let them pick places that are slightly more inland than on the coast. Let their intuition and their dreams to their safe haven or home itself. Everything west of the Rockies, including the Jewel of the North, will disappear. On the eastern seaboard, it will not be so severe. There just will be flooding; gradual in some places, and inundated with water in other places. In the Caribbean, you can expect tsunami to take large cruise liners and move them inland a few miles. Then this will drain.

Expect these occurrences to happen and then dissipate, not to be permanent. When the Earth rests, or comes to its proper orbit - for there will come a day when the sun will rise from the west, you see - in those days, the planet will be calm and subtle. But until those times, expect more wobbling and flooding in this general area that you have given us. When you have reports of tsunami effected from Spain, or here, from that of the Congo on the western coast of Africa, and when you have reports of volcanic activity along that of the Brazilian coast, and even into that of the Caribbean (this is to the Mexican area), you will find yourself becoming aware of what is going to happen in your own home or own state. Be not afraid. Be prepared. For what is going to happen will happen; in some places gradually, in other places suddenly. But we see everyone in this room will have some preparation or knowledge of what is going to take place. Act upon what you know. Do not debate it, contemplate it, or procrastinate. Be prepared. Above all, pray to God Almighty. But you will be spared, and you will be of service, and there is no doubt you would be pre-warned that you will be safe.

From the spiritual perspective, understand that as one gains this information about changes in the world, the renovations in that of the scientific, religious, arts, political and commercial worlds, there can be some fear. But from the spiritual, there is no fear. Self meeting self; self meeting those conditions that it has aligned itself with. Do not be afraid. Be aware. No harm will come to those who obey. Remember Noah. Remember others. They survived because they listened. They survived because they were prepared. They survived because they were in harmony with the Godhead or the Christos itself. We offer the same counsel.

You will be armed with warnings and dreams and visions. For this is a time in the great revelation, the great awakening, that in divers places the old and the young will come forth, dreaming dreams and visions and they, properly interpreted or used, will see the race, will see the peoples survive and thrive. Be not afraid. For if thy God is with thee, who can be against thee? Be aware. Be enthusiastic for life. Be prepared. And live your life fully. For those that have ears, let them hear.

QUANTUM MEDITATION SESSION
DECEMBER 10, 2014 (RD QUESTIONING)

AS PART OF THE END OF THIS AGE, IS THE HEAT AND THE FIRE GOING TO HAPPEN BEFORE THE EARTH TILTS ON ITS AXIS, OR AFTERWARDS?

It is happening currently. You will find that the heating of the oceans is an indication of what is taking place beneath the surface of the crust. Understand the Earth is a very complex planet. The crust itself is weak, like bakery crust on a pie. The molten mantle of the Earth is rotating at a different speed than the crust. The difference between the inner Earth or crust and mantle is causing friction to occur. Also because of the instability, because of this movement or rotation, there is a bubbling up of pressures internally. These are volcanic activity as the end result, or as the result of this bubbling up, and of course magma, volcanic lava, and volcanic ash are added to the planet. There are many parts of the world at this point in time that are experiencing the increase in volcanic activity, both above the surface of the ocean and below the surface of the oceans (more below than above). The fortunate part of volcanic activity below is that the volcanic ash is not spewed into the atmosphere. But make no mistake, there is buckling, there is movement in the Earth's crust.

From a two-dimensional viewpoint, there will be separations or earthquakes. There will be fissures and caverns and crevices created or expanded. Looking to the mountains in which there have been long-standing volcanic activity, but dormant activity in recent past, these will tend to become active, for they were vent-holes or release points when there was the previous contraction of the crust. Planet rotation is already affected. There is movement of the north pole towards the Bering Strait. The weather patterns are moving southwardly that should have been in a northward direction. In the top of the planet – in Norway, for instance – the stars are changing their locations. In fact, it is the Earth already changing.

To the question: look around that you would see, even now, heat and fire (volcanic activity, if you will) is afoot. Heat, in the predictions or prophecies, is already here. The oceans are heating up. There are those complaining of global warming and they are attempting to blame it on ozone or industrial gases or whatever. Currently there are scientific groupings who are attempting to bring to light the volcanic activity – more exactly, the volcanic ash in the higher atmosphere – which is causing more heat and more difficulties with growing cycles. This will continue to be a bigger problem until it will rain dust. In the western part of [the North American] continent, there will be a wall of flame. It will stretch from the north to the south and that that is west of the Rockies will disappear, including Alaska. Now, when this occurs, the Earth will open up and there will be a mountain – a wave, if you will – of lava, ash and heat. This will occur in other parts of the world where you would see prehistoric or historical volcanoes that have caused catastrophe in not-too-distant times.

You will find large islands bubbling up, that will be of the size of the continent of Australia. This will effect change the pressures and some of the cracks or fissures will allow substances that are below the ground to burn (oil and gas, you see). The effect is heat. These are the sources. These are the steps that the planet itself will be shifting, even now. The rotation of the planet will stop. As the sun goes to set in the west, then the planet will rotate in the opposite direction and the sun will rise in the west. This will be the time in which the planet will have slipped on its axis. The wobbling effects are now occurring, and they are quite severe; and you would find that the heating of the planet is already occurring. Therefore, to the question, the heat will come before the planet flips or changes rotation. But it is already occurring.

THERE IS THE STATEMENT MADE THAT THE HEAT COULD ALSO COME FROM SOLAR INFLUENCES, SPECIFICALLY MASS CORONAL EJECTION. IS THERE ANY TRUTH OR ACCURACY TO THIS STATEMENT?

Look to the *Sol* itself and you would find already eruptions that have never been seen before; the so-called "jack o'lantern effect" on the sun. This should be taken more serious, not to be made fun. These explosions are gigantic. That of the waves of energy from the sun are bending over the protective shields on the Earth. You can expect heat, but not a roasting, from the sun. Yes, it is added to the unusual times. The sun has already changed its polarity. This seemingly has been a curiosity. But look what is happening with solar flares and explosions. It is like any internally-combustible engine. Explosions are occurring. It will be settling down in some time yet to come. There is no fear of the sun going nova. But, here, it is not a cohesive ball of flame. It is, rather, folding in on itself – a foliation, you might call it. As it changes its polarity, it is changing the outside to the inside and the inside to the outside. A curious phenomenon.

Until this settles down you can expect more bombardment, more heat to emanate from *Sol* itself. This is already occurring, to some degree. We do not see a roasting of the planet, but certainly there would be continued inundations of solar flare activity or bombardment of particles from the sun. Look to the pictures and you would see the planet itself being like a candle, and someone blowing on the wick with that of the protective coating of the Earth trailing out behind. This will expose the planet to great radiations and the peoples to be disoriented, weak, and disease to be prominent.

IN PREVIOUS COMMUNICATIONS, YOU HAVE MENTIONED A CELESTIAL EVENT OCCURRING WITH THE EARTH AT THE APEX OF A LETTER Y AND SOME PLANETS LINING UP ON THE LEFT OF THE Y, AND OTHERS ON THE RIGHT. COULD YOU PLEASE GIVE THE NAMES OF THOSE PLANETS ON THE LEFT AND THE RIGHT?

Jupiter and Saturn on the left. Neptune and the lesser planets on the right. Direction.

AND JUST TO CONFIRM, THE SUN IS GOING TO BE IN THE MIDST OF ALL THIS?

The sun will be behind the Earth; the Earth will be in front of the sun, and even that of the moon will be in alignment in front of the Earth. This will be a strong three-way tug-of-war (shall we call it). This has already been close, as the planets have lined up in this configuration, but not exactly. Projecting the rotation, you will see the planets themselves, the larger ones on the left, a large and then lesser planets on the right. However, the effects will be not at that moment. The effects will start as the alignments occur. And if you look back, you will see, on several occasions, where there were alignments of the planets, almost in a straight row from the planet Earth, that there were effects upon the planet; the geo-planetary effects, the weather, and the social and political effects, as well. All they need to do is to look to the sky.

There are monumental occurrences taking place. This is a time of great opportunity. This is a time in which the universe is aligning the solar system. This is a new era. Like never before has there been seen such a time as this. Being prepared would be like being prepared for a storm. It will come, and will pass. But after the storm will come great growth. There will be further understanding of gravity and how to control it. There will be increased understanding in electrical or electricity and lightning effects upon the growth of food. There will be seen the greater understanding of how the awareness of the small points or the cells of the body can be manipulated to the good or betterment of health and the ridding of disease.

The contentious issues of warfare and greed, these will seem to subside as there is more interest in survival and cooperation out of necessity. The arrogance of humankind will be tested. The meek will inherit the Earth. The Sons of the Law of One will come forth, and unite the world in groups with similar purpose. The Sons of those that would be of Belize or Belgal, they shall surely suffer.

However, ye will survive, as would be others. The meek, the faithful, and those who are of service, who are associated with the Hallower will be a light that will illuminate other lights. Remember: thy God is a loving and just God. There are no injustices in the world or the universe (as you know it). Each receives exactly that that they give forth. Justice is blind. But justice is supreme. It is the only way for the existence or function of humans (as you know humans) can evolve the higher realms of consciousness, enlightenment, and a return from whence they came.

Fear not. Enjoy the extremes. But remember they are extreme. Try to find a middle road. It will take cooperation and action from those who would be prepared to avoid this time of duress. Like those who would have wood in the fireplace and wood beside the fireplace to burn later, and those who would have cans of food in the pantry and extra blankets on the shelves. They would be comforted as the storm passes. This is a monumental time in the universe. Enjoy it, for it does not come often, you know. Fear not. Ye will survive.

I NOTICE IN THE MARKET THAT GOLD IS QUITE VOLATILE. SHOULD GOLD COINS STILL BE HELD ONTO TO BE USED DURING THE UPCOMING UPHEAVALS TO PAY FOR THE NECESSITIES OF LIFE?

Buy more. They are currency, are they not? And as you look to the world itself, you will find more governments are now insisting on payments in real gold. As it once was, from one government to another, the only accepted value was gold. The paper money was supposed to be a convenience that you would not have to carry heavy coins or that there would be some form of equalization that would overcome the bartering system. Likewise, exchanging commodities in the marketplace. This has led to the adulteration of the concept that the paper monies would be backed up by gold and silver; commonly traded metals that would be precious. Because of this, now the world's marketplaces or countries that mistrust each other and because of the manipulation even unto the greatest exchanges or markets in the world, now there is an insistence on exchanging metals rather than paper vehicles.

The purpose that you would hang onto the metals would be to use as currency in the future. For those that would be your legacy (your inheritors, if you will), if you wish to profit by the metals, then it would be only advisable to sell the metals when you would be paying debts. For to have no debts is paramount. For those who have debts will be controlled by others and will be enslaved. To some degree, it is taking place now. Having the metals and keeping them, to exchange or to pay for things in the future would be the ideal (and the reason or purpose to do so). The current metal price is based on dollars. At some time in the future, it will be based on what it can buy or what value it has for commodity or product or item or circumstance. It will not be compared to dollars and then exchanged for dollars and then the dollar spent on the item. It will be directly spent on the item, or bartered for, you see. Buy more.

The metals are fluctuating and they will increase or ascend shortly. But this is, as we have indicated before, the manipulation of the metals is not by market supply and demand but by manipulation of those organizations, those people who are supposed to protect the public from any adulteration or gouging or (call it) misbehaviour, and yet they are the ones doing the same. When the trust is lost, chaos ensues. For the short term, those who would profit and gain do gain well. But the expense or the price that others pay is enormous. This cannot last. The manipulation of the markets is coming to an end as governments are warring with each other. In the currency wars now that are somewhat understood, or seen, or are remarked about by the general public. In the future, this will be looked back upon as a time of great war, the average citizen unaware, but governments fully aware that their currencies are being attacked, and their economies being depleted. As power shifts from the West to the East, remember there are no injustices. The injustice or that of the actions of the West against those in the East is now being compensated and the East will retaliate for long-term sufferings that have been imposed. However, this is digressing from the question.

Silver and gold coins should be held for use of purchasing things in the future. See them as currency. However, if you want to profit by them in the short term, they may be cashed in and the monies gained can be used to pay down debts or to buy things; more property, more items, more supplies, more seeds, more equipment for those who would expect to be self-sufficient in the coming generations. In the future, factories will be spaced far apart. It will be a precaution against Earth changes or catastrophes of weather and quake and volcanic activity. Naturally it would be done so. This will necessitate devices or vehicles that would float through the air at high speed. This is what will make communities spaced out, like on a grid. They will have their own economies within the cities, and it would be the precious metals that they would exchange between centers (and between each other, for that matter). But there is a move towards a cashless society, which is now almost there. As a matter of fact, there are some countries that are declaring that they will no longer print monies. As this "convenience" spreads to other countries, what would you have left, but coins that would be precious. Perhaps ingots and bars and other slabs of gold and silver, palladium and platinum; or perhaps, if you would have nickel and copper. But this is all you would have.

For those that have ears, let them hear. Remember in the past, as recently as Roman times, before coins, there were nuggets of precious metal. The coins became a way of measuring the metal, and also signifying how much as well as how refined the metals were. Of course, there was some adulteration of this, as always, but it ensured, at that point in time, some continuity or consistency that the metal that was given was of a certain weight, a certain caliber, a certain value, a certain integrity. This day is coming again. Humans, as you know humans, will figure out a way of trading with each other, but the days of money are declining in the sense of paper money, paper certificate, *et cetera*.

APPENDIX II

≪✤≫

The Scope of Quantum Meditation

By Robert Appel, B.A., B.C.L., L.L.B.

Although Douglas James Cottrell's contribution to humankind from his talent is clearly within the medical field, it must be underscored that the questions capable of being fielded in the context of the Quantum Meditation are not necessarily limited, as to scope or topic. Quite the contrary. In the case of Edgar Cayce, for example, 85% of his readings were medical or health-oriented. With Douglas, the number is much higher, perhaps in the 98% range. But that 2% can get pretty darn interesting.

In 1982, for example, Douglas signed on as "consultant" to a film project then in the works entitled *Lorne Greene's Atlantis*, a docudrama on the lost continent, hosted by the famous T.V. Western star. To understand how this came about, you need to recall the context of the day. Author Jeff Goodman had just completed his fascinating work on the use of Remote Viewing to assist in finding lost artifacts on archeology digs [Goodman, J. *Psychic Archeology: Time Machine to the Past.* Berkeley Publishing Group, 1980], and the book had been surprisingly well received by the media of the era. Even better, unlike other so-called "intuitive" phenomena, this form of experimentation produced easily verifiable results. If a psychic or viewer said, "dig here to find a twelve-inch golden widget," and digging in that precise spot revealed such a widget, then the value of the technique was clearly hard to question.

This series of circumstances also enabled us to push Douglas, and the Quantum Meditation, to limits never tested before. For example, during the film project, published best-selling author David Zink [*Stones of Atlantis*, and others] was preparing a book about an individual who, under hypnosis, regressed to a past life and claimed to speak "Atlantean." Zink was intrigued with Douglas's ability and asked for assistance. The tapes were first passed to a professor of linguistics at the University of Toronto, who concluded, in writing, that the language was "not glossallallia" (i.e. not "fake") and had roots in both proto-Semitic and Native American dialects. Still, no one could make sense of the tapes. When these tapes were played to Douglas in Quantum Meditation, however, he claimed to be able to translate them from Atlantean to English! [Students of eclectic pseudoscience will want to note that Douglas, in the meditative trance, specifically said that the dialect or accent on the tape was considered to be "low-caste Atlantean, not well educated." A check with Zink later revealed that his hypnotic subject claimed to have been a low-ranking soldier/guard, stationed at one of the farthest points of the empire!]

In another experiment, Douglas, in Quantum Meditation, was directed to locate an individual who, at the precise time of the reading, was holding in his hand a printed facsimile of the strange, indecipherable glyphs then (and currently) on file with the official government archives in Rio de Janeiro [*Manuscript No. 512*, Biblioteca Nacional]. The glyphs were recorded by a 1734 Portuguese expedition into the Matto Grosso of Brazil. The survivors of the trek claimed to have discovered a "lost city" with peculiar markings on the buildings. These glyphs were also the inspiration for the "lost" expedition led by Colonel Percy Fawcett almost two centuries later, in 1925, when he set to rediscover that same city [aside: the Harrison Ford character in *Raiders of the Lost Ark* was based on the life of Col. Percy Fawcett].

In the Quantum Meditation, Douglas claimed to be able to translate these glyphs. He said they were essentially "building names" but written in "different languages" because the lost city in South America from which they came was a "melting pot" for "ancient cultures from both the Atlantic and Pacific areas." Although Douglas was given no warning before the session, this dove-tailed with comments of scholars who had previously studied these glyphs and came away confused, because, even though they supposedly all came from the same "lost city," the language was not consistent from one to the other - giving rise to speculation that the Portuguese adventurers, who had barely made it out of the jungle alive, were "delirious," or had made the whole thing up.

In another instance of "pushing" the Quantum Meditation, a very educated and intelligent woman came to Douglas for a dream interpretation. As was the case with Cayce, Douglas cannot only interpret dreams via the Quantum Meditation, but does so with specific reference to the singular and specific "archetypal library" of the individual being read. That is quite a feat all by itself. In this particular case, however, the client had forgotten the ending of the dream and was frustrated. This writer was present during the session and, on a hunch, suggested that Douglas locate the "record" of the dream, based on the arcane notion that even thoughts can, in theory, leave a residue on the universal parchment, or those mysterious "Akashic Records" that Cayce himself had referred to. Douglas then proceeded to fill the missing ending of the "forgotten" dream, which the woman agreed was fully accurate. After filling in the blanks, Douglas proceeded to interpret the dream which, in this particular instance, was quite anticlimactic.

And then there is the "sound and feel" of the Quantum Meditation. It can be unsettling, even to a seasoned experimenter. Douglas's natural tone, grammar, and syntax all sharpen up significantly. Even more extraordinary is the speed at which information leaves his lips (lips which, given his low respiration and heart rate, should not be able to talk at all). While today, aspiring toastmasters and speakers consider themselves lucky if they can get through a dinner salutation without an "um" or "err," Douglas, in the Quantum Meditation trance, dumps information on the listener in an almost non-stop, contiguous fashion, pausing only to breathe.

And for those who choose to attend the Quantum Meditation in person and discourse with him (they don't have to, of course), there is the disturbing phenomenon of having to interact with someone who not only knows more about most things than you do; but, to an uncomfortable degree, knows more about YOU than you do. [Often, when doing the Quantum Meditation with the client in the room, Douglas will demur from the written questions the client is nervously reading from, and instead move ahead, offering to answer "the question held in the mind of the questioner."]

And finally there is the fact that Douglas, as did Cayce, handles the Quantum Meditation entirely in the first person plural. The explanation for this? Here is an "urban legend" popular within the para-psychological community — and one which is probably based in fact. A man spends years learning to acquire a deeper and deeper trance state to experience "freedom from attachment." One day, with his wife and friends in the room, he achieves his goal. His wife then asks him, in the trance, if he has a message for her. He opens his mouth to speak and then seems to get "stuck" with his mouth wide open. This lasts for several minutes, until his worried spouse panics and brings him out of the trance. When awake, she asks him what happened. The fellow remembers the whole event (itself fairly uncommon, as most trance practitioners do not remember anything of the experience) and explains, "I tried to say the words I LOVE YOU, but there was no word for I."

When you clear the mind of ego, there is no word for I!

So what can we learn from Douglas and the Quantum Meditation? Perhaps the solution to the riddle is not to look a gift horse in the mouth, but rather do what we can with the information the readings provide. Over the years, quietly, without fanfare, Douglas has done about twenty-five thousand viewings on health and disease. What emerges from these is an approach to human well-being which is refreshingly clear and unfettered with dogma.

Take arthritis for example. Here is a condition that tortures millions, yet which, like most major illnesses, is listed in the literature as "idiopathic" (meaning "cause unknown"). On the condition itself, Douglas is typically succinct:

> ...the body tends to store toxins or sediments in every nook and cranny. They can be placed on the shelf, so to speak, out of the way of the important organs and the endocrine system. The affected individual is unable to secrete or otherwise eliminate these; therefore the body does the next best thing. In order to protect the heart, liver, kidney, lungs, etc., the body inserts these into spaces between the joints. The waste then tends to adhere and harden onto the bone, and ultimately encase the joint. This is rheumatoid arthritis.

For a young woman who suffered from a constant ringing in the ear, another medical mystery, Douglas offered an explanation that had nothing to do with the ear:

The answer lies in an examination of the lymph system. There is a degree of movement of (lymph) fluid in the inner ear. Understand that vibration or sound travels better through fluid than through air. Therefore, a blockage anywhere within the system, whether in the chest or the throat or the inner ear, makes the lymph fluid 'grind' its way through the nodes. Assuming additional congestion within the ear, or at the base of the brain, this is again amplified, and causes the ringing.

Nor, as we have already seen, do Douglas's viewings need to be client-centric. Here, for example, his view of how the body works "at the cellular level" can provide us with invaluable insights of benefit to a very wide audience:

Crack and cocaine toxify the system and decrease the functioning of the immune system. Residues are left in the cells and in the bone. Ultimately the body will react negatively to more and more things in the day-to-day environment. Joint pain, reproductive difficulties, respiratory problems and weak hearts, cardiovascular troubles will develop early in life. Mental health, sanity, will suffer. Expect also hair loss, reduced vision, loss of smell and taste as well. Definitely premature aging. Life-span will be shortened considerably.

When asked if aluminum causes Alzheimer's disease, Douglas, in Quantum Meditation, opined on more than one occasion:

> *There are many causes. If you would regard all the causes as a pie, and you would cut that pie into three equal slices, then aluminum would represent two of the three slices. The body is conditioned to deliver elements, minerals, directly to the brain to assist in the electrical processes which take place there. Unlike other, beneficial substances, aluminum, once it reaches the brain, is not dissolved by normal processes. A residue remains, which is toxic to the cells, causing, if you like, a short-circuiting of the electrical processes. This residue eventually pollutes not only the brain matter, but even the bone of the skull itself. If you were to test for aluminum in the bone of people with this condition, you would find aluminum present.*

Concerning Alzheimer's specifically, scientists have noted peculiar scarring in the brain matter of advanced patients, but have no explanation. Douglas does:

> *The 'holes' in the brain that are seen in the pathology of [Alzheimer's patients] are the result of the decomposing brain tissue, caused by the deposits of aluminum. At the cell level, aluminum causes these tissues to actually be 'burned' away over a period of time — but this is figure of speech only, as the brain cannot feel pain.*

Today there is an ongoing controversy about the effect of power transmission grids on the local community. On this topic, Douglas had this to say:

There are disturbances that go about and along these wires. The electrical current that is transmitted does not, in fact, go 'through' these wires, but rather spirals around them. Any curve or bend in hydroelectric wires will cause some distortion or leakage into the air. That is why the towers are laid out in a straight line; to minimize these effects. Notice that when you drive under hydro lines with your radio on, you will find a spot of severe interference. This is the spill-over. These waves, similar in many respects to sound waves, will affect the cells of people who expose themselves to them. Specifically, some of the normally more active cells are slowed down, while other, more inactive cells are speeded up. The effect of this imbalance, generally, is a lowering of the immune system, permitting a greater likelihood of disease and susceptibility to viral conditions. Cancers are a direct result of these distortions.

And finally, as was precisely the case with Edgar Cayce, a "cosmic" sense of humor may invariably pop up, even within the complex cosmology of a Quantum Meditation reading. For example, when doing a session on a long-term client who had "broken all the rules" by allowing mental depression to aggravate his physical problems (at the time of the reading, the poor fellow needed a cane simply to get from the bedroom to the bathroom), the session commented almost absently, "the body does not need a recovery; it needs a rescue!"

The Legacy of Quantum Meditation

So, can anyone do what Douglas James Cottrell does? Seems a simple question, but it is not. The correct answer is "Yes... and no!" The more detailed answer....

Yes. And in fact, the readings do insist on this, over and over. The ability to contact the High Mind, as taught in many esoteric religions (Huna being the clearest) is available to everyone; and, in fact, we are all in touch with this portion of our mind on a regular basis, although – compared to the clarity of Douglas's connection – the "robustness" of the link, to use modern computer lingo, is perhaps not what it should be.

No. No, for the same reason that Bill Gates is Bill Gates and the rest of us are not. Each time you adjust the Preferences in any computer program you own, or adjust a Control Panel in Windows, you are essentially repeating the very same skill that made Bill Gates the number one richest man in the world. Except that, in all probability, you will not attain the same lofty heights he did. Why? Drive, ambition, circumstance, timing – these are all factors. In the case of Douglas, he was "tipped" at an early age, by a credentialed trance-medium, to the fact that he had a latent talent in this field. Motivated by a powerful desire to save his child, he then threw himself into a training period that lasted literally years. He persevered. He struggled. He learned to put up with the physical, societal, and emotional stresses involved with "being asleep" for most of his working day, and being called names by critics and fools. He not only tolerated these events but, much as a pearl is produced by "stressing" its host, he used them as an opportunity to improve, and, ultimately, become virtually the best at what he does.

None of the above should be taken to say that it is not worth-while, or interesting, or educational, for each of us to pursue these skills at our own pace, under our own terms. For clearly ours is a society sadly lacking in intuitive, empathetic, or common-sense skills. Were it otherwise, we would perhaps not be aggressively poisoning ourselves and our planet, while at the same time trying to obliterate selected portions of our neighbors.

Consider this for a moment: scientists and clinicians use the term "twilight sleep" to describe that portion of the sleep cycle where the "ball is handed," so to speak, from the conscious to the unconscious mind, and then true sleep immediately follows. For the average person, in the average night, this process is both seamless and transparent. However, every now and then – and this has happened to almost each of us at one time or another – we become "aware" of the process itself, and the effect is so jarring and startling that it wakes us up. Generally, if one had to describe the effect to a third party, one would note that the mind was suddenly filled with images or objects or people or events that were "illogical," or (this is the phrase most often used) "I just don't know how that stuff got into my head."

Now consider this: that unsettling transitional phase or twilight sleep referred to above, when the reassuring control mechanism of "logic" is removed from our mental processes, and the subconscious takes over, is the very realm – the domain – in which Douglas spends (and has spent) most of his adult life!

Those who have studied trance mediums (and the research is scant, and spotty) have suggested that, if the flow of questions to the medium should cease or stop, the process is actually "painful" to the medium because, lacking the conscious thought process associated with the ego, the medium is floating on an "ocean of information," without a clue as to where to swim to next. The very introduction of the next question itself gives purpose and meaning to the process and allows the medium to "breathe," if you will. [Note: Douglas in Quantum Meditation almost always ends an answer with a request for yet another question. He says "Direction?" There is method to this.]

Just as there are those who attempt to emulate Bill Gates or Warren Buffett, you can, with work, possibly achieve some of Douglas's skill on your own. Over the last decades, "schools" that attempt to teach this have come and gone. These organizations effectively teach you how to separate your conscious from your subconscious and, for the most part, their "graduation exercises" generally involve some sort of psychic reading on a total stranger. Interviews with graduates of these programs suggest that the intensive training they offer is useful, and most students, to their own shock and amazement, do pass the graduation exam. However, follow-ups also suggest that, without constant, day-to-day use, these newly-learned skills soon atrophy and disappear.

APPENDIX III

 formatting_ornament

The Master Mind:
A Working Hypothesis of Quantum Meditation

By Robert Appel, B.A., B.C.L., L.L.B.

During one "test" of Douglas James Cottrell, done in a hotel room in Toronto, Ontario in the early 1990s, a medical doctor read the names and addresses of five of his patients – as was done with Edgar Cayce – and Douglas, to the doctor's satisfaction, discussed the symptomology of each. Students of Cayce lore will immediately observe that this test duplicated a key test of Cayce at a turning point in his own career. At the tail end of that session, the M.D., a specialist in diabetes research, mentioned to Douglas, still in the state of meditative trance (or what he now calls Quantum Meditation), that they were testing two protocols for pancreas transplants – one with extraneous fatty tissue still attached, and one without. Which would do better? "The one with the fatty tissue," Douglas replied. Several weeks later, the good doctor was kind enough to contact the writer to confirm that Douglas was correct.

All of which begs the question, how much time could have been saved, if scientists and researchers sought Douglas out before their tests, to solve these problems...in advance?

And then there is the plain, won't-go-away fact that what Douglas does is not very sexy or "Hollywood." In fact, for many experiencing the Quantum Meditation for the first time, it is downright spooky and uncomfortable. For someone dealing with the Quantum Meditation for the very first time – assuming you choose to be present in the room and not be read "remotely" – the impact can be jarring.

So, the question begs for an audience, is there any "capital-S science" to this?

MINDREACH

The simplest – but clearly incomplete – explanation for what Douglas does is to classify it merely as an exponent of the MINDREACH phenomenon, named after the book of the selfsame name by Doctors Targ and Puthoff. This seminal work, published in 1977 by Delacorte Press, established via respected, double-blind testing protocols, that it is possible to "send" the mind of one person to a given geographical location, and have that person report on what he or she "sees" there. In its own way, it is probably the strongest single argument for E.S.P. advanced within the last century. Ironically, it received little press coverage when first published, and even less interest from the public at large.

[Note: the experiments in the original MINDREACH series used map co-ordinates almost exclusively to provide a "scent" for their psychics. Later iterations of these protocols, however, were much looser – using names, dates, historical events, etc. Douglas -- as did Cayce – relies almost exclusively on the individual's name, but with a street address to "boost" the signal, or amplify the name, if you like. Why a name? Because in the annals of esoteric literature dating back to the beginning of history, one's name is the most intimate connection an intuitive can latch onto. This is why, for example, the so-called elite "psychic societies," so prominent in 19th Century Europe, required new members to immediately assume a pseudonym, or initials, and never use their given names. This was to protect them from enemies known and unknown. The children's fairy tale, "Rumpelstiltskin" tells the same story in a different, but equally compelling way – that discovering someone's true name is the ultimate way to control that person.]

In fact, it would be almost a decade later before the implications of what Drs. Targ and Puthoff had achieved reached the mass (media) mind. In 1989, the top-rated U.S. drama T.V. series *Columbo* devoted an entire episode to a murderer who "fooled" the U.S. government into hiring him by falsely replicating the MINDREACH phenomenon.

So, as to the question of whether life imitates art, or vice versa, the answer may possibly be found in the mid-1990s, when no less than *Time* magazine did a surprise cover story "exposing" the U.S. government's top-secret ten-year-old research program into deploying the MINDREACH protocol for military purposes. [The headline read "The Vision Thing - Ten Years And $20 Million Later, The Pentagon Discovers That Psychics Are Unreliable Spies."] Students of conspiracy theory were delighted to note that, simultaneous to the *Time* "exposé," was the news that the U.S. government had determined there was, seemingly, no real value in the protocol, and was promptly disbanding its programs.

Coincidence? Disinformation? True or not, it was clear, nonetheless, that the U.S. was in fact disbanding something, as, over the following years, a plethora of hereto unknown writers began to come forward, each claiming they had been within the "inner circle" of the U.S. Government's Remote Viewing Project (one of its many names) and, via their books, proceeded to share their top-secret experiences with millions of readers (such as the popular *Psychic Warrior,* and its sequel, both written by ex-remote viewer and self-proclaimed spy, David Morehouse).

Of course, to simply label Douglas's talent an extension of MINDREACH ultimately begs the question. It tells us how he gets to where he is going, but not how he finds the information with which to answer questions about what he has found. For that, we can perhaps benefit from several hints that Edgar Cayce himself left in his own trance sessions. Many times, replying to the suggestion that he was "channeling" (something that Douglas has been accused of as well), Cayce would reply with the information that, in fact, it was his own "superconscious" that questioners were in contact with.

The A.R.E. itself, the research organization founded by the Cayce family after Edgar's death in 1945, says of their founder: "His own higher self – or his superconscious mind – was the source of the information. So it was not a non-physical being speaking through Edgar Cayce, but his own superconscious mind that generally obtained the information from the individual getting the reading, or from what he called the Akashic Records. These records can be briefly described as a history of every soul since the dawn of creation." Unfortunately, other than the above-quoted synopsis, the A.R.E. has not expounded further on what precisely this ability might be, or why the hypnotic trance is the "key" to unlocking it. To solve that riddle, we must dig a bit deeper.

THE SUPERCONSCIOUS

The "superconscious" as a concept is as old as Man, and appears to have been a valid precept of some of the oldest religions on the planet – including that of Tibet, India and Egypt – where it is identified with the following names: High Self, Overself, High Conscious, and Superconscious, among others. Abstractly, it represents a specific portion of the construct of a living being. Not just any portion, mind you, but the most important portion – the "soul" portion, if you like – the part that is immortal, the part that transcends time and space, the part that is in touch with the corresponding "ourselves" of all other beings, living or dead, that have ever existed, or will ever exist.

All fine and dandy, of course, but our era is, first and foremost, an "I'm from Missouri, show me!" era. So, the question has to be asked, what "practical" or "tangible" evidence do we have that this energy exists, or, more importantly, that it can provide the basis to explain the Cayce/Cottrell phenomenon? First, let's look at the collected works of Max Freedom Long, originally published in the mid-Twentieth Century, and recently reprinted, who spent his entire life in Hawaii studying Huna.

What is Huna? Huna is believed to be one of the oldest – if not THE oldest – practicing religions on the planet. Its roots are unknown, just as are the origins of the Hawaiian people themselves. Hawaiian legends not only speak of a time when their islands were a single landmass – a postulate that staggers the imagination, and is beyond the scope of this article – but also, according to Long, when the natives shared common beliefs and rituals with the ancient Egyptians. With the advent of aggressive Christianity in the late Nineteenth and early Twentieth Century, Huna was banned by local government and went underground. That, however, did not prevent Long, during his lifetime, from contacting the living Huna masters – "kahunas" – and attempting to preserve their beliefs in his books.

Convinced that Huna was not only the oldest surviving religion, but also the most practical, Long revealed how, centuries before

Freud took his first breath, Huna broke down the human condition into three distinct parts: the Conscious, the Subsonscious, and the Superconscious. The Conscious is that we use from the moment we wake up each morning to the moment we go to sleep at night. It is functional and logical but lacking in two characteristics otherwise essential to our survival – memory and emotion. For those, we need access to the Subconscious, which is the root of both these attributes. Unfortunately, lacking in logic, the Subconscious is far too easily in-fluenced, and much too quick to lose perspective. Were it not con-trolled by the Conscious, Long suggests, we as a race mightn't last until Tuesday.

[When one can't recall a thing or a name, and it "pops" into awareness minutes or hours later, even when we have "consciously" lost interest in the original question, that, according to Long, is an example of the Conscious accessing data from the Subconscious. This is a semi-mechanical process, he suggests, which takes some time to complete. Long wrote long before the invention of the computer, but had he been aware of the technology, it is likely he would have read-ily espoused the metaphor of "database access" to describe this process.]

The Superconscious was another kettle of fish. In language eerily reminiscent of Cayce readings (done early in the Twentieth Century, but almost certainly unavailable to Long, whose research represents a completely independent "thread") Huna masters talked about a "common point" of awareness at which not only did all minds, living and dead, past and future, "merge," but at which all information from all sources was available as pure stream of con-sciousness.

If, therefore, there was any portion of an individual's life-en-ergy that survived death (a topic, which, it seems, has somehow reached the mainstream in recent years!) then that portion would have to be mated in some way to the Superconscious, the pure-soul portion [which, of course, opens the doorway to a further discussion of reincarnation, or "the continual and sequential use of the soul of human identities to achieve specific goals." Like Cayce before him, Douglas in Quantum Meditation can, on demand, "read" the incarnation record of any individual who asks for it, and even provide eerily specific How-Did-He-Know-That? "points of resonance" between the current life and the past one. This is a topic, of course, beyond the scope of this current work!]. Back to our search for a "connection" between the Quantum Meditation process and access to the Higher Self.

Turns out there is one! And a big one indeed! All of Long's lengthy works on Huna emphasize his conclusion that the "most sacred secret" of Huna was also, by no mere coincidence, the most well-kept secret of the mystical and psychic societies of earlier eras - namely, that to access the Superconscious, you first had to go through the Subconscious; as, for example, by an altered state induced by drugs, ceremony, prayer, ritual, or – of course – hypnosis. [You could never reach the Superconscious from the Conscious waking state. On this, Long was adamant. You couldn't get there from here!]

Interestingly – if this hypothesis is correct – then, in theory, this phenomenon is much greater than the Cayce/Cottrell iteration of it, and there should be some evidence of Quantum Meditation-like manifestations outside the areas of pseudoscience and intuitive medical readings. And there is!

THE MASTER MIND

For many years, among practicing psychologists and psychiatrists, there were anecdotal stories circulating about attempts to "integrate" patients with Multiple Personality Disorder (M.P.D.) going "peculiarly" awry. The gossip was that, every now and again, during personality reintegration, a dominant or master personality would emerge under hypnosis, which seemed to not only be fully aware of all the other personality fragments – itself unusual – but also seemed to be aware of the doctor, the doctor's own family, the doctor's personal friends, and, generally, a veritable encyclopedia of information it should not have had access to in the first place, under any conditions.

Sound familiar? Practicing physician Dr. Ralph B. Allison, M.D., even gave a name to this phenomenon – "the Inner Self Helper," or, alternatively, the "Multiple Mind" or the "Master Mind" – and wrote a book about it [Allison, Dr. Ralph B., *Minds in Many Pieces*, C.I.E. Publishing, 1998]. Surely, even to the casual reader, what Dr. Allison found sounds suspiciously like a precursor to the Quantum Meditation phenomena of Edgar Cayce and Douglas James Cottrell!

And finally – the most difficult thesis of them all – and the one almost completely lacking in objective proof – there is the notion of "cellular intelligence" (i.e. an awareness and push toward capital-L "life" within each of our cells). Douglas the person, not the meditative reader, has said of his own work on more than one occasion, "It's as though the body really wants to get rid of [the disease] and all it needs is a little push." In the opinion of this writer, cellular intelligence, notwithstanding that we have no proof here - totally anyway - may well turn out to be the "missing link" in all this. Science gives little credit to the so-called "autonomic" nervous system, other than to suggest that it can keep your heart beating and your lungs breathing without conscious effort. But could there be more?

The metaphysical literature is rife with anecdotal stories of people who were "warned" of potential health problems in dreams, and thereby given the opportunity to prepare for the coming crisis. Warned by whom? Where did the messages originate? In 1991, Irish-born electrical engineer Michael Sheridan had a series of peculiar experiences which caused him to devote the rest of his life to exploring purely spiritual themes. He founded the Aisling Dream Institute in Dublin, and continues, to this day; his mission to show people how understanding their dreams can change their lives. On the subject of warnings in dreams, Sheridan is very clear, "When we ignore aspects of our functioning, our dreams will redress the balance by giving 'symbolic' expression to these aspects, while at the same time attempting to give healing for the 'conditions' which cause us to ignore these aspects in the first place."

Pursuing this premise to its logical conclusion, we can envision an invisible intelligence within each of us that monitors various conditions and attempts to repair them. Sometimes, it simply can't – and asks us for our help – usually in a dream, a sudden insight, or perhaps a "hunch." But, compared to what Douglas does in the Quantum Meditation, that is a flawed communication. When Douglas "reads" someone in the Quantum Meditation, it is more than possible he is plugging directly into that invisible and benevolent intelligence, and working with it to solve the problem.

And there is even more evidence, albeit equally circumstantial. Today, one of the hottest new "holistic" practices is known as Kinesiology. Kinesiology was originally developed by Dr. George Goodheart, a chiropractor, in the early 1960s. He discovered the relationship between Chinese meridians (also used by practitioners of Chinese medicine, including acupunturists) and muscle groups, glands, and organs in the body. By testing the resistance of a muscle, when a small amount of pressure is applied to it, weaknesses and imbalances in its corresponding meridian could be discerned. To say that this technique is "popular" would be an understatement. There are currently practitioners in every corner of the globe serving millions of patients. Even M.D.s are involved. The science of Kinesiology is currently taught as a full-credit course in dozens of North American universities. However, the term "Kinesiology" is not standardized from practitioner to practitioner. While some practice the more mundane forms, many are experimenting with a more esoteric practice, whereby potentially inhibiting foods, gems, metals, or other items are placed in the hand of the patient to determine if muscle groups weaken on contact. If they do, patients are advised to avoid the item, or foodstuff, in the future. Nowhere, however, in the literature on the topic, is there much of an explanation for this aspect of the doctrine. If pressed, practitioners suggest that the "subconscious" of the patient has made contact with the item and has reacted to it. Sound familiar?

This is, of course, a significantly cruder version of what Douglas does, and is most obviously comparable to Douglas's ability to give chapter and verse on the good/bad effects of a vitamin or medicine when held in the hand of a person being "read." [The late Brenda Carlin, wife of the famous comedian George Carlin, once flew to Canada for a private session with Douglas. In the course of her reading, she held in her hand a new and experimental drug she had recently been prescribed, and asked Douglas to, first, "locate" it, and then to list the positive and negative effects it was having on her body. After listing the positive effects, Douglas said one of the negatives was that it was constricting small arteries, reducing blood flow to the limbs, and making Brenda feel cold. At this point in the session, Brenda jumped out of her chair and said that, on the plane from

L.A., she had asked for a blanket for the first time ever, and had been feeling cold since she had started to take the medication!]

And the explanation in both instances has to be – must be – the same. A distinct and present intelligence at the cell level of the host, capable of being "contacted." There is simply no other answer that will pass muster. Where does all this lead? And can we form a working hypothesis on the functioning of the Quantum Meditation from all this?

We can. For one who is prepared to work hard at achieving deeper and deeper levels of dissociation, to truly abandon the ego in the search for a larger consciousness, hypnotic induction may indeed be the "gateway" to not only higher powers of mind (such as remote viewing, E.S.P., empathy, clairvoyance, clairaudience, etc.) but also to that "merge-point" at which all consciousness and knowledge is shared – but at which, ironically, time and space themselves would have very little meaning. This "merging of minds" in the absence of time/space constraints is, exactly as Edgar Cayce said, the key.

Of course, as with all great riddles, sometimes finding the answer only ends up raising new questions. If "merging minds" provide the answer, then whose minds, which minds, minds from where? Both Douglas Cottrell and Edgar Cayce are fully in agreement on this point also - the answer is "all minds," independent of the cycle of birth and death as we know it.

Which brings us back, full circle, to the issue of the Super-conscious or Overself – the only metaphysical "launch pad" from which these sorts of contacts are believed to be possible, according, at least, to the most ancient texts on the planet. Interestingly, in the classic *Yoga Sutras of Patanjali* (Second Century B.C.) the Superconscious is specifically referred to, literally, as the "rain cloud of all knowable things."

But let us not fool ourselves – these topics can never be proved conclusively, any more than one can prove, in a laboratory setting, the existence of the soul, or life after death [with full apologies to the Hollywood writing community, who, nonetheless, seem to be able to accomplish these impossible tasks every few weeks, within the pages of a movie or T.V. script!]. What we can do, however, is create a working postulate and then see if the evidence supports it.

And, in fact, that is precisely what appears to be happening. In a special reading done by Douglas for this article, I took the opportunity to "challenge" Douglas, yet again, by, in the course of the reading, asking him to locate a herbal tea, held in the questioner's own hand at the time of the session, given me by a Chinese acupuncturist who spoke almost no English.

"What effect on my body is this substance having?" I asked.

"Give us the name," said Douglas in Quantum Meditation, after acknowledging that he had "located" the herbs held in my hand, while the question was being asked.

"I don't have a name. It is a Chinese compound, and I was not given the name."

There was a three- or four-second pause; always an indication that "something is happening" in the context of the Quantum Meditation. "We have consulted with a mind knowledgeable in Chinese herbs," said Douglas. "This compound has the quality of thinning the blood, increasing blood flow, and allowing those substances that weigh heavily in the system – the drosses, the excesses – to be more readily carried to the organs of elimination."

The next day, I asked the acupuncturist what the tea was for. "Improves circulation," was his succinct two-word answer.

Similarly, working with the Quantum Meditation, we must

resist the urge to allow the strangeness of the phenomenon to put us off what is really important. We must, at the same time, expand our cosmology not only to include the Superconscious, and those so-called Akashic Records – a cosmic chalk board, if you like, that records everything we do and think – but we must, at the same time, learn to give up our fear of death, for in Douglas's world, ideas and the souls that created them never die.

At one level – a level arguably outside the scope of this work – Cayce and Cottrell are clearly demonstrating, via their unique abilities, the immortality of the soul, beyond our parochial notions of time and space, to a degree that leaves even those intuitives who "talk to the dead" standing in the cosmic dust, so to speak.

APPENDIX IV

֍

Suggested Reading

ANCIENT CIVILIZATIONS

Hapgood, Charles H. *Maps of the Ancient Sea Kings* (1966)

Cayce, Edgar and Hugh Lynn Cayce. *Edgar Cayce on Atlantis* (1968)

EARTH CHANGES

Cayce, Edgar. *Earth Changes: Historical, Economical, Political, and Global* (2013)

Goodman, Jeffrey. *Earthquake Generation: A Psychic-Scientific Prediction* (1979)

Hutton, William. *Coming Earth Changes: The Latest Evidence* (1996)

Lindsey, Hal. *Late Great Planet Earth* (1970)

Noone, Richard W. *Ice: The Ultimate Disaster: Revised Edition* (1997)

Velikovsky, Immanuel. *Worlds in Collision* (1950)

Wheeler, W. Alexander. *Prophetic Revelations of Paul Solomon: Earthward Toward a Heavenly Light* (2013)

FUTURE EARTH MAPS

www.bibliotecapleyades.net/profecias/esp_profecia_mapas.htm

2012rising.com/article/post-pole-shift-map-of-earth-changes-between-2012-2015

QUANTUM MEDITATION

Cayce, Edgar. *My Life as a Seer: The Lost Memoirs* (1997)

Spraggett, Allen. *Ross Peterson: The New Edgar Cayce* (1977)

Stearn, Jess. *Edgar Cayce: The Sleeping Prophet* (1967)

Sugrue, Thomas. *There Is A River: The Story of Edgar Cayce* (1942)

ALSO BY DOUGLAS JAMES COTTRELL

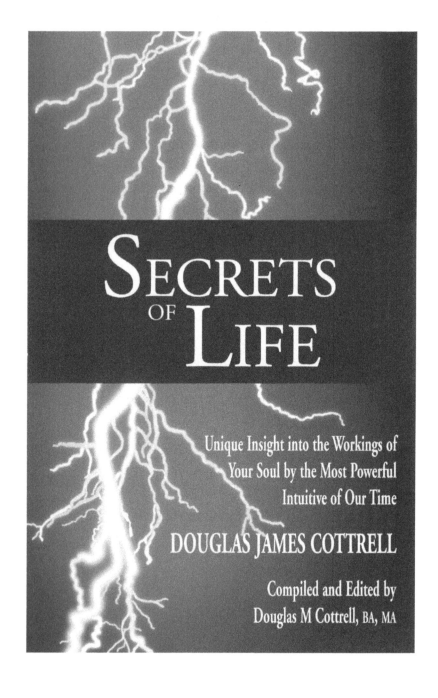

SECRETS OF LIFE

Unique Insight into the Workings of
Your Soul by the Most Powerful
Intuitive of Our Time

DOUGLAS JAMES COTTRELL

Compiled and Edited by
Douglas M Cottrell, BA, MA

ALSO BY DOUGLAS JAMES COTTRELL

VOLUME ONE

THE
COMPLEAT
NEW AGE
HEALTH
GUIDE

BASED ON THE REMARKABLE DEEP TRANCE MEDITATION READINGS OF

DOUGLAS JAMES COTTRELL Ph.D.

CO-AUTHORED AND EDITED BY

DOUGLAS M COTTRELL B.A., M.A.

ALSO BY DOUGLAS JAMES COTTRELL

DOUGLAS JAMES COTTRELL

ATLANTIS
REVISITED